Philosophy of Right

G. W. F. Hegel

Translated by
S. W. Dyde

DOVER PUBLICATIONS, INC.
Mineola, New York

DOVER PHILOSOPHICAL CLASSICS

Bibliographical Note

This Dover edition, first published in 2005, is an unabridged republication of the S. W. Dyde translation, originally published by George Bell & Sons, London, in 1896. The original German work was first published in Berlin in 1821 under the title *Grundlinien der Philosophie des Rechts.*

Library of Congress Cataloging-in-Publication Data

Hegel, Georg Wilhelm Friedrich, 1770–1831.
  [Grundlinien der Philosophie des Rechts. English]
  Philosophy of right / G.W.F. Hegel ; translated by S.W. Dyde.
      p. cm. — (Dover philosophical classics)
  Originally published: Hegel's Philosophy of right. London : G. Bell, 1896.
  Includes index.
  ISBN-13: 978-0-486-44563-2 (pbk.)
  ISBN-10: 0-486-44563-1 (pbk.)
  1. Law—Philosophy. 2. Natural law. 3. State, The. 4. Political science. 5. Ethics.
I. Dyde, S. W. (Samuel Waters), b. 1862. II. Title. III. Series.

K230.H43G7813 2005
320'.01'1—dc22

2005040107

Manufactured in the United States by Courier Corporation
44563104   2015
www.doverpublications.com

WITH THE NAME OF

PROFESSOR WATSON,

WHO GAVE ME
MY FIRST LESSONS, NOT IN HEGEL ONLY, BUT IN
PHILOSOPHY, IT GIVES ME PLEASURE TO
CONNECT THIS TRANSLATION.

Contents

Third Part: Ethical Observance
§§142–360.

Translator's Preface

IN HIS PREFACE, Hegel's editor, Professor Eduard Gans, makes some interesting remarks upon the "Philosophy of Right," and informs us as to the way in which the matter of the book had been put together. He dates his preface May 29th, 1833, thirteen years, lacking one month, later than Hegel's date for the completion of his own preface, and eighteen months after the philosopher's death. Hegel had, it would appear, lived to see the outbreak of unusual opposition to his political conceptions, and so Dr. Gans begins: "The wide-spread misunderstanding, which prevents the recognition of the real value of the present work, and stands in the way of its general acceptance, urges me, now that an enlarged edition of it has been prepared, to touch upon some things, which I would rather have left simply to increasing philosophic insight." He goes on to give three reasons for placing great value upon this work of Hegel's.

1. He thinks that the highest praise is due to the author for the way in which he does justice to every side of the subject, even investigating questions which have only a slight bearing upon the matter in hand, and thus erecting a marvellously complete structure. This fact is more striking, thinks Dr. Gans, than the foundation of the work, which had been already in a measure laid by Kant and Rousseau.

2. A second achievement of the "Philosophy of Right" is the abolition of the distinction, so prominent in the seventeenth and eighteenth centuries, between law and politics. Even in our own time, remarks the editor, many think of law as the skeleton, as it were, of the different forms of the state, as an abstract thing devoid of life and movement. Politics, again, they conceive to be more mobile and a function of a living thing. Law is thus said to stand to politics as anatomy to physiology. This divergence, which was unknown to Plato and Aristotle, had its origin in the separatist character of the Middle Ages, and was brought to completion in the seventeenth and eighteenth centuries. Hegel, gathering up the

experience of centuries, returns to the form of the ancient state, and counts law and politics as organic phases of one single whole.

3. The "Philosophy of Right" suggests a two-fold place for the principle of natural right. In its scientific treatment this principle precedes the philosophy of right, and it also comes at the close. That part of the "Encyclopædia of the Philosophical Sciences," which precedes the discussion there given of right, morality, and the ethical system, is designated the subjective mind or spirit, and from that ground natural right proceeds. Skipping over the region occupied by the "Philosophy of Right," dealing with the objective spirit, natural right reappears in world-history. Dr. Gans means that the right of the world-spirit, transcending, as it does, the individual and the nation, is a return at a higher level to natural right. Nations are, as he says, so many streams discharging themselves into the world-ocean of history.

The three points of Professor Gans may be summarized thus: (1.) Hegel is thorough and systematic; (2.) He has so clear and penetrating a conception of his main idea that he is able to unify sciences, which had seemed to be mutually exclusive; (3.) A right of nature may be viewed as a phase of any stage of an expanding idea, and can be understood only by reference to the exact stage which the exposition has reached. Hence a right of nature, like subjectivity or objectivity, may mean quite different things at different points in the unfolding of the system.

The single word here added is meant to accent what is implied in the third of these remarks. The "Philosophy of Right" is really only one part of a system. In the third part of his "Encyclopaedia," when he reaches the subject of Right, Hegel says *(note* to §487) that he may deal briefly with this topic, since he has already gone exhaustively into it in his "Philosophy of Right." Hence as this work treats of an essential stage in the evolution of spirit, whose whole nature is unfolded scene by scene in the "Encyclopaedia," it is not accurate to speak of Hegel's ethical principles as based upon his logic. The more concrete categories of the "Philosophy of Right" are related each to the next in the same way as are the more abstract categories treated of in the logic. But the relation of the ethics to the logic is not that of superstructure to foundation or of application to principle, but of the more concrete to the less concrete stage of evolution. One single life runs through the whole organism of the work. Hence, Dr. Gans is not wrong in stating that this work is an essential part of Hegel's philosophy, and adding that with the entire system it must stand or fall. Rather, correcting the dramatic tone of the remark, he says in effect that standing and falling are not the only possibilities in the case of a great philosophy. Nor, again, can the different works of a genuine philosopher be separated into those that are gold and those that are alloy. His work as a whole becomes a common possession, and in that way makes ready, as Dr. Gans say, for a higher thought. The unqualified rejection of any part of a philosopher's work is a challenge to his claim to rank as a great thinker. But the only challenge which he could himself accept as genuine, is the one which is prepared to call in question the basis of his entire system.

Perhaps in the "Philosophy of Right" the average philosophical worker comes more quickly to understand something of Hegel than in his other writings. At least Hegel in this book is more likely to collide directly with the reader's prepossessions, and therefore more speedily stimulates him to form his own view. No genuine philosopher will hesitate to show what form his principles assume in relation to tangible human interests. Hegel exhibits philosophic breadth by dressing up his ideas for the thoroughfare, where the every-day thinker finds it possible to hob and nob with the master. Yet the student must be again cautioned not to fancy that, because he "feels sure" that Hegel's conception of the family, of the monarch, or of war is defective, he has left his author behind. Such a feeling is at best only a first step, and the student must go on to know how these practical ideas of Hegel are necessitated by his general conception of the process of spirit. And the sure feeling can survive only if it is transformed into a consistent criticism of this fundamental process. The stronghold of Hegel may not be impregnable, but it will not fall on a mere summons to surrender.

The object of the translator is to let Hegel speak at large for himself. What liberties have been taken with the Hegelian vocabulary are illustrated by the index of words to be found at the close of this volume. It has been considered quite within the province of a translator to ameliorate Hegel's rigid phraseology. Even as it is the English would read more smoothly, had the words "the individual," "the subject," etc., been more frequently used instead of "particularity" and "subjectivity," but the substitution casts a different shade over Hegel's thought. Apart from the words, the reader of German will miss also Hegel's brackets and italics.

As Dr. Gans has pointed out, the present work is in form made up of three elements, the paragraphs proper, the notes and the additions. The paragraphs comprised the entire book as it was originally issued. Then Hegel added what he in all his references to them calls *Notes*, although they are not expressly so designated in the German text. For the sake of simplicity this term has been used throughout the book. After these notes by Hegel are frequently found *Additions* made by students of Hegel from his oral lectures and comments. It is but bare justice to the editors to say that these additions usually cast a welcome light upon the text. Yet as they are mere additions, not even supervised by Hegel, it is no matter of surprise that the student, in beginning a new paragraph must, in order to get the direct connection, revert to the closing sentences not of the addition or note but of the preceding paragraph. It ought to be some comfort to the earnest reader to have in his hand all that Hegel on this subject thought to be worth saying. Mistakes the translator has no doubt made, and it would be for him fortunate if workers in this department were sufficiently interested in this translation to point them out.

S. W. DYDE.

QUEEN'S UNIVERSITY,
   KINGSTON, CANADA,
      March 23rd, 1896.

Author's Preface

THE IMMEDIATE occasion for publishing these outlines is the need of placing in the hands of my hearers a guide to my professional lectures upon the Philosophy of Right. Hitherto I have used as lectures that portion of the "Encyclopaedia of the Philosophic Sciences" (Heidelberg, 1817), which deals with this subject. The present work covers the same ground in a more detailed and systematic way.

But now that these outlines are to be printed and given to the general public, there is an opportunity of explaining points which in lecturing would be commented on orally. Thus the *notes* are enlarged in order to include cognate or conflicting ideas, further consequences of the theory advocated, and the like. These expanded notes will, it is hoped, throw light upon the more abstract substance of the text, and present a more complete view of some of the ideas current in our own time. Moreover, there is also subjoined, as far as was compatible with the purpose of a compendium, a number of notes, ranging over a still greater latitude. A compendium proper, like a science, has its subject-matter accurately laid out. With the exception, possibly, of one or two slight additions, its chief task is to arrange the essential phases of its material. This material is regarded as fixed and known, just as the form is assumed to be governed by well-ascertained rules. A treatise in philosophy is usually not expected to be constructed on such a pattern, perhaps because people suppose that a philosophical product is a Penelope's web which must be started anew every day.

This treatise differs from the ordinary compendium mainly in its method of procedure. It must be understood at the outset that the philosophic way of advancing from one matter to another, the general speculative method, which is the only kind of scientific proof available in philosophy, is essentially different from every other. Only a clear insight into the necessity for this difference can snatch philosophy out of the ignominious condition into which it has fallen in our day. True, the logical rules, such as those of definition, classification, and inference are now generally recognized to be inadequate for speculative science. Perhaps it is nearer the mark to say that the inadequacy of the rules has been felt rather than recognized, because they have been counted as mere fetters, and thrown aside to make room for free speech from the heart, fancy and random intuition. But when reflection and relations of thought were required, people unconsciously fell back upon the old-fashioned method of inference and formal reasoning.—In my "Science of Logic" I have developed the nature of speculative science in detail. Hence in this treatise an explanation of method will be added only here and there. In a work which is concrete, and presents such a diversity of phases, we may safely neglect to display at every turn the logical process, and may take for granted an acquaintance with the scientific procedure. Besides, it may readily be observed that the work as a whole, and also the construction of the parts, rest upon the logical spirit. From this standpoint, especially, is it that I would like this treatise to be understood and judged. In such a work as this we are dealing with a science, and in a science the matter must not be separated from the form.

Some, who are thought to be taking a profound view, are heard to say that everything turns upon the subject-matter, and that the form may be ignored. The business of any writer, and especially of the philosopher, is, as they say, to discover, utter, and diffuse truth and adequate conceptions. In actual practice this business usually consists in warming up and distributing on all sides the same old cabbage. Perhaps the result of this operation may be to fashion and arouse the feelings; though even this small merit may be regarded as superfluous, for "they have Moses and the prophets: let them hear them." Indeed, we have great cause to be amazed at the pretentious tone of those who take this view. They seem to suppose that up till now the dissemination of truth throughout the world has been feeble. They think that the warmed-up cabbage contains new truths, especially to be laid to heart at the present time. And yet we see that what is on one side announced as true, is driven out and swept away by the same kind of worn-out truth. Out of this hurly-burly of opinions, that which is neither new nor old, but permanent, cannot be rescued and preserved except by science.

Further, as to rights, ethical observances, and the state, the truth is as old as that in which it is openly displayed and recognized, namely, the law, morality, and religion. But as the thinking spirit is not satisfied with possessing the truth in this simple way, it must conceive it, and thus acquire a rational form for a content which is already rational implicitly. In this way the substance is justified before the bar of free thought. Free thought cannot be satisfied with what is given to it, whether by the external positive authority of the state or human agreement, or by the authority of internal feelings, the heart, and the witness of the spirit, which coincides unquestioningly with the heart. It is the nature of free thought rather to proceed out of its own self, and hence to demand that it should know itself as thoroughly one with truth.

The ingenuous mind adheres with simple conviction to the truth which is publicly acknowledged. On this foundation it builds its conduct and way of life. In opposition to this naïve view of things rises the supposed difficulty of detecting amidst the endless differences of opinion anything of universal application. This trouble may easily be supposed to spring from a spirit of earnest inquiry. But in point of fact those who pride themselves upon the existence of this obstacle are in the plight of him who cannot see the woods for the trees. The confusion is all of their own making. Nay, more: this confusion is an indication that they are in fact not seeking for what is universally valid in right and the ethical order. If they were at pains to find that out, and refused to busy themselves with empty opinion and minute detail, they would adhere to and act in accordance with substantive right, namely the commands of the state and the claims of society. But a further difficulty lies in the fact that man thinks, and seeks freedom and a basis for conduct in thought. Divine as his right to act in this way is, it becomes a wrong, when it takes the place of thinking. Thought then regards itself as free only when it is conscious of being at variance with what is generally recognized, and of setting itself up as something original.

The idea that freedom of thought and mind is indicated only by deviation from, or even hostility to what is everywhere recognized, is most persistent with regard to the state. The essential task of a philosophy of the state would thus seem to be the discovery and publication of a new and original theory. When we examine this idea and the way it is applied, we are almost led to think that no state or constitution has ever existed, or now exists. We are tempted to suppose that we must now begin and keep on beginning afresh for ever. We are to fancy that the founding of the social order has depended upon present devices and discoveries. As to nature, philosophy, it is admitted, has to understand it as it is. The philosophers' stone must be concealed somewhere, we say, in nature itself, as nature is in itself rational. Knowledge must, therefore, examine, apprehend and conceive the reason actually present in nature. Not with the superficial shapes and accidents of nature, but with its eternal harmony, that is to say, its inherent law and essence, knowledge has to cope. But the ethical world or the state, which is in fact reason potently and permanently actualized in self-consciousness, is not permitted to enjoy the happiness of being reason at all.[1] On the contrary the spiritual uni-

---

[1]There are two kinds of laws, laws of nature and laws of right. The laws of nature are simply there, and are valid as they are. They cannot be gainsaid, although in certain cases they may be transgressed. In order to know laws of nature, we must set to work to ascertain

verse is looked upon as abandoned by God, and given over as a prey to
accident and chance. As in this way the divine is eliminated from the ethical world, truth must be sought outside of it. And since at the same time
reason should and does belong to the ethical world, truth, being divorced
from reason, is reduced to a mere speculation. Thus seems to arise the
necessity and duty of every thinker to pursue a career of his own. Not
that he needs to seek for the philosophers' stone, since the philosophizing of our day has saved him the trouble, and every would-be thinker is
convinced that he possesses the stone already without search. But these
erratic pretensions are, as it indeed happens, ridiculed by all who, whether

them, for they are true, and only our ideas of them can be false. Of these laws the measure is outside of us. Our knowledge adds nothing to them, and does not further their
operation. Only our knowledge of them expands. The knowledge of right is partly of
the same nature and partly different. The laws of right also are simply there, and we have
to become acquainted with them. In this way the citizen has a more or less firm hold of
them as they are given to him, and the jurist also abides by the same standpoint. But there
is also a distinction. In connection with the laws of right the spirit of investigation is
stirred up, and our attention is turned to the fact that the laws, because they are different,
are not absolute. Laws of right are established and handed down by men. The inner voice
must necessarily collide or agree with them. Man cannot be limited to what is presented
to him, but maintains that he has the standard of right within himself. He may be subject to the necessity and force of external authority, but not in the same way as he is to
the necessity of nature; for always his inner being says to him how a thing ought to be,
and within himself he finds the confirmation or lack of confirmation of what is generally accepted. In nature the highest truth is that a law is. In right a thing is not valid because it is, since every one demands that it shall conform to his standard. Hence arises a
possible conflict between what is and what ought to be, between absolute unchanging
right and the arbitrary decision of what ought to be right. Such division and strife occur
only on the soil of the spirit. Thus the unique privilege of the spirit would appear to lead
to discontent and unhappiness, and frequently we are directed to nature in contrast with
the fluctuations of life. But it is exactly in the opposition arising between absolute right,
and that which the arbitrary will seeks to make right, that the need lies of knowing thoroughly what right is. Men must openly meet and face their reason, and consider the rationality of right. This is the subject-matter of our science in contrast with jurisprudence,
which often has to do merely with contradictions. Moreover the world of to-day has an
imperative need to make this investigation. In ancient times respect and reverence for the
law were universal. But now the fashion of the time has taken another turn, and thought
confronts everything which has been approved. Theories now set themselves in opposition to reality, and make as though they were absolutely true and necessary. And there is
now more pressing need to know and conceive the thoughts upon right. Since thought
has exalted itself as the essential form, we must now be careful to apprehend right also as
thought. It would look as though the door were thrown open for every casual opinion,
when thought is thus made to supervene upon right. But true thought of a thing is not
an opinion, but the conception of the thing itself. The conception of the thing does not
come to us by nature. Every man has fingers, and may have brush and colours, but he is
not by reason of that a painter. So is it with thought. The thought of right is not a thing
which every man has at first hand. True thinking is thorough acquaintance with the object. Hence our knowledge must be scientific.

they are aware of it or not, are conditioned in their lives by the state, and find their minds and wills satisfied in it. These, who include the majority if not all, regard the occupation of philosophers as a game, sometimes playful, sometimes earnest, sometimes entertaining, sometimes dangerous, but always as a mere game. Both this restless and frivolous reflection and also this treatment accorded to it might safely be left to take their own course, were it not that betwixt them philosophy is brought into discredit and contempt. The most cruel despite is done when every one is convinced of his ability to pass judgment upon, and discard philosophy without any special study. No such scorn is heaped upon any other art or science.

In point of fact the pretentious utterances of recent philosophy regarding the state have been enough to justify any one who cared to meddle with the question, in the conviction that he could prove himself a philosopher by weaving a philosophy out of his own brain. Notwithstanding this conviction, that which passes for philosophy has openly announced that truth cannot be known. The truth with regard to ethical ideals, the state, the government and the constitution ascends, so it declares, out of each man's heart, feeling, and enthusiasm. Such declarations have been poured especially into the eager ears of the young. The words "God giveth truth to his chosen in sleep" have been applied to science; hence every sleeper has numbered himself amongst the chosen. But what he deals with in sleep is only the wares of sleep. Mr. Fries,[2] one of the leaders of this shallow-minded host of philosophers, on a public festive occasion, now become celebrated, has not hesitated to give utterance to the following notion of the state and constitution: "When a nation is ruled by a common spirit, then from below, out of the people, will come life sufficient for the discharge of all public business. Living associations, united indissolubly by the holy bond of friendship, will devote themselves to every side of national service, and every means for educating the people." This is the last degree of shallowness, because in it science is looked upon as developing, not out of thought or conception, but out of direct perception and random fancy. Now the organic connection of the manifold branches of the social system is the architectonic of the state's rationality, and in this supreme science of state architecture the strength of the whole is made to depend upon the harmony of all the clearly marked phases of public life, and the stability of every pillar, arch, and buttress of the social edifice. And yet the shallow doctrine, of which we have spoken, permits this elaborate structure to melt and lose itself in the brew and stew of the "heart, friendship, and inspiration." Epicurus, it is

---

[2] I have already had occasion to notice the shallowness of his science. See "Science of Logic" (Nürnberg, 1812), Introduction, p. 17.

said, believed that the world generally should be given over to each individual's opinions and whims; and according to the view we are criticising the ethical fabric should be treated in the same way. By this old
wives' decoction, which consists in founding upon the feelings what has
been for many centuries the labour of reason and understanding, we no
longer need the guidance of any ruling conception of thought. On this
point Goethe's Mephistopheles, and the poet is a good authority, has a
remark, which I have already used elsewhere:

> "Verachte nur Verstand und Wissenschaft,
>   des Menschen allerhöchste Gaben—
> So hast dem Teufel dich ergeben
>   und musst zu Grunde gehn."

It is no surprise that the view just criticised should appear in the form
of piety. Where, indeed, has this whirlwind of impulse not sought to justify itself? In godliness and the Bible it has imagined itself able to find authority for despising order and law. And, in fact, it is piety of a sort which
has reduced the whole organized system of truth to elementary intuition
and feeling. But piety of the right kind leaves this obscure region, and
comes out into the daylight, where the idea unfolds and reveals itself. Out
of its sanctuary it brings a reverence for the law and truth which are absolute and exalted above all subjective feeling.

The particular kind of evil consciousness developed by the wishy-
washy eloquence already alluded to, may be detected in the following
way. It is most unspiritual, when it speaks most of the spirit. It is the most
dead and leathern, when it talks of the scope of life. When it is exhibiting the greatest self-seeking and vanity it has most on its tongue the
words "people" and "nation." But its peculiar mark, found on its very
forehead, is its hatred of law. Right and ethical principle, the actual world
of right and ethical life, are apprehended in thought, and by thought are
given definite, general, and rational form, and this reasoned right finds
expression in law. But feeling, which seeks its own pleasure, and conscience, which finds right in private conviction, regard the law as their
most bitter foe. The right, which takes the shape of law and duty, is by
feeling looked upon as a shackle or dead cold letter. In this law it does
not recognize itself and does not find itself free. Yet the law is the reason
of the object, and refuses to feeling the privilege of warming itself at its
private hearth. Hence the law, as we shall occasionally observe, is the
Shibboleth, by means of which are detected the false brethren and friends
of the so-called people.

Inasmuch as the purest charlatanism has won the name of philosophy,
and has succeeded in convincing the public that its practices are philosophy, it has now become almost a disgrace to speak in a philosophic way

about the state. Nor can it be taken ill, if honest men become impatient, when the subject is broached. Still less is it a surprise that the government has at last turned its attention to this false philosophizing. With us philosophy is not practised as a private art, as it was by the Greeks, but has a public place, and should therefore be employed only in the service of the state. The government has, up till now, shown such confidence in the scholars in this department as to leave the subject matter of philosophy wholly in their hands. Here and there, perhaps, has been shown to this science not confidence so much as indifference, and professorships have been retained as a matter of tradition. In France, as far as I am aware, the professional teaching of metaphysics at least has fallen into desuetude. In any case the confidence of the state has been ill requited by the teachers of this subject. Or, if we prefer to see in the state not confidence, but indifference, the decay of fundamental knowledge must be looked upon as a severe penance. Indeed, shallowness is to all appearance most endurable and most in harmony with the maintenance of order and peace, when it does not touch or hint at any real issue. Hence it would not be necessary to bring it under public control, if the state did not require deeper teaching and insight, and expect science to satisfy the need. Yet this shallowness, notwithstanding its seeming innocence, does bear upon social life, right and duty generally, advancing principles which are the very essence of superficiality. These, as we have learned so decidedly from Plato, are the principles of the Sophists, according to which the basis of right is subjective aims and opinions, subjective feeling and private conviction. The result of such principles is quite as much the destruction of the ethical system, of the upright conscience, of love and right, in private persons, as of public order and the institutions of the state. The significance of these facts for the authorities will not be obscured by the claim that the holder of these perilous doctrines should be trusted, or by the immunity of office. The authorities will not be deterred by the demand that they should protect and give free play to a theory which strikes at the substantial basis of conduct, namely, universal principles, and that they should disregard insolence on the ground of its being the exercise of the teacher's function. *To him, to whom God gives office, He gives also understanding* is a well-worn jest, which no one in our time would like to take seriously.

In the methods of teaching philosophy, which have under the circumstances been reanimated by the government, the important element of protection and support cannot be ignored. The study of philosophy is in many ways in need of such assistance. Frequently in scientific, religious, and other works may be read a contempt for philosophy. Some, who have no conspicuous education and are total strangers to philosophy, treat it as a cast-off garment. They even rail against it, and regard as foolishness and sinful presumption its efforts to conceive of God and physical and spiritual nature. They scout its endeavour to know the truth. Reason, and again reason, and reason in endless iteration is by them accused, despised, condemned. Free expression, also, is given by a large number of those, who are supposed to be cultivating scientific research, to their annoyance at the unassailable claims of the conception. When we, I say, are confronted with such phenomena as these, we are tempted to harbour the thought that old traditions of tolerance have fallen out of use, and no longer assure to philosophy a place and public recognition.[3]

These presumptuous utterances, which are in vogue in our time, are, strange to say, in a measure justified by the shallowness of the current philosophy. Yet, on the other hand, they have sprung from the same root as that against which they so thanklessly direct their attacks. Since that self-named philosophizing has declared that to know the truth is vain, it has reduced all matter of thought to the same level, resembling in this way the despotism of the Roman Empire, which equalized noble and slave, virtue and vice, honour and dishonour, knowledge and ignorance. In such a view the conceptions of truth and the laws of ethical observance are simply opinions and subjective convictions, and the most criminal principles, provided only that they are convictions, are put on a level with these laws. Thus, too, any paltry special object, be it never so flimsy, is given the same value as an interest common to all thinking men and the bonds of the established social world.

Hence it is for science a piece of good fortune that that kind of philosophizing, which might, like scholasticism, have continued to spin its notions within itself, has been brought into contact with reality. Indeed, such contact was, as we have said, inevitable. The real world is in earnest with the principles of right and duty, and in the full light of a consciousness of these principles it lives. With this world of reality philosophic cob-web spinning has come into open rupture. Now, as to genuine philosophy it is precisely its attitude to reality which has been misapprehended. Philosophy is, as I have already observed, an inquisition into the rational, and therefore the apprehension of the real and present. Hence it cannot be the exposition of a world beyond, which is merely a castle in the air, having no existence except in the terror of a one-sided

[3]The same view finds expression in a letter of Joh. v. Müller ("Works," Part VIII., p. 56), who, speaking of the condition of Rome in the year 1803, when the city was under French rule, writes, "A professor, asked how the public academies were doing, answered, 'On les tolère comme les bordels!'" Similarly the so-called theory of reason or logic we may still hear commended, perhaps under the belief that it is too dry and unfruitful a science to claim any one's attention, or, if it be pursued here and there, that its formulae are without content, and, though not of much good, can be of no great harm. Hence the recommendation, so it is thought, if useless, can do no injury.

and empty formalism of thought. In the following treatise I have remarked that even Plato's "Republic," now regarded as the byword for an
empty ideal, has grasped the essential nature of the ethical observances of
the Greeks. He knew that there was breaking in upon Greek life a deeper
principle, which could directly manifest itself only as an unsatisfied longing and therefore as ruin. Moved by the same longing Plato had to seek
help against it, but had to conceive of the help as coming down from
above, and hoped at last to have found it in an external special form of
Greek ethical observance. He exhausted himself in contriving how by
means of this new society to stem the tide of ruin, but succeeded only
in injuring more fatally its deeper motive, the free infinite personality. Yet
he has proved himself to be a great mind because the very principle and
central distinguishing feature of his idea is the pivot upon which the
world-wide revolution then in process turned:

> What is rational is real;
> And what is real is rational.

Upon this conviction stand not philosophy only but even every unsophisticated consciousness. From it also proceeds the view now under
contemplation that the spiritual universe is the natural. When reflection,
feeling, or whatever other form the subjective consciousness may assume,
regards the present as vanity, and thinks itself to be beyond it and wiser,
it finds itself in emptiness, and, as it has actuality only in the present, it is
vanity throughout. Against the doctrine that the idea is a mere idea, fig-
ment or opinion, philosophy preserves the more profound view that
nothing is real except the idea. Hence arises the effort to recognize in the
temporal and transient the substance, which is immanent, and the eternal, which is present. The rational is synonymous with the idea, because
in realizing itself it passes into external existence. It thus appears in an
endless wealth of forms, figures and phenomena. It wraps its kernel
round with a robe of many colours, in which consciousness finds itself at
home. Through this varied husk the conception first of all penetrates, in
order to touch the pulse, and then feel it throbbing in its external manifestations. To bring to order the endlessly varied relations, which constitute the outer appearance of the rational essence is not the task of philosophy. Such material is not suitable for it, and it can well abstain from
giving good advice about these things. Plato could refrain from recom-
mending to the nurses not to stand still with children, but always to dan-
dle them in their arms. So could Fichte forbear to construe, as they say,
the supervision of passports to such a point as to demand of all suspects
that not only a description of them but also their photograph, should be
inserted in the pass. Philosophy now exhibits no trace of such details.
These superfine concerns it may neglect all the more safely, since it shows

itself of the most liberal spirit in its attitude towards the endless mass of objects and circumstances. By such a course science will escape the hate which is visited upon a multitude of circumstances and institutions by the vanity of a better knowledge. In this hate bitterness of mind finds the greatest pleasure, as it can in no other way attain to a feeling of self-esteem.

This treatise, in so far as it contains a political science, is nothing more than an attempt to conceive of and present the state as in itself rational. As a philosophic writing it must be on its guard against constructing a state as it ought to be. Philosophy cannot teach the state what it should be, but only how it, the ethical universe, is to be known.

> Ἰδοὺ Ῥόδος, ἰδοὺ καὶ τὸ πήδημα.
> *Hic* Rhodus, *hic* saltus.

To apprehend what is is the task of philosophy, because what is is reason. As for the individual, every one is a son of his time; so philosophy also is its time apprehended in thoughts. It is just as foolish to fancy that any philosophy can transcend its present world, as that an individual could leap out of his time or jump over Rhodes. If a theory transgresses its time, and builds up a world as it ought to be, it has an existence merely in the unstable element of opinion, which gives room to every wandering fancy.

With little change the above saying would read:

> *Here* is the rose, *here* dance.

The barrier which stands between reason, as self-conscious spirit, and reason as present reality, and does not permit spirit to find satisfaction in reality, is some abstraction, which is not free to be conceived. To recognize reason as the rose in the cross of the present, and to find delight in it, is a rational insight which implies reconciliation with reality. This reconciliation philosophy grants to those who have felt the inward demand to conceive clearly, to preserve subjective freedom while present in substantive reality, and yet though possessing this freedom to stand not upon the particular and contingent, but upon what is self-originated and self-completed.

This also is the more concrete meaning of what was a moment ago more abstractly called the unity of form and content. Form in its most concrete significance is reason, as an intellectual apprehension which conceives its object. Content, again, is reason as the substantive essence of social order and nature. The conscious identity of form and content is the philosophical idea.

It is a self-assertion, which does honour to man, to recognize nothing in sentiment which is not justified by thought. This self-will is a feature of modern times, being indeed the peculiar principle of Protestantism. What was initiated by Luther as faith in feeling and the witness of the spirit, the more mature mind strives to apprehend in conception. In that way it seeks to free itself in the present, and so find there itself. It is a celebrated saying that a half philosophy leads away from God, while a true philosophy leads to God. (It is the same halfness, I may say in passing, which regards knowledge as an approximation to truth.) This saying is applicable to the science of the state. Reason cannot content itself with a mere approximation, something which is neither cold nor hot, and must be spued out of the mouth. As little can it be contented with the cold scepticism that in this world of time things go badly, or at best only moderately well, and that we must keep the peace with reality, merely because there is nothing better to be had. Knowledge creates a much more vital peace.

Only one word more concerning the desire to teach the world what it ought to be. For such a purpose philosophy at least always comes too late. Philosophy, as the thought of the world, does not appear until reality has completed its formative process, and made itself ready. History thus corroborates the teaching of the conception that only in the maturity of reality does the ideal appear as counterpart to the real, apprehends the real world in its substance, and shapes it into an intellectual kingdom. When philosophy paints its grey in grey, one form of life has become old, and by means of grey it cannot be rejuvenated, but only known. The owl of Minerva takes its flight only when the shades of night are gathering.

But it is time to close this preface. As a preface it is its place to speak only externally and subjectively of the standpoint of the work which it introduces. A philosophical account of the essential content needs a scientific and objective treatment. So, too, criticisms, other than those which proceed from such a treatment, must be viewed by the author as unreflective convictions. Such subjective criticisms must be for him a matter of indifference.

BERLIN, *June 25th,* 1820.

Introduction

1. THE PHILOSOPHIC SCIENCE of right has as its object the idea of right, *i.e.,* the conception of right and the realization of the conception.

Note.—Philosophy has to do with ideas or realized thoughts, and hence not with what we have been accustomed to call mere conceptions. It has indeed to exhibit the one-sidedness and untruth of these mere conceptions, and to show that, while that which commonly bears the name "conception," is only an abstract product of the understanding, the true conception alone has reality and gives this reality to itself. Everything, other than the reality which is established by the conception, is transient surface existence, external accident, opinion, appearance void of essence, untruth, delusion, and so forth. Through the actual shape, which it takes upon itself in actuality, is the conception itself understood. This shape is the other essential element of the idea, and is to be distinguished from the form, which exists only as conception.

Addition.—The conception and its existence are two sides, distinct yet united, like soul and body. The body is the same life as the soul, and yet the two can be named independently. A soul without a body would not be a living thing, and *vice versâ.* Thus the visible existence of the conception is its body, just as the body obeys the soul which produced it. Seeds contain the tree and its whole power, though they are not the tree itself; the tree corresponds accurately to the simple structure of the seed. If the body does not correspond to the soul, it is defective. The unity of visible existence and conception, of body and soul, is the idea. It is not a mere harmony of the two, but their complete interpenetration. There lives nothing, which is not in some way idea. The idea of right is freedom, which, if it is to be apprehended truly, must be known both in its conception and in the embodiment of the conception.

2. The science of right is a part of philosophy. Hence it must develop the idea, which is the reason of an object, out of the conception. It is the same thing to say that it must regard the peculiar internal development of the thing itself. Since it is a part, it has a definite beginning, which is

the result and truth of what goes before, and this, that goes before, constitutes its so-called proof. Hence the origin of the conception of right falls outside of the science of right. The deduction of the conception is presupposed in this treatise, and is to be considered as already given.

Addition.—Philosophy forms a circle. It has, since it must somehow make a beginning, a primary, directly given matter, which is not proved and is not a result. But this starting-point is simply relative, since from another point of view it appears as a result. Philosophy is a consequence, which does not hang in the air or form a directly new beginning, but is self-enclosed.

According to the formal unphilosophic method of the sciences, definition is the first desideratum, as regards, at least, the external scientific form. The positive science of right, however, is little concerned with definition, since its special aim is to give what it is that is right, and also the particular phases of the laws. For this reason it has been said as a warning, *Omnis definitio in jure civili periculosa;* and in fact the more disconnected and contradictory the phases of a right are, the less possible is a definition of it. A definition should contain only universal features; but these forthwith bring to light contradictions, which in the case of law are injustice, in all their nakedness. Thus in Roman law, for instance, no definition of man was possible, because it excluded the slave. The conception of man was destroyed by the fact of slavery. In the same way to have defined property and owner would have appeared to be perilous to many relations.—But definitions may perhaps be derived from etymology, for the reason, principally, that in this way special cases are avoided, and a basis is found in the feeling and imaginative thought of men. The correctness of a definition would thus consist in its agreement with existing ideas. By such a method everything essentially scientific is cast aside. As regards the content there is cast aside the necessity of the self-contained and self-developed object, and as regards the form there is discarded the nature of the conception. In philosophic knowledge the necessity of a conception is the main thing, and the process, by which it, as a result, has come into being, is the proof and deduction. After the content is seen to be necessary independently, the second point is to look about for that which corresponds to it in existing ideas and modes of speech. But the way in which a conception exists in its truth, and the way it presents itself in random ideas not only are but must be different both in form and structure. If a notion is not in its content false, the conception can be shown to be contained in it and to be already there in its essential traits. A notion may thus be raised to the form of a conception. But so little is any notion the measure and criterion of an independently necessary and true conception, that it must accept truth from the conception, be justified by it, and know itself through it.—If the method of knowing, which proceeds by formal definition, inference and proof, has more or less disappeared, a worse one has come to take its place. This new method maintains that ideas, as, *e.g.,* the idea of right in all its aspects, are to be directly apprehended as mere facts of consciousness, and that natural feeling, or that heightened form of it which is known as the inspiration of one's own breast, is the source of right. This method may be the most convenient of all, but it is also the most unphilosophic. Other features of this view, referring not merely to knowledge but directly to action, need not detain us here. While the first or formal method went so far as to require in definition the form of the conception, and in proof the form of a necessity of knowledge, the method of the intuitive consciousness and feeling takes for its principle the arbitrary contingent consciousness of the subject.—In this treatise we take for granted the scientific procedure of philosophy, which has been set forth in the philosophic logic.

3. Right is positive in general (*a*) in its form, since it has validity in a state; and this established authority is the principle for the knowledge of right. Hence we have the positive science of right. (*b*) On the side of content this right receives a positive element (α) through the particular character of a nation, the stage of its historical development, and the interconnection of all the relations which are necessitated by nature: (β) through the necessity that a system of legalized right must contain the application of the universal conception to objects and cases whose qualities are given externally. Such an application is not the speculative thought or the development of the conception, but a subsumption made by the understanding: (γ) through the ultimate nature of a decision which has become a reality.

Note.—Philosophy at least cannot recognize the authority of feeling, inclination and caprice, when they are set in opposition to positive right and the laws.—It is an accident, external to the nature of positive right, when force or tyranny becomes an element of it. It will be shown later (§§211–214), at what point right must become positive. The general phases which are there deduced, are here only mentioned, in order to indicate the limit of philosophic right, and also to forestall the idea or indeed the demand that by a systematic development of right should be produced a law-book, such as would be needed by an actual state.—To convert the differences between right of nature and positive right, or those between philosophic right and positive right, into open antagonism would be a complete misunderstanding. Natural right or philosophic right stands to positive right as institutions to pandects.—With regard to the historical element in positive right, referred to in the paragraph, it may be said that the true historical view and genuine philosophic standpoint have been presented by Montesquieu. He regards legislation and its specific traits not in an isolated and abstract way, but rather as a dependent element of one totality, connecting it with all the other elements which form the character of a nation and an epoch. In this interrelation the various elements receive their meaning and justification.—The purely historical treatment of the phases of right, as they develop in time, and a comparison of their results with existing relations of right have their own value; but they are out of place in a philosophic treatise, except in so far as the development out of historic grounds coincides with the development out of the conception, and the historical exposition and justification can be made to cover a justification which is valid in itself and independently. This distinction is as manifest as it is weighty. A phase of right may be shown to rest upon and follow from the circumstances and existing institutions of right, and yet may be absolutely unreasonable and void of right. This is the case in Roman law with many aspects of private right, which were the logical results of its interpretation of paternal power and of marriage. Further, if the aspects of right are really right and reasonable, it is one thing to point out what with regard to them can truly take place through the conception, and quite another thing to portray the manner of their appearance in history, along with the circumstances, cases, wants and events, which they have called forth. Such a demonstration and deduction from nearer or more remote historic causes, which is the occupation of pragmatic history, is frequently called exposition, or preferably conception, under the opinion that in such an indication of the historic elements is found all that is essential to a conception of law and institutions of right. In point of fact that which is truly essential, the conception of the matter, has not been so much as mentioned.—So also we are accustomed to hear of Roman or German conceptions of right, and of conceptions of right as they are laid down in this or that statute-book, when indeed nothing about conceptions can be found in them, but only general phases of right, propositions derived from the understanding, general maxims, and laws.—By neglect of the distinction, just alluded to, the true standpoint is obscured and the question of a valid justification is shifted into a justification based upon circumstances; results are founded on presuppositions, which in themselves are of little value; and in general the relative is put in place of the absolute, and external appearance in place of the nature of the thing. When the historical vindication substitutes the external origin for the origin from the conception, it unconsciously does the opposite of what it intends. Suppose that an institution, originating under definite circumstances, is shown to be necessary and to answer its purpose, and that it accomplishes all that is required of it by the historical standpoint. When such a proof is made to stand for a justification of the thing itself, it follows that, when the circumstances are removed, the institution has lost its meaning and its right. When, e.g., it is sought to support and defend cloisters on the grounds that they have served to clear and people the wilderness and by teaching and transcribing to preserve scholarship, it follows that just in so far as the circumstances are changed, cloisters have become aimless and superfluous.—In so far as the historic significance, or the historical exposition and interpretation of the origin of anything is in different spheres at home with the philosophic view of the origin and conception of the thing, one might tolerate the other. But, in illustration of the fact that they neither here nor in science, preserve this peaceful attitude, I quote from Mr. Hugo's "Lehrbuch der Geschichte des römischen Rechts."[4] In this work Mr. Hugo says (5th edition §53) that "Cicero praises the twelve tables with a side glance at philosophy," "but the philosopher Phavorinus treats them exactly as many a great philosopher since has treated positive right." Mr. Hugo makes the ultimate reply to such a method as that of Phavorinus, when he says of him that he "understood the twelve tables just as little as the philosophers understood positive right."—The correction of the philosopher Phavorinus by the jurist Sextus Cæcilius (Gellius, "Noct. Attic." xx. 1) expresses the lasting and true principle of the justification of that which is in its content merely positive. "Non ignoras," as Cæcilius felicitously remarks to Phavorinus, "legum opportunitates et medelas pro temporum moribus, et pro rerum publicarum generibus, ac pro utilitatum præsentium rationibus, proque vitiorum, quibus medendum est, fervoribus mutari ac flecti, neque uno statu consistere, quin, ut facies cœli et maris, ita rerum atque fortunæ tempestatibus varientur. Quid salubrius visum est rogatione illa Stolonis, etc., quid utilius plebiscito Voconio, etc., quid tam necessarium existimatum est, quam lex Licinia, etc.? Omnia tamen hæc obliterata et operta sunt civitatis opulentia," etc.—These laws are positive so far as they have meaning and appropriateness under the circumstances, and thus have only an historic value. For this reason they are in their nature transient. Whether the legislator or government was wise or not in what it did for its own immediate time and circumstances is a matter quite by itself and is for history to say. History will the more profoundly recognize the action of the legislator in proportion as its estimate receives support from the philosophic standpoint.—From the vindications of the twelve tables against the judgment of Phavorinus I shall give further examples, because in them Cæcilius furnishes an illustration of the fraud which is indissolubly bound up with the methods of the understanding and its reasonings. He adduces a good reason for a bad thing, and supposes that he has in that way justified the thing. Take the horrible law which permitted a creditor, after the lapse of a fixed term of respite, to kill a debtor or sell him into slavery. Nay, further, if there were

---

[4]"Text-book of the History of Roman Law."

several creditors, they were permitted to cut pieces off the debtor, and thus divide him amongst them, with the proviso that if any one of them should cut off too much or too little, no action should be taken against him. It was this clause, it may be noticed, which stood Shakespeare's Shylock in "The Merchant of Venice" in such good stead, and was by him most thankfully accepted. Well, for this law Cæcilius adduces the good argument that by it trust and credit were more firmly secured, and also that, by reason of the very horror of the law, it never had to be enforced. Not only does he in his want of thought fail to observe that by the severity of the law that very intention of securing trust and credit was defeated, but he forthwith himself gives an illustration of the way in which the disproportionate punishment caused the law to be inoperative, namely through the habit of giving false witness.—But the remark of Mr. Hugo that Phavorinus had not understood the law is not to be passed over. Now any school-boy can understand the law just quoted, and better than anyone else would Shylock have understood what was to him of such advantage. Hence, by "understand" Mr. Hugo must mean that form of understanding which consists in bringing to the support of a law a good reason.—Another failure to understand, asserted by Cæcilius of Phavorinus, a philosopher at any rate may without blushing acknowledge: *jumentum*, which without any *arcera* was the only legal way to bring a sick man into court as a witness, was held to mean not only a horse but also a carriage or wagon. Further on in this law Cæcilius found more evidence of the excellence and accuracy of the old statutes, which for the purpose of non-suiting a sick man at court distinguished not only between a horse and a wagon, but also, as Cæcilius explains, between a wagon covered and cushioned and one not so comfortably equipped. Thus one would have the choice between utter severity on one side, and on the other senseless details. But to exhibit fully the absurdity of these laws and the pedantic defence offered in their behalf would give rise to an invincible repugnance to all scholarship of that kind.

But in his manual Mr. Hugo speaks also of rationality in connection with Roman law, and I have been struck with the following remarks. He first of all treats of the epoch extending from the origin of the Republic to the twelve tables (§§38, 39), noticing that in Rome people had many wants, and were compelled in their labour to use draught animals and beasts of burden, as we ourselves do, and that the ground was an alternation of hill and valley, and that the city was set upon a hill, etc. These statements might, perhaps, have answered to the sense of Montesquieu's thought, though in them it would be well-nigh impossible to find his genius. But after these preliminary paragraphs, he goes on to say in §40, that the condition of the law was still very far from satisfying the highest demands of reason. This remark is wholly in place, as the Roman family-right, slavery, etc., give no satisfaction to the smallest demands of reason. Yet when discussing the succeeding epochs, Mr. Hugo forgets to tell us in what particulars, if any, the Roman law has satisfactorily met the highest demands of reason. Still of the classic jurists, who flourished in the era of the greatest expansion of Roman law as a science, it is said (§289) that "it has been long since been observed that the Roman jurists were educated in philosophy," but "few know" (more will know now through the numerous editions of Mr. Hugo's manual) "that there is no class of writers, who, as regards deduction from principles, deserved to be placed beside the mathematicians, and also, as regards the quite remarkable way in which they develop their conceptions, beside the modern founder of metaphysic; as voucher for this assertion is the notable fact that nowhere do so many trichotomies occur as in the classic jurists and in Kant." This form of logical reasoning, extolled by Leibnitz, is certainly an essential feature of the science of right, as it is of mathematics and every other intelligible science; but the logical procedure of the mere understanding, spoken of by Mr. Hugo, has nothing to do with the satisfaction of the claims of reason and with philosophic science. Moreover, the very lack of logical procedure, which is characteristic of the Roman jurists and prætors, is to be esteemed as one of their chief virtues, since by means of it they obviated the consequences of unrighteous and horrible institutions. Through their want of logic they were compelled *callide* to put sense into mere verbal distinctions, as they did when they identified *Bonorum possessio* with inheritance, and also into silly evasions, for silliness is a defect of logic, in order to save the letter of the tables, as was done in the *fictio* or ὑπόκρισις that a *filia patroni* was a *filius* (Heinecc. "Antiq. Rom.," lib. i. tit. ii. §24). But it is absurd to place the classic jurists, with their use of trichotomy, along with Kant, and in that way to discern in them the promise of the development of conceptions.

4. The territory of right is in general the spiritual, and its more definite place and origin is the will, which is free. Thus freedom constitutes the substance and essential character of the will, and the system of right is the kingdom of actualized freedom. It is the world of spirit, which is produced out of itself, and is a second nature.

Addition.—Freedom of will is best explained by reference to physical nature. Freedom is a fundamental phase of will, as weight is of bodies. When it is said that matter is heavy, it might be meant that the predicate is an accident; but such is not the case, for in matter there is nothing which has not weight; in fact, matter is weight. That which is heavy constitutes the body, and is the body. Just so is it with freedom and the will; that which is free is the will. Will without freedom is an empty word, and freedom becomes actual only as will, as subject. A remark may also be made as to the connection of willing and thinking. Spirit, in general, is thought, and by thought man is distinguished from the animal. But we must not imagine that man is on one side thinking and on another side willing, as though he had will in one pocket and thought in another. Such an idea is vain. The distinction between thought and will is only that between a theoretical and a practical relation. They are not two separate faculties. The will is a special way of thinking; it is thought translating itself into reality; it is the impulse of thought to give itself reality. The distinction between thought and will may be expressed in this way. When I think an object, I make of it a thought, and take from it the sensible. Thus I make of it something which is essentially and directly mine. Only in thought am I self-contained. Conception is the penetration of the object, which is then no longer opposed to me. From it I have taken its own peculiar nature, which it had as an independent object in opposition to me. As Adam said to Eve, "thou art flesh of my flesh and bone of my bone," so says the spirit, "This object is spirit of my spirit, and all alienation has disappeared." Any idea is a universalizing, and this process belongs to thinking. To make something universal is to think. The "I" is thought and the universal. When I say "I," I let fall all particularity of character, natural endowment, knowledge, age. The I is empty, a point and simple, but in its simplicity active. The gaily coloured world is before me; I stand opposed to it, and in this relation I cancel and transcend the opposition, and make the content my own. The I is at home in the world, when it knows it, and still more when it has conceived it.

So much for the theoretical relation. The practical, on the other hand, begins with thinking, with the I itself. It thus appears first of all as placed in opposition, because it exhibits, as it were, a separation. As I am practical, I am active; I act and determine myself; and to determine myself means to set up a distinction. But these distinctions are again mine, my own determinations come to me; and the ends are mine, to which I am impelled. Even when I let these distinctions and determinations go, setting them in the so-called external world, they remain mine. They are that which I have done and made, and bear the trace of my spirit. That is the distinction to be drawn between the theoretical and the practical relations.

And now the connection of the two must be also stated. The theoretical is essentially contained in the practical. Against the idea that the two are separate runs the fact that man has no will without intelligence. The will holds within itself the theoretical, the will determines itself, and this determination is in the first instance internal. That which I will I place before my mind, and it is an object for me. The animal acts according to instinct, is impelled by something internal, and so is also practical. But it has no will, because it cannot place before its mind what it desires. Similarly man cannot use his theoretic faculty or think without will, for in thinking we are active. The content of what is thought receives, indeed, the form of something existing, but this existence is occasioned by our activity and by it established. These distinctions of theoretical and practical are inseparable; they are one and the same; and in every activity, whether of thought or will, both these elements are found.

It is worth while to recall the older way of proceeding with regard to the freedom of the will. First of all, the idea of the will was assumed, and then an effort was made to deduce from it and establish a definition of the will. Next, the method of the older empirical psychology was adopted, and different perceptions and general phenomena of the ordinary consciousness were collected, such as remorse, guilt, and the like, on the ground that these could be explained only as proceeding out of a will that is free. Then from these phenomena was deduced the so-called proof that the will is free. But it is more convenient to take a short cut and hold that freedom is given as a fact of consciousness, and must be believed in.

The nature of the will and of freedom, and the proof that the will is free, can be shown, as has already been observed (§2), only in connection with the whole. The ground principles of the premises—that spirit is in the first instance intelligence, and that the phases, through which it passes in its development, namely from feeling, through imaginative thinking to thought, are the way by which it produces itself as will, which, in turn, as the practical spirit in general, is the most direct truth of intelligence— I have presented in my "Encyclopædia of the Philosophical Sciences" (Heidelberg, 1817), and hope some day to be able to give of them a more complete exposition. There is, to my mind, so much the more need for me to give my contribution to, as I hope, the more thorough knowledge of the nature of spirit, since, as I have there said, it would be difficult to find a philosophic science in a more neglected and evil plight than is that theory of spirit, which is commonly called psychology.—Some elements of the conception of will, resulting from the premises enumerated above are mentioned in this and the following paragraphs. As to these, appeal may moreover be made to every individual to see them in his own self-consciousness. Everyone will, in the first place, find in himself the ability to abstract himself from all that he is, and in this way prove himself able of himself to set every content within himself, and thus have in his own consciousness an illustration of all the subsequent phases.

5. The will contains (a) the element of pure indeterminateness, *i.e.,* the pure doubling of the I back in thought upon itself. In this process every limit or content, present though it be directly by way of nature, as in want, appetite or impulse, or given in any specific way, is dissolved. Thus we have the limitless infinitude of absolute abstraction, or universality, the pure thought of itself.

Note.—Those who treat thinking and willing as two special, peculiar, and separate faculties, and, further, look upon thought as detrimental to the will, especially the good will, show from the very start that they know nothing of the nature of willing—a remark which we shall be called upon to make a number of times upon the same attitude of mind.—The will on one side is the possibility of abstraction from every aspect in which the I finds itself or has set itself up. It reckons any content as a limit, and flees from it. This is one of the forms of the self-direction of the will, and is by imaginative thinking insisted upon as of itself freedom. It is the negative side of the will, or freedom as apprehended by the understanding. This freedom is that of the void, which has taken actual shape, and is stirred to passion. It, while remaining purely theoretical, appears in Hindu religion as the fanaticism of pure contemplation; but becoming actual it assumes both in politics and religion the form of a fanaticism, which would destroy the established social order, remove all individuals suspected of desiring any kind of order, and demolish any organization which then sought to rise out of the ruins. Only in devastation does the negative will feel that it has reality. It intends, indeed, to bring to pass some positive social condition, such as universal equality or universal religious life. But in fact it does not will the positive reality of any such condition, since that would carry in its train a system, and introduce a separation by way of institutions and between individuals. But classification and objective system attain self-consciousness only by destroying negative freedom. Negative freedom is actuated by a mere solitary abstract idea, whose realization is nothing but the fury of desolation.

Addition.—This phase of will implies that I break loose from everything, give up all ends, and bury myself in abstraction. It is man alone who can let go everything, even life. He can commit suicide, an act impossible for the animal, which always remains only negative, abiding in a state foreign to itself, to which it must merely get accustomed. Man is pure thought of himself, and only in thinking has he the power to give himself universality and to extinguish in himself all that is particular and definite. Negative freedom, or freedom of the understanding, is one-sided, yet as this one-sidedness contains an essential feature, it is not to be discarded. But the defect of the understanding is that it exalts its one-sidedness to the sole and highest place. This form of freedom frequently occurs in history. By the Hindus, *e.g.*, the highest freedom is declared to be persistence in the consciousness of one's simple identity with himself, to abide in the empty space of one's own inner being, like the colourless light of pure intuition, and to renounce every activity of life, every purpose and every idea. In this way man becomes Brahma; there is no longer any distinction between finite man and Brahma, every difference having been swallowed up in this universality. A more concrete manifestation of this freedom is the fanaticism of political and religious life. Of this nature was the terrible epoch of the French Revolution, by which all distinctions in talent and authority were to have been superseded. In this time of upheaval and commotion any specific thing was intolerable. Fanaticism wills an abstraction and not an articulate association. It finds all distinctions antagonistic to its indefiniteness, and supersedes them. Hence in the French Revolution the people abolished the institutions which they themselves had set up, since every institution is inimical to the abstract self-consciousness of equality.

6. (β) The I is also the transition from blank indefiniteness to the distinct and definite establishment of a definite content and object, whether this content be given by nature or produced out of the conception of spirit. Through this establishment of itself as a definite thing the I becomes a reality. This is the absolute element of the finitude or specialization of the I.

Note. This second element in the characterization of the I is just as negative as the first, since it annuls and replaces the first abstract negativity. As the particular is contained in the universal, so this second phase is contained already in the first, and is only an establishing of what the first is implicitly. The first phase, if taken independently, is not the true infinitude, *i.e.,* the concrete universal, or the conception, but limited and one-sided. In that it is the abstraction from all definite character, it has a definite character. Its abstract and one-sided nature constitutes its definite character, its defect and finitude.

The distinct characterization of these two phases of the I is found in the philosophy of Fichte as also in that of Kant. Only, in the exposition of Fichte the I, when taken as unlimited, as it is in the first proposition of his "Wissenschaftslehre," is merely positive. It is the universality and identity made by the understanding. Hence this abstract I is in its independence to be taken as the truth, to which by way of mere addition comes in the second proposition, the limitation, or the negative in general, whether it be in the form of a given external limit or of an activity of the I.—To apprehend the negative as immanent in the universal or self-identical, and also as in the I, was the next step, which speculative philosophy had to make. Of this want they have no presentiment, who like Fichte never apprehend that the infinite and finite are, if separated, abstract, and must be seen as immanent one in the other.

Addition.—This second element makes its appearance as the opposite of the first; it is to be understood in its general form: it belongs to freedom but does not constitute the whole of it. Here the I passes over from blank indeterminateness to the distinct establishment of a specific character as a content or object. I do not will merely, but I will something. Such a will, as is analysed in the preceding paragraph, wills only the abstract universal, and therefore wills nothing. Hence it is not a will. The particular thing, which the will wills is a limitation, since the will, in order to be a will, must in general limit itself. Limit or negation consists in the will willing something. Particularizing is thus as a rule named finitude. Ordinary reflection holds the first element, that of the indefinite, for the absolute and higher, and the limited for a mere negation of this indefiniteness. But this indefiniteness is itself only a negation, in contrast with the definite and finite. The I is solitude and absolute negation. The indefinite will is thus quite as much one-sided as the will, which continues merely in the definite.

7. (γ) The will is the unity of these two elements. It is particularity turned back within itself and thus led back to universality; it is individuality; it is the self-direction of the I. Thus at one and the same time it establishes itself as its own negation, that is to say, as definite and limited, and it also abides by itself, in its self-identity and universality, and in this position remains purely self-enclosed.—The I determines itself in so far as it is the reference of negativity to itself; and yet in this self-reference it is indifferent to its own definite character. This it knows as its own, that is, as an ideal or a mere possibility, by which it is not bound, but rather exists in it merely because it establishes itself there.—This is the freedom of the will, constituting its conception or substantive reality. It is its gravity, as it were, just as gravity is the substantive reality of a body.

Note.—Every self-consciousness knows itself as at once universal, or the possibility of abstracting itself from everything definite, and as particular, with a fixed object, content or aim. These two elements, however, are only abstractions. The concrete and true,—and all that is true is concrete,—is the universality, to which the particular is at first opposed, but, when it has been turned back into itself, is in the end made equal.— This unity is individuality, but it is not a simple unit as is the individuality of imaginative thought, but a unit in terms of the conception ("Encyclopædia of the Philosophical Sciences," §§112–114). In other words, this individuality is properly nothing else than the conception. The first two elements of the will, that it can abstract itself from everything, and that it is definite through either its own activity or something else, are easily admitted and comprehended, because in their separation they are untrue, and characteristic of the mere understanding. But into the third, the true and speculative—and all truth, as far as it is conceived, must be thought speculatively—the understanding declines to venture, always calling the conception the inconceivable. The proof and more detailed explanation of this inmost reserve of speculation, of infinitude as the negativity which refers itself to itself, and of this ultimate source of all activity, life and consciousness, belong to logic, as the purely speculative philosophy. Here it can be noticed only in passing that, in the sentences, "The will is universal," "The will directs itself," the will is already regarded as presupposed subject or substratum; but it is not something finished and universal before it determines itself, nor yet before this determination is superseded and idealized. It is will only when its activity is self-occasioned, and it has returned into itself.

Addition.—What we properly call will contains the two above-mentioned elements. The I is, first of all, as such, pure activity, the universal which is by itself. Next this universal determines itself, and so far is no longer by itself, but establishes itself as another, and ceases to be the universal. The third step is that the will, while in this limitation, *i.e.,* in this other, is by itself. While it limits itself, it yet remains with itself, and does not lose its hold of the universal. This is, then, the concrete conception of freedom, while the other two elements have been thoroughly abstract and one-sided. But this concrete freedom we already have in the form of perception, as in friendship and love. Here a man is not one-sided, but limits himself willingly in reference to another, and yet in this limitation knows himself as himself. In this determination he does not feel himself determined, but in the contemplation of the other as another has the feeling of himself. Freedom also lies neither in indeterminateness nor in determinateness, but in both. The wilful man has a will which limits itself wholly to a particular object, and if he has not this will, he supposes himself not to be free. But the will is not bound to a particular object, but must go further, for the nature of the will is not to be one-sided and confined. Free will consists in willing a definite object, but in so doing to be by itself and to return again into the universal.

8. If we define this particularizing (β §6) further, we reach a distinction in the forms of the will. (*a*) In so far as the definite character of the will consists in the formal opposition of the subjective to the objective or external direct existence, we have the formal will as a self consciousness, which finds an outer world before it. The process by which individuality turns back in its definiteness into itself, is the translation of the subjective end, through the intervention of an activity and a means, into objectivity. In the absolute spirit, in which all definite character is thoroughly its own and true ("Encyclop." §363), consciousness is only one side, namely, the manifestation or appearance of the will, a phase which does not require detailed consideration here.

Addition.—The consideration of the definite nature of the will belongs to the understanding, and is not in the first instance speculative. The will as a whole, not only in the sense of its content, but also in the sense of its form, is determined. Determinate character on the side of form is the end, and the execution of the end. The end is at first merely something internal to me and subjective, but it is to be also objective and to cast away the defect of mere subjectivity. It may be asked, why it has this defect. When that which is deficient does not at the same time transcend its defect, the defect is for it not a defect at all. The animal is to us defective, but not for itself. The end, in so far as it is at first merely ours, is for us a defect, since freedom and will are for us the unity of subjective and objective. The end must also be established as objective; but does not in that way attain a new one-sided character, but rather its realization.

9 (*b*). In so far as the definite phases of will are its own peculiar property or its particularization turned back into itself, they are content. This content, as content of the will, is for it, by virtue of the form given in (*a*), an end, which exists on its inner or subjective side as the imaginative will, but by the operation of the activity, which converts the subjective into the objective, it is realized, completed end.

10. The content or determinate phase of will is in the first instance direct or immediate. Then the will is free only in itself or for us, *i.e.,* it is the will in its conception. Only when it has itself as an object is it also for itself, and its implicit freedom becomes realized.

Note.—At this standpoint the finite implies that whatever is in itself, or according to its conception, has an existence or manifestation different from what it is for itself. For example the abstract separateness of nature is in itself space, but for itself time. Here, two things are to be observed, (1) that because the truth is the idea, when any object or phase is apprehended only as it is in itself or in conception, it is not as yet apprehended in its truth, and yet (2) that, whatever exists as conception or in itself, at the same time exists, and this existence is a peculiar form of the object, as *e.g.* space. The separation of existence-in-itself or implicit existence from existence-for-itself or explicit existence is a characteristic of the finite, and constitutes its appearance or merely external reality. An example of this is to hand in the separation of the natural will from formal right. The understanding adheres to mere implicit existence, and in accordance with this position calls freedom a capacity, since it is at this point only a possibility. But the understanding regards this phase as absolute and perennial, and considers the relation of the will to what it wills or reality as an application to a given material, which does not belong to the essence of freedom. In this way the understanding occupies itself with mere abstractions, and not with the idea and truth.

Addition.—The will, which is will only according to the conception, is free implicitly, but is at the same time not free. To be truly free, it must have a truly fixed content; then it is explicitly free, has freedom for its object, and is freedom. What is at first merely in conception, *i.e.,* implicit, is only direct and natural. We are familiar with this in pictorial thought also. The child is implicitly a man, at first has reason implicitly, and is at first the possibility of reason and freedom. He is thus free merely according to the conception. That which is only implicit does not yet exist in actuality. A man, who is implicitly rational, must create himself by working through and out of himself and by reconstructing himself within himself, before he can become also explicitly rational.

11. The will, which is at first only implicitly free, is the direct or natural will. The distinctive phases, which the self-determining conception sets up in the will, appear in the direct will, as a directly present content. They are impulses, appetites, inclinations, by which the will finds itself determined by nature. Now this content, with all its attendant phases, proceeds from the rationality of the will, and is therefore implicitly rational; but let loose in its immediate directness it has not as yet the form of rationality. The content is indeed for me and my own, but the form and the content are yet different. The will is thus in itself finite.

Note.—Empirical psychology enumerates and describes these impulses and inclinations, and the wants which are based upon them. It takes, or imagines that it takes this material from experience, and then seeks to classify it in the usual way. It will be stated below, what the objective side of impulse is, and what impulse is in its truth, apart from the form of irrationality which it has as an impulse, and also what shape it assumes when it reaches existence.

Addition.—Impulse, appetite, inclination are possessed by the animal also, but it has not will; it must obey impulse, if there is no external obstacle. Man, however, is the completely undetermined, and stands above impulse, and may fix and set it up as his. Impulse is in nature, but it depends on my will whether I establish it in the I. Nor can the will be unconditionally called to this action by the fact that the impulse lies in nature.

12. The system of this content, as it occurs directly in the will, exists only as a multitude or multiplicity of impulses, every one of which is mine in a general way along with others, but is at the same time universal and undetermined, having many objects and ways of satisfaction. The will, by giving itself in this two-fold indefiniteness the form of individuality (§7), resolves, and only as resolving is it actual.

Note.—Instead of to "resolve," *i.e.* to supersede the indefinite condition in which a content is merely possible, our language has the expression "decide" ("unfold itself"). The indeterminate condition of the will, as neutral but infinitely fruitful germ of all existence, contains within itself its definite character and ends, and brings them forth solely out of itself.

13. By resolution will fixes itself as the will of a definite individual, and as thereby distinguishing itself from another. However apart from this finite character which it has as consciousness (§8), the immediate will is in virtue of the distinction between its form and its content formal. Hence

its resolution as such is abstract, and its content is not yet the content and work of its freedom.

Note.—To the intelligence, as thinking, the object or content remains universal; the intelligence retains the form merely of a universal activity. Now the universal signifies in will that which is mine, *i.e.* it is individuality. And yet, also, the direct and formal will is abstract; its individuality is not yet filled with its free universality. Hence at the beginning the peculiar finitude of the intelligence is in will, and only by exalting itself again to thought and giving itself intrinsic universality does the will transcend the distinction of form and content and make itself objective infinite will. It is therefore a misunderstanding of the nature of thought and will to suppose that in the will man is infinite, while in thought and even in reason he is limited. In so far as thought and will are still distinct, the reverse is rather the case, and thinking reason, when it becomes will, assigns itself to finitude.

Addition.—A will which resolves nothing, is not an actual will; that which is devoid of definite character never reaches a volition. The reason for hesitation may lie in a sensitiveness, which is aware that in determining itself it is engaged with what is finite, is assigning itself a limit, and abandoning its infinity; it may thus hold to its decision not to renounce the totality which it intends. Such a feeling is dead, even when it aims to be something beautiful. "Who will be great," says Goethe, "must be able to limit himself." By volition alone man enters actuality, however distasteful it may be to him; for indolence will not desert its own self-brooding, in which it clings to a universal possibility. But possibility is not yet actuality. Hence the will, which is secure simply of itself, does not as yet lose itself in any definite reality.

14. The finite will, which has merely from the standpoint of form doubled itself back upon itself, and has become the infinite and self-secluded I (§5), stands above its content of different impulses and also above the several ways by which they are realized and satisfied. At the same time, as it is only formally infinite, it is confined to this very content as the decisive feature of its nature and external actuality, although it is undetermined and not confined to one content rather than another (§§6, 11). As to the return of the I into itself such a will is only a possible will, which may or may not be mine, and the I is only the possibility of deputing itself to this or that object. Hence amongst these definite phases, which in this light are for the I external, the will chooses.

15. Freedom of the will is in this view of it caprice, in which are contained both a reflection, which is free and abstracted from everything, and a dependence upon a content or matter either internally or externally provided. Since the content is in itself or implicitly necessary as an end,

and in opposition to this reflection is a definite possibility, caprice, when it is will, is in its nature contingent.

Note.—The usual idea of freedom is that of caprice. It is a midway stage of reflection between the will as merely natural impulse and the will as free absolutely. When it is said that freedom as a general thing consists in doing what one likes, such an idea must be taken to imply an utter lack of developed thought, containing as yet not even a suspicion of what is meant by the absolutely free will, right, the ethical system, etc. Reflection, being the formal universality and unity of self-consciousness, is the will's abstract certitude of its freedom, but it is not yet the truth of it, because it has not as yet itself for content and end; the subjective side is still different from the objective. Thus the content in such a case remains purely and completely finite. Caprice, instead of being will in its truth, is rather will in its contradiction.

In the controversy carried on, especially at the time of the metaphysic of Wolf, as to whether the will is really free, or our consciousness of its freedom is a delusion, it was this caprice which was in the minds of both parties. Against the certitude of abstract self-direction, determinism rightly opposed a content, which was externally presented, and not being contained in this certitude came from without. It did not matter whether this "without" were impulse, imagination, or in general a consciousness so filled that the content was not the peculiar possession of the self-determining activity as such. Since only the formal element of free self-direction is immanent in caprice, while the other element is something given to it from without, to take caprice as freedom may fairly be named a delusion. Freedom in every philosophy of reflection, whether it be the Kantian or the Friesian, which is the Kantian superficialized, is nothing more than this formal self-activity.

Addition.—Since I have the possibility of determining myself in this or that way, since I have the power of choice, I possess caprice, or what is commonly called freedom. This choice is due to the universality of the will, enabling me to make my own this thing or another. This possession is a particular content, which is therefore not adequate to me, but separated from me, and is mine only in possibility; just as I am the possibility of bringing myself into coincidence with it. Hence choice is due to the indeterminateness of the I, and to the determinateness of a content. But as to this content the will is not free, although it has in itself formally the side of infinitude. No such content corresponds to will; in no content can it truly find itself. In caprice it is involved that the content is not formed by the nature of my will, but by contingency. I am dependent upon this content. This is the contradiction contained in caprice. Ordinary man believes that he is free, when he is allowed to act capriciously, but precisely in caprice is it inherent that he is not free. When I will the rational, I do not act as a particular individual but according to the conception of ethical observance in general. In an ethical act I establish not myself but the thing. A man, who acts perversely, exhibits particularity. The rational is the highway on which every one travels, and no one is specially marked. When a great artist finishes a work we say: "It must be so." The particularity of the artist has wholly disappeared and the work shows no mannerism. Phidias has no mannerism; the statue itself lives and moves. But the poorer is the artist, the more easily we discern himself, his particularity and caprice. If we adhere to the consideration that in caprice a man can will what he pleases, we have certainly freedom of a kind; but again, if we hold to the view that the content is given, then man must be determined by it, and in this light is no longer free.

16. What is resolved upon and chosen (§14) the will may again give up (§5). Yet, even with the possibility of transcending any other content which it may substitute, and of proceeding in this way *ad infinitum,* the will does not advance beyond finitude, because every content in turn is different from the form and is finite. The opposite aspect, namely indeterminateness, irresolution or abstraction, is also one-sided.

17. Since the contradiction involved in caprice (§15) is the dialectic of the impulses and inclinations, it is manifested in their mutual antagonism. The satisfaction of one demands the subjection and sacrifice of the satisfaction of another. Since an impulse is merely the simple tendency of its own essential nature, and has no measure in itself, to subject or sacrifice the satisfaction of any impulse is a contingent decision of caprice. In such a case caprice may act upon the calculation as to which impulse will bring the greater satisfaction, or may have some other similar purpose.

Addition.—Impulses and inclinations are in the first instance the content of will, and only reflection transcends them. But these impulses are self-directing, crowding upon and jostling one another, and all seeking to be satisfied. To set all but one in the background, and put myself into this one, is to limit and distort myself, since I, in so doing, renounce my universality, which is a system of all the impulses. Just as little help is found in a mere subordination of them, a course usually followed by the understanding. There is available no criterion by which to make such an arrangement, and hence the demand for a subordination is usually sustained by tedious and irrelevant allusions to general sayings.

18. With regard to the moral estimate of impulses, dialectic appears in this form. The phases of the direct or natural will are immanent and positive, and thus good. Hence man is by nature good. But natural characteristics, since they are opposed to freedom and the conception of the spirit, and are, hence, negative, must be eradicated. Thus man is by nature evil. To decide for either view is a matter of subjective caprice.

Addition.—The Christian doctrine that man is by nature evil is loftier than the opposite that he is naturally good, and is to be interpreted philosophically in this way. Man as spirit is a free being, who need not give way to impulse. Hence in his direct and unformed condition, man is in a situation in which he ought not to be, and he must free himself. This is the meaning of the doctrine of original sin, without which Christianity would not be the religion of freedom.

19. In the demand that impulses must be purified is found the general idea that they must be freed from the form of direct subjection to nature, and from a content that is subjective and contingent, and must be restored to their substantive essence. The truth contained in this indefinite demand is that impulses should be phases of will in a rational system. To apprehend them in this way as proceeding from the conception is the content of the science of right.

Note.—The content of this science may, in all its several elements, right, property, morality, family, state, be represented in this way, that man has by nature the impulse to right, the impulse to property, to morality, to sexual love, and to social life. If instead of this form, which belongs to empirical psychology, a philosophic form be preferred, it may be obtained cheap from what in modern times was reputed and still is reputed to be philosophy. He will then say that man finds in himself as a fact of consciousness that he wills right, property, the state, etc. Later will be given still another form of the content which appears here in the shape of impulses, that, namely, of duties.

20. The reflection which is brought to bear upon impulses, placing them before itself, estimating them, comparing them with one another, and contrasting them with their means and consequences, and also with a whole of satisfaction, namely happiness, brings the formal universal to this material, and in an external way purifies it of its crudity and barbarism. This propulsion by the universality of thought is the absolute worth of civilization (§187).

Addition.—In happiness thought has already the upper hand with the force of natural impulse, since it is not satisfied with what is momentary, but requires happiness as a whole. This happiness is dependent upon civilization to the extent to which civilization confirms the universal. But in the ideal of happiness there are two elements. There is (1) a universal that is higher than all particulars; yet, as the content of this universal is in turn only universal pleasure, there arises once more the individual, particular and finite, and retreat must be made to impulse; (2) Since the content of happiness lies in the subjective perception of each individual, this universal end is again particular; nor is there present in it any true unity of content and form.

21. But the truth of this formal universality, which taken by itself is

undetermined and finds definite character in externally given material, is the self-directing universality which is will or freedom. Since the will has as its object, content and end, universality itself, and thus assumes the form of the infinite, it is free not only in itself or implicitly, but for itself or explicitly. It is the true idea.

Note.—The self-consciousness of the will in the form of appetite or impulse is sensible, the sensible in general indicating the externality of self-consciousness, or that condition in which self-consciousness is outside of itself. Now this sensible side is one of the two elements of the reflecting will, and the other is the abstract universality of thought. But the absolute will has as its object the will itself as such in its pure universality. In this universality the directness of the natural will is superseded, and so also is the private individuality which is produced by reflection and infects the natural condition. But to supersede these and lift them into the universal, constitutes the activity of thought. Thus the self-consciousness, which purifies its object, content or end, and exalts it to universality, is thought carrying itself through into will. It is at this point that it becomes clear that the will is true and free only as thinking intelligence. The slave knows not his essence, his infinitude, his freedom; he does not know himself in his essence, and not to know himself is not to think himself. The self-consciousness, which by thought apprehends that itself is essence, and thus puts away from itself the accidental and untrue, constitutes the principle of right, morality, and all forms of ethical observance. They who, in speaking philosophically of right, morality, and ethical observance, would exclude thought and turn to feeling, the heart, the breast, and inspiration, express the deepest contempt for thought and science. And science itself, overwhelmed with despair and utter insipidity, makes barbarism and absence of thought a principle, and so far as in it lay robbed men of all truth, dignity, and worth.

Addition.—In philosophy truth is had when the conception corresponds to reality. A body is the reality, and soul is the conception. Soul and body should be adequate to each other. A dead man is still an existence, but no longer a true existence; it is a reality void of conception. For that reason the dead body decays. So with the true will; that which it wills, namely, its content, is identical with it, and so freedom wills freedom.

22. The will which exists absolutely is truly infinite, because its object being the will itself, is for it not another or a limitation. In the object the will has simply reverted into itself. Moreover, it is not mere possibility, capacity, potentiality (*potentia*), but infinitely actual (*infinitum actu*), because the reality of the conception or its visible externality is internal to itself.

Note.—Hence when the free will is spoken of without the qualification of absolute freedom, only the capacity of freedom is meant, or the natural and finite will (§11), and, notwithstanding all words and opinions to the contrary, not the free will. Since the understanding comprehends the infinite only in its negative aspect, and hence as a beyond, it thinks to do the infinite all the more honour the farther it removes it into the vague distance, and the more it takes it as a foreign thing. In free will the true infinite is present and real; it is itself the actually present self-contained idea.

Addition.—The infinite has rightly been represented as a circle. The straight line goes out farther and farther, and symbolizes the merely negative and bad infinite, which, unlike the true, does not return into itself. The free will is truly infinite, for it is not a mere possibility or disposition. Its external reality is its own inner nature, itself.

23. Only in this freedom is the will wholly by itself, because it refers to nothing but itself, and all dependence upon any other thing falls away.—The will is true, or rather truth itself, because its character consists in its being in its manifested reality, or correlative opposite, what it is in its conception. In other words, the pure conception has the perception or intuition of itself as its end and reality.

24. The will is universal, because in it all limitation and particular individuality are superseded. These one-sided phases are found only in the difference between the conception and its object or content, or, from another standpoint, in the difference between the conscious independent existence of the subject, and the will's implicit, or self-involved existence, or between its excluding and concluding individuality, and its universality.

Note.—The different phases of universality are tabulated in the logic ("Encyclop. of the Phil. Sciences," §§118–126). Imaginative thinking always takes universality in an abstract and external way. But absolute universality is not to be thought of either as the universality of reflection, which is a kind of concensus or generality, or, as the abstract universality and self-identity, which is fashioned by the understanding (§6, *note)*, and keeps aloof from the individual. It is rather the concrete, self-contained, and self-referring universality, which is the substance, intrinsic genus, or immanent idea of self-consciousness. It is a conception of free will as the universal, transcending its object, passing through and beyond its own specific character, and then becoming identical with itself.—This absolute universal is what is in general called the rational, and is to be apprehended only in this speculative way.

25. The subjective side of the will is the side of its self-consciousness and individuality (§7), as distinguished from its implicit conception. This subjectivity is (α) pure form or absolute unity of self-consciousness with itself. This unity is the equation "I = I," consciousness being characterized by a thoroughly inward and abstract self-dependence. It is pure

certitude of itself in contrast with the truth; (β) particularity of will, as caprice with its accidental content of pleasurable ends; (γ) in general a one-sided form (§8), in so far as that which is willed is at first an unfulfilled end, or a content which simply belongs to self-consciousness.

26. (α) In so far as the will is determined by itself, and is in accord with its conception and true, it is wholly objective will. (β) But objective self-consciousness, which has not the form of the infinite, is a will sunk in its object or condition, whatever the content of that may be. It is the will of the child, or the will present in slavery or superstition, (γ) Objectivity is finally a one-sided form in opposition to the subjective phase of will; it is direct reality, or external existence. In this sense the will becomes objective only by the execution of its ends.

Note.—These logical phases of subjectivity and objectivity, since they are often made use of in the sequel, are here exposed, with the express purpose of noting that it happens with them as with other distinctions and opposed aspects of reflection; they by virtue of their finite and dialectic character pass over into their opposites. For imagination and understanding the meanings of antithetic phases are not convertible, because their identity is still internal. But in will, on the contrary, these phases, which ought to be at once abstract and yet also sides of that which can be known only as concrete, lead of themselves to identity, and to an exchange of meanings. To the understanding this is unintelligible.—Thus, *e.g.,* the will, as a freedom which exists in itself, is subjectivity itself; thus subjectivity is the conception of the will, and therefore its objectivity. But subjectivity is finite in opposition to objectivity, yet in this opposition the will is not isolated, but in intricate union with the object; and thus its finitude consists quite as much in its not being subjective, etc.—What in the sequel is to be meant by the subjective or the objective side of the will, has each time to be made clear from the context, which will supply their positions in relation to the totality.

Addition.—It is ordinarily supposed that subjective and objective are blank opposites; but this is not the case. Rather do they pass into one another, for they are not abstract aspects like positive and negative, but have already a concrete significance. To consider in the first instance the expression "subjective;" this may mean an end which is merely the end of a certain subject. In this sense a poor work of art, that is not adequate to the thing, is merely subjective. But, further, this expression may point to the content of the will, and is then of about the same meaning as capricious; the subjective content then is that which belongs merely to the subject. In this sense bad acts are merely subjective. Further, the pure, empty I may be called subjective, as it has only itself as an object, and possesses the power of abstraction from all further content. Subjectivity has, moreover, a wholly particular and correct meaning in accordance with which anything, in order to win recognition from me, has to become mine and seek validity in me. This is the infinite avarice of subjectivity, eager to comprehend and consume everything within the simple and pure I.

Similarly we may take the objective in different ways. By it we may understand anything to which we give existence in contrast to ourselves, whether it be an actual thing or a mere thought, which we place over against ourselves. By it also we understand the direct reality, in which the end is to be realized. Although the end itself is quite particular and subjective, we yet name it objective after it has made its appearance. Further, the objective will is also that in which truth is; thus, God's will, the ethical will also, are objective. Lastly, we may call the will objective, when it is wholly submerged in its object, as, *e.g.,* the child's will, which is confiding and without subjective freedom, and the slave's will, which does not know itself as free, and is thus a will-less will. In this sense any will is objective, if it is guided in its action by a foreign authority, and has not yet completed the infinite return into itself.

27. The absolute character or, if you like, the absolute impulse of the free spirit (§21) is, as has been observed, that its freedom shall be for it an object. It is to be objective in a two-fold sense: it is the rational system of itself, and this system is to be directly real (§26). There is thus actualized as idea what the will is implicitly. Hence, the abstract conception of the idea of the will is in general the free will which wills the free will.

28. The activity of the will, directed to the task of transcending the contradiction between subjectivity and objectivity, of transferring its end from subjectivity into objectivity, and yet while in objectivity of remaining with itself, is beyond the formal method of consciousness (§8), in which objectivity is only direct actuality. This activity is the essential development of the substantive content of the idea (§21). In this development the conception moulds the idea, which is in the first instance abstract, into the totality of a system. This totality as substantive is independent of the opposition between mere subjective end and its realization, and in both of these forms is the same.

29. That a reality is the realization of the free will, this is what is meant by a right. Right, therefore, is, in general, freedom as idea.

Note.—In the Kantian doctrine (Introduction to Kant's "Theory of Right"), now generally accepted, "the highest factor is a limitation of my freedom or caprice, in order that it may be able to subsist alongside of every other individual's caprice in accordance with a universal law." This doctrine contains only a negative phase, that of limitation. And besides, the positive phase, the universal law or so-called law of reason, consisting in the agreement of the caprice of one with that of another, goes beyond the well-known formal identity and the proposition of contradiction.

The definition of right, just quoted, contains the view which has especially since Rousseau spread widely. According to this view neither the absolute and rational will, nor the true spirit, but the will and spirit of the particular individual in their peculiar caprice, are the substantive and primary basis. When once this principle is accepted, the rational can announce itself only as limiting this freedom. Hence it is not an inherent rationality, but only a mere external and formal universal. This view is accordingly devoid of speculative thought, and is rejected by the philosophic conception. In the minds of men and in the actual world it has assumed a shape, whose horror is without a parallel, except in the shallowness of the thoughts upon which it was founded.

30. Right in general is something holy, because it is the embodiment of the absolute conception and self-conscious freedom. But the formalism of right, and after a while of duty also, is due to distinctions arising out of the development of the conception of freedom. In contrast with the more formal, abstract and limited right, there is that sphere or stage of the spirit, in which spirit has brought to definite actuality the further elements contained in the idea. This stage is the richer and more concrete; it is truly universal and has therefore a higher right.

Note.—Every step in the development of the idea of freedom has its peculiar right, because it is the embodiment of a phase of freedom. When morality and ethical observance are spoken of in opposition to right, only the first or formal right of the abstract personality is meant. Morality, ethical observance, a state-interest, are every one a special right, because each of these is a definite realization of freedom. They can come into collision only in so far as they occupy the same plane. If the moral standpoint of spirit were not also a right and one of the forms of freedom, it could not collide with the right of personality or any other right. A right contains the conception of freedom which is the highest phase of spirit, and in opposition to it any other kind of thing is lacking in real substance. Yet collision also implies a limit and a subordination of one phase to another. Only the right of the world-spirit is the unlimited absolute.

31. The scientific method by which the conception is self-evolved, and its phases self-developed and self-produced, is not first of all an assurance that certain relations are given from somewhere or other, and then the application to this foreign material of the universal. The true process is found in the logic, and here is presupposed.

Note.—The efficient or motive principle, which is not merely the analysis but the production of the several elements of the universal, I call dialectic. Dialectic is not that process in which an object or proposition, presented to feeling or the direct consciousness, is analyzed, entangled, taken hither and thither, until at last its contrary is derived. Such a merely negative method appears frequently in Plato. It may fix the opposite of any notion, or reveal the contradiction contained in it, as did the ancient scepticism, or it may in a feeble way consider an approximation to truth, or modern half-and-half attainment of it, as its goal. But the higher dialectic of the conception does not merely apprehend any phase as a limit and opposite, but produces out of this negative a positive content and result. Only by such a course is there development and inherent progress. Hence this dialectic is not the external agency of subjective thinking, but the private soul of the content, which unfolds its branches and fruit organically. Thought regards this development of the idea and of the peculiar activity of the reason of the idea as only subjective, but is on its side unable to make any addition. To consider anything rationally is not to bring reason to it from the outside, and work it up in this way, but to count it as itself reasonable. Here it is spirit in its freedom, the summit of self-conscious reason, which gives itself actuality, and produces itself as the existing world. The business of science is simply to bring the specific work of the reason, which is in the thing, to consciousness.

32. The phases of the development of the conception are themselves conceptions. And yet, because the conception is essentially the idea, they have the form of manifestations. Hence the sequence of the conceptions, which arise in this way, is at the same time a sequence of realizations, and are to be by science so considered.

Note.—In a speculative sense the way, in which a conception is manifested in reality, is identical with a definite phase of the conception. But it is noteworthy that, in the scientific development of the idea, the elements, which result in a further definite form, although preceding this result as phases of the conception, do not in the temporal development go before it as concrete realizations. Thus, as will be seen later, that stage of the idea which is the family presupposes phases of the conception, whose result it is. But that these internal presuppositions should be present in such visible realizations as right of property, contract, morality, etc., this is the other side of the process, which only in a highly developed civilization has attained to a specific realization of its elements.

Addition.—The idea must always go on determining itself within itself, since at the beginning it is only abstract conception. However, this initial abstract conception is never given up, but only becomes inwardly richer, the last phase being the richest. The earlier and merely implicit phases reach in this way free self-dependence, but in such a manner that the conception remains the soul which holds everything together, and only through a procedure immanent within itself arrives at its own distinctions. Hence the last phase falls again into a unity with the first, and it cannot be said that the conception ever comes to something new. Although the elements of the conception appear to have fallen apart when they enter reality, this is only a mere appearance. Its superficial character is revealed in the process, since all the particulars finally turn back again into the conception of the universal. The empirical sciences usually analyze what they find in pictorial ideas, and if the individual is successfully brought back to the general, the general property is then called the conception. But this is not our procedure. We desire only to observe how the conception determines itself, and compels us to keep at a distance everything of our own spinning and thinking. But what we get in this way is one series of thoughts and another series of realized forms. As to these two series, it may happen that the order of time of the actual manifestations is partly different from the order of the conception. Thus it cannot, *e.g.,* be said that property existed before the family, and yet, in spite of that it is discussed before the family is discussed. The question might also be raised here, Why do we not begin with the highest, *i.e.,* with concrete truth? The answer is, because we desire to see truth in the form of a result, and it is an essential part of the process to conceive the conception first of all as abstract. The actual series of realizations of the conception is thus for us in due course as follows, even although in actuality the order should be the same. Our process is this, that the abstract forms reveal themselves not as self-subsistent but as untrue.

Division of the Work

33. According to the stages in the development of the idea of the absolutely free will,

A. The will is direct or immediate; its conception is therefore abstract, *i.e.,* personality, and its embodied reality is a direct external thing. This is the sphere of abstract or formal right.

B. The will, passing out of external reality, turns back into itself. Its phase is subjective individuality, and it is contrasted with the universal. This universal is on its internal side the good, and on its external side a presented world, and these two sides are occasioned only by means of each other. In this sphere the idea is divided, and exists in separate elements. The right of the subjective will is in a relation of contrast to the right of the world, or the right of the idea. Here, however, the idea exists only implicitly. This is the sphere of morality.

C. The unity and truth of these two abstract elements. The thought idea of the good is realized both in the will turned back into itself, and also in the external world. Thus freedom exists as real substance, which is quite as much actuality and necessity as it is subjective will. The idea here is its absolutely universal existence, viz., ethical observance. This ethical substance is again,

a. Natural spirit; the family,

b. The civic community, or spirit in its dual existence and mere appearance,

c. The state, or freedom, which, while established in the free self-dependence of the particular will is also universal and objective. This actual and organic spirit (α) is the spirit of a nation, (β) is found in the relation to one another of national spirits, and (γ) passing through and beyond this relation is actualized and revealed in world history as the universal world-spirit, whose right is the highest.

Note.—It is to be found in the speculative logic, and here is presupposed, that a thing or content, which is established first of all according to its conception, or implicitly, has the form of direct existence. The conception, however, when it has the form of the conception is explicit, and no longer is a direct existence. So, too, the principle, upon which the division of this work proceeds, is presupposed. The divisions might be regarded as already settled by history, since the different stages must be viewed as elements in the development of the idea, and therefore as springing from the nature of the content itself. A philosophic division is not an external classification of any given material, such a classification as would be made according to one or several schemes picked up at random, but the inherent distinctions of the conception itself. Morality and ethical observance, which are usually supposed to mean the same thing, are here taken in essentially different meanings. Meanwhile even imaginative thought seems to make a distinction between them. In the usage of Kant the preference is given to the term morality, and the practical principles of his philosophy limit themselves wholly to this standpoint, making impossible the standpoint of ethical observance, and indeed expressly destroying and abolishing it. Although morality and ethics have the same meaning according to their etymology, yet these different words may be used for different conceptions.

Addition.—When we speak of right, we mean not only civil right, which is the usual significance of the word, but also morality, ethical observance and world-history. These belong to this realm, because the conception taking them in their truth, brings them all together. Free will, in order not to remain abstract, must in the first instance give itself reality; the sensible materials of this reality are objects, *i.e.,* external things. This first phase of freedom we shall know as property. This is the sphere of formal and abstract right, to which belong property in the more developed form of contract and also the injury of right, *i.e.,* crime and punishment. The freedom, we have here, we name person, or, in other words, the subject who is free, and indeed free independently, and gives himself a reality in things. But this direct reality is not adequate to freedom, and the negation of this phase is morality. In morality I am beyond the freedom found directly in this thing, and have a freedom in which this directness is superseded. I am free in myself, *i.e.,* in the subjective. In this sphere we come upon my insight, intention, and end, and externality is established as indifferent. The good is now the universal end, which is not to remain merely internal to me, but to realize itself. The subjective will demands that its inward character, or purpose, shall receive external reality, and also that the good shall be brought to completion in external existence. Morality, like formal right, is also an abstraction, whose truth is reached only in ethical observance. Hence ethical observance is the unity of the will in its conception with the will of the individual or subject. The primary reality of ethical observance is in its turn natural, taking the form of love and feeling. This is the family. In it the individual has transcended his prudish personality, and finds himself with his consciousness in a totality. In the next stage is seen the loss of this peculiar ethical existence and substantive unity. Here the family falls asunder, and the members become independent one of another, being now held together merely by the bond of mutual need. This is the stage of the civic community, which has frequently been taken for the state. But the state does not arise until we reach the third stage, that stage of ethical observance or spirit, in which both individual independence and universal substantivity are found in gigantic union. The right of the state is, therefore, higher than that of the other stages. It is freedom in its most concrete embodiment, which yields to nothing but the highest absolute truth of the world-spirit.

FIRST PART
ABSTRACT RIGHT

34. The completely free will, when it is conceived abstractly, is in a condition of self-involved simplicity. What actuality it has when taken in this abstract way, consists in a negative attitude towards reality, and a bare abstract reference of itself to itself. Such an abstract will is the individual will of a subject. It, as particular, has definite ends, and, as exclusive and individual, has these ends before itself as an externally and directly presented world.

Addition.—The remark that the completely free will, when it is taken abstractly, is in a condition of self-involved simplicity must be understood in this way. The completed idea of the will is found when the conception has realized itself fully, and in such a manner that the embodiment of the conception is nothing but the development of the conception itself. But at the outset the conception is abstract. All its future characters are implied in it, it is true, but as yet no more than implied. They are, in other words, potential, and are not yet developed into an articulate whole. If I say, "I am free," the I, here, is still implicit and has no real object opposed to it. But from the standpoint of morality as contrasted with abstract right there is opposition, because there I am a particular will, while the good, though within me, is the universal. Hence, at that stage, the will contains within itself the contrast between particular and universal, and in that way is made definite. But at the beginning such a distinction does not occur, because in the first abstract unity there is as yet no progress or modification of any kind. That is what is meant by saying that the will has the mark of self-involved simplicity or immediate being. The chief thing to notice at this point is that this very absence of definite features is itself a definite feature. Absence of determinate character exists where there is as yet no distinction between the will and its content. But when this lack of definiteness is set in opposition to the definite, it becomes itself something definite. In other words, abstract identity becomes the distinguishing feature of the will, and the will thereby becomes an individual will or person.

1

35. This consciously free will has a universal side, which consists in a formal, simple and pure reference to itself as a separate and independent unit. This reference is also a self-conscious one though it has no further content. The subject is thus so far a person. It is implied in personality that I, as a distinct being, am on all sides completely bounded and limited, on the side of inner caprice, impulse and appetite, as well as in my direct and visible outer life. But it is implied likewise that I stand in absolutely pure relation to myself. Hence it is that in this finitude I know myself as infinite, universal and free.

Note.—Personality does not arise till the subject has not merely a general consciousness of himself in some determinate mode of concrete existence, but rather a consciousness of himself as a completely abstract I, in which all concrete limits and values are negated and declared invalid. Hence personality involves the knowledge of oneself as an object, raised, however, by thought into the realm of pure infinitude, a realm, that is, in which it is purely identical with itself. Individuals and peoples have no personality, if they have not reached this pure thought and self-consciousness. In this way, too, the absolute or completed mind or spirit may be distinguished from its mere semblance. The semblance, though self-conscious, is aware of itself only as a merely natural will with its external objects. The other, as an abstract and pure I, has itself as its end and object, and is therefore a person.

Addition.—The abstract will, the will which exists for itself, is a person. The highest aim of man is to be a person, and yet again the mere abstraction "person" is not held in high esteem. Person is essentially different from subject. Subject is only the possibility of personality. Any living thing at all is a subject, while person is a subject which has its subjectivity as an object. As a person I exist for myself. Personality is the free being in pure self-conscious isolation. I as a person am conscious of freedom. I can abstract myself from everything, since nothing is before me except pure personality. Notwithstanding all this I am as a particular person completely limited. I am of a certain age, height, in this space, and so on. Thus a person is at one and the same time so exalted and so lowly a thing. In him is the unity of infinite and finite, of limit and unlimited. The dignity of personality can sustain a contradiction, which neither contains nor could tolerate anything natural.

36. (1) Personality implies, in general, a capacity to possess rights, and constitutes the conception and abstract basis of abstract right. This right, being abstract, must be formal also. Its mandate is: Be a person and respect others as persons.

37. (2) The particularity of the will, that phase of the will, namely, which implies a consciousness of my specific interests, is doubtless an element of the whole consciousness of the will (§34), but it is not con-

tained in mere abstract personality. It is indeed present in the form of appetite, want, impulse and random desire, but is distinct as yet from the personality, which is the essence of freedom.—In treating of formal right therefore, we do not trench upon special interests, such as my advantage or my well-being, nor have we here to do with any special reason or intention of the will.

Addition.—Since the particular phases of the person have not as yet attained the form of freedom, everything relating to these elements is so far a matter of indifference. When anyone bases a claim upon his mere formal right, he may be wholly selfish, and often such a claim comes from a contracted heart and mind. Uncivilized man, in general, holds fast to his rights, while a more generous disposition is alert to see all sides of the question. Abstract right is, moreover, the first mere possibility, and in contrast with the whole context of a given relation is still formal. The possession of a right gives a certain authority, it is true, but it is not, therefore, absolutely necessary that I insist upon a right, which is only one aspect of the whole matter. In a word, possibility is something, which means that it either may or may not exist.

38. In contrast with the deeper significance of a concrete act in all its moral and social bearings, abstract right is only a possibility. Such a right is, therefore, only a permission or indication of legal power. Because of this abstract character of right the only rule which is unconditionally its own is merely the negative principle not to injure personality or anything which of necessity belongs to it. Hence we have here only prohibitions, the positive form of command having in the last resort a prohibition as its basis.

39. (3) A person in his direct and definite individuality is related to a given external nature. To this outer world the personality is opposed as something subjective. But to confine to mere subjectivity the personality, which is meant to be infinite and universal, contradicts and destroys its nature. It bestirs itself to abrogate the limitation by giving itself reality, and proceeds to make the outer visible existence its own.

40. Right is at first the simple and direct concrete existence which freedom gives itself directly. This unmodified existence is

(*a*) Possession or property. Here freedom is that of the abstract will in general, or of a separate person who relates himself only to himself.

(*b*) A person by distinguishing himself from himself becomes related to another person, although the two have no fixed existence for each other except as owners. Their implicit identity becomes realized through a transference of property by mutual consent, and with the preservation of their rights. This is contract.

(*c*) The will in its reference to itself, as in (*a*), may be at variance not with some other person, (*b*), but within itself. As a particular will it may differ from and be in opposition to its true and absolute self. This is wrong and crime.

Note.—The division of rights into personal right, real right, and right to actions is, like many other divisions, intended to systematize the mass of unorganized material. But this division utterly confuses rights which presuppose such concrete relations as the family or the state with those which refer to mere abstract personality. An example of this confusion is the classification, made popular by Kant, of rights into Real Rights, Personal Rights, and Personal Rights that are Real in kind. It would take us too far afield to show how contorted and irrational is the classification of rights into personal and real, a classification which lies at the foundation of Roman law. The right to actions concerns the administration of justice, and does not fall under this branch of the subject. Clearly it is only personality which gives us a right to things, and therefore personal right is in essence real right. A thing must be taken in its universal sense as the external opposite of freedom, so that in this sense my body and my life are things. Thus real right is the right of personality as such. In the interpretation of personal right, found in Roman law, a man is not a person till he has reached a certain status (Heineccii "Elem. Jur. Civ.," §lxxv.). In Roman law personality is an attribute of a class and is contrasted with slavery. The so-called personal right of Roman law includes not only a right to slaves, a class to which probably belong the children, not only a right over the class which has been deprived of right (*capitis diminutio*), but also family relations. With Kant, family relations are wholly personal rights which are real in kind.—The Roman personal right is not the right of a person as such, but of a special person. It will be afterwards shown that the family relation is really based upon the renunciation of personality. It cannot but seem an inverted method to treat of the rights of persons who belong to definite classes before the universal right of personality.—According to Kant personal rights arise out of a contract or agreement that I should give or perform something; this is the *jus ad rem* of Roman law which has its source in an *obligatio*. Only a person, it is true, can perform a thing through contract; and further, only a person can acquire the right to such a performance. Yet we cannot, therefore, call such a right personal. Every sort of right is right of a person; but a right, which springs out of contract, is not a right to a person, but only to something external to him, or to be disposed of by him; and this is always a thing.

FIRST SECTION
Property

41. A person must give to his freedom an external sphere, in order that he may reach the completeness implied in the idea. Since a person is as

yet the first abstract phase of the completely existent, infinite will, the external sphere of freedom is not only distinguishable from him but directly different and separable.

Addition.—The reasonableness of property consists not in its satisfying our needs, but in its superseding and replacing the subjective phase of personality. It is in possession first of all that the person becomes rational. The first realization of my freedom in an external object is an imperfect one, it is true, but it is the only realization possible so long as the abstract personality has this firsthand relation to its object.

42. That which is defined as different from the free spirit is both in its own nature and also for this spirit the external. It is an object, something not free, impersonal and without rights.

Note.—"Thing," like "objective," has two opposite meanings. When we say "That is the thing or fact," "It depends on the thing itself, not on the person," we mean by "thing" that which is real and substantive. But it is also contrasted with person, which here includes more than a particular subject, and then it means the opposite of the real and substantive, and is something merely external.—What is external for the free spirit, which is different from mere consciousness, is absolutely external. Hence nature is to be conceived as that which is external in its very self.

Addition.—Since a thing has no subjectivity it is external not merely to a subject, but to itself. Space and time are external. I, as sensible, am external, spatial, and temporal. My faculty of sense-perception is external to itself. An animal may perceive, but the soul of the animal has as its object not itself, but something external.

43. The person in his direct conception and as a separate individual has an existence which is purely natural. This existence is something partly inalienable, partly akin in its nature to the external world.—As the individual is considered in his first abstract simplicity, reference is here made only to those features of personality with which he is directly endowed, not to those which he might proceed to acquire by voluntary effort.

Note.—Mental endowments, science, art, such matters of religion as sermons, masses, prayers, blessings of consecrated utensils, inventions also, are objects of exchange, recognized things to be bought and sold. It is possible to ask, also, if an artist or scholar is in legal possession of his art, science, or capacity to preach or read mass; and the question is put on the presumption that these objects are things. Yet one hesitates to call such gifts, knowledge, powers, mere things, because although they may be bargained for as a thing, they have an inner spiritual side. Hence the understanding becomes confused as to how they are to be regarded at law. Before the understanding always arises an exclusive disjunction, which in this case is that something must be either a thing or not a thing. It is like the disjunctive judgment that a thing must be either finite or infinite. But, though knowledge, talents, etc., are the possession of the free mind, and therefore internal to it, they may be relinquished and given an external existence. (See below.) They would then fall under the category of things. They are not direct objects at the first, but the spirit lowers its inner side to the level of the directly external.

According to the unjust and immoral finding of the Roman law, children were things for their father, and he was in legal possession of them. At the same time he was related to them ethically by the tie of love, although the value of this relation was much weakened by the legal usage. In this legal relation there occurs a completely wrong union of thing and not-thing.

The essential feature of abstract right is that its object is the person as such, with only those elements added which, belonging to the external and visible embodiment of his freedom, are directly different from him and separable. Other phases it can include only after the conscious operation of the subjective will. Mental endowments, the sciences, etc., come up for treatment only from the standpoint of legal possession. The possession of the body and the mind, which is acquired by education, study and habit, is an inward property of the spirit, and does not fall to be considered here. The process by which a mental possession passes into the external world and comes under the category of a legal property, will be taken up later, under *relinquishment*.

44. A person has the right to direct his will upon any object, as his real and positive end. The object thus becomes his. As it has no end in itself, it receives its meaning and soul from his will. Mankind has the absolute right to appropriate all that is a thing.

Note.—There is a philosophy which ascribes to the impersonal, to separate things, as they are directly apprehended, an independent and absolutely complete reality. There is also a philosophy which affirms that the mind cannot know what the truth or the thing in itself is. These philosophies are directly contradicted by the attitude of the free will to these things. Although the so-called external things seem to have an independent reality in consciousness as perceiving and imagining, the free will is the idealization or truth of such reality.

Addition.—A man may own anything, because he is a free will, and is therefore self-contained and self-dependent. But the mere object is of an opposite nature. Every man has the right to turn his will upon a thing or make the thing an object of his will, that is to say, to set aside the mere thing and recreate it as his own. As the thing is in its nature external, it has no purpose of its own and contains no infinite reference to itself; it is external to itself. An animal also is external to itself, and is, so far, a thing. Only the will is the unlimited and absolute, while all other things in contrast with the will are merely relative. To appropriate is at bottom only to manifest the majesty of my will towards things, by demonstrating that they are not self-complete and have no purpose of their own. This is brought about by my instilling into the object another end than that which it primarily had. When the living thing becomes my property it gets another soul than it had. I give it my will. Free will is thus the idealism which refuses to hold that things as they are can be self-complete. Realism on the other hand declares them to be absolute in their finite form. But this realistic philosophy is not shared in by the animal, which by consuming things proves that they are not absolutely independent.

45. To have something in my power, even though it be externally, is possession. The special fact that I make something my own through natural want, impulse or caprice, is the special interest of possession. But, when I as a free will am in possession of something, I get a tangible existence, and in this way first became an actual will. This is the true and legal nature of property, and constitutes its distinctive character.

Note.—Since our wants are looked upon as primary, the possession of property appears at first to be a means to their satisfaction; but it is really the first embodiment of freedom and an independent end.

46. Since property makes objective my personal individual will, it is rightly described as a private possession. On the other hand, common property, which may be possessed by a number of separate individuals, is a mark of a loosely joined company, in which a man may or may not allow his share to remain at his own choice.

Note.—The elements of nature cannot become private property.—In the agrarian laws of Rome may be found a conflict between collective and private ownership of land. Private possession is the more reasonable, and, even at the expense of other rights, must win the victory.—Property bound up with family trusts contains an element which is opposed to the right of personality and private ownership. Yet private possession must be kept subject to the higher spheres of right, to a corporate body, *e.g.,* or to the state, as happens when private ownership is entrusted to a so-called moral person, as in mortmain. Yet these exceptions are not to be based on chance, private caprice or personal benefit, but only on the rational organization of the state. The idea of Plato's "Republic" does a wrong to the person, in regarding him as unable to hold property. The theory of a pious, friendly, or even compulsory brotherhood of men, who are to possess all their goods in common, and to banish the principle of private ownership, easily presents itself to one who fails to understand the nature of freedom of spirit, and the nature of right, through mistaking their definite phases. There is a moral or religious side, also. When the friends of Epicurus proposed to establish a community of goods, he dissuaded them on the ground that the plan indicated a lack of confidence in one another, and that those who mistrusted one another could not be friends ("Diog. Laërt." l. x. n. vi).

Addition.—In property my will is personal. But the person, it must be observed, is this particular individual, and, thus, property is the embodiment of this particular will. Since property gives visible existence to my will, it must be regarded as "this" and hence as "mine." This is the important doctrine of the necessity of private property. If exceptions may be made by the state, the state alone can be suffered to make them. But frequently, and especially in our time, it has restored private possession. Thus, for instance, many states have rightly abolished cloisters, because persons, living together in these institutions, have ultimately no such right to property, as the person has.

47. As a person, I am an individual in only its simplest aspect; more definitely, I am alive in a particular bodily organism. My body is as to its content my universal undifferentiated external existence; it is the real possibility of all definite phases. But also as a person I have my life and body, as I have other things only in so far as they express my will.

Note.—The view that the individual, not in his actualized existence but in his direct conception, is to be taken simply as living and having a physical organism follows from the conception of that phase of life and spirit, which we know as soul. The details of this conception are found in the philosophy of nature.

I have organs and life only so far as I will. The animal cannot mutilate or kill itself, but a human being can.

Addition.—Animals do in a manner possess themselves. Their soul is in possession of their body. But they have no right to their life, because they do not will it.

48. The body, merely as it stands, is not adequate to spirit. In order to be a willing instrument and vitalized means, it must first be taken possession of by the spirit (§57). Still for others I am essentially a free being in my body, as I directly have it.

Note.—It is only because I in my living body am a free being, that my body cannot be used as a beast of burden. In so far as the I lives, the soul, which conceives and, what is more, is free, is not separated from the body. The body is the outward embodiment of freedom, and in it the I is sensible. It is an irrational and sophistic doctrine, which separates body and soul, calling the soul the thing in itself and maintaining that it is not touched or hurt when the body is wrongly treated, or when the existence of a person is subject to the power of another. I can indeed withdraw out of my existence into myself and make my existence something external. I can regard any present feeling as something apart from my real self, and may in this way be free even in chains. But that is an affair of my will. I exist for others in my body; that I am free for others is the same thing as that I am free in this outward life. If my body is treated roughly by others, I am treated roughly.

Since it is I that am sensible, violence offered to my body touches me instantly and directly. This is the difference between personal assault and injury to any external property. In property my will is not so vividly present as it is in my body.

49. In my relation to external things, the rational element is that it is I who own property. But the particular element on the other hand is concerned with ends, wants, caprices, talents, external circumstances, etc. (§45). Upon them, it is true, mere abstract possession depends, but they in this sphere of abstract personality are not yet identical with freedom. Hence what and how much I possess is from the standpoint of right a matter of indifference.

Note.—If we can speak of several persons, when as yet no distinction has been drawn between one person and another, we may say that in personality all persons are equal. But this is an empty tautological proposition, since a person abstractedly considered is not as yet separate from others, and has no distinguishing attribute. Equality is the abstract identity set up by the mere understanding. Upon this principle mere reflecting thought, or, in other words, spirit in its middle ranges, is apt to fall, when before it there arises the relation of unity to difference. This equality would be only the equality of abstract persons as such, and would exclude all reference to possession, which is the basis of inequality. Sometimes the demand is made for equality in the division of the soil of the earth, and even of other kinds of wealth. Such a claim is superficial, because differences of wealth are due not only to the accidents of external nature but also to the infinite variety and difference of mind and character. In short, the quality of an individual's possessions depends upon his reason, developed into an organic whole. We cannot say that nature is unjust in distributing wealth and property unequally, because nature is not free and, therefore, neither just nor unjust. It is in part a moral desire that all men should have sufficient income for their wants, and when the wish is left in this indefinite form it is well-meant, although it, like everything merely well-meant, has no counterpart in reality. But, further, income is different from possession and belongs to another sphere, that of the civic community.

Addition.—Since wealth depends upon application, equality in the distribution of goods would, if introduced, soon be disturbed again. What does not permit of being carried out, ought not to be attempted. Men are equal, it is true, but only as persons, that is, only with reference to the source of possession. Accordingly every one must have property. This is the only kind of equality which it is possible to consider. Beyond this is found the region of particular persons, and the question for the first time comes up, How much do I possess? Here the assertion that the property of every man ought in justice to be equal to that of every other is false, since justice demands merely that every one should have property. Indeed, amongst persons variously endowed inequality must occur, and equality would be wrong. It is quite true that men often desire the goods of others; but this desire is wrong, for right is unconcerned about differences in individuals.

50. It is a self-evident and, indeed, almost superfluous remark that an object belongs to him who is accidentally first in possession of it. A second person cannot take into possession what is already the property of another.

Addition.—So far we have been chiefly concerned with the proposition that personality must find an embodiment in property. From what has been said, it follows that he who is first in possession is likewise owner. He is rightful owner, not because he is first, but because he is a free will. He is not first till some one comes after him.

51. In order to fix property as the outward symbol of my personality, it is not enough that I represent it as mine and internally will it to be mine; I must also take it over into my possession. The embodiment of my will can then be recognized by others as mine. That the object, of which I take possession be unowned is a self-evident, negative condition (§50). Rather it is more than a bare negative, since it anticipates a relation to others.

Addition.—A person's putting his will into an object is the conception of property, and the next step is the realizing of it. The inner act of my will, which says that something is mine, must be made recognizable for others. When I make an object mine, I give it a predicate, which must be manifested in its outer form, and not remain merely in my inner will. Children often affirm this earlier act of will against the real possessing of a thing by others. But for adults such a will is not enough. The form of subjectivity must be removed by working itself out into something objective.

52. Active possession makes the material of an object my property, since the material is not independently its own.

Note.—The material opposes itself to me. Indeed its very nature is to furnish opposition to me. It exhibits its abstract independence to my abstract or sentient consciousness. The sentient imagination, it may be said in passing, puts the truth upside down when it regards the sentient side of mind as concrete, and the rational as abstract. In reference therefore to the will and property this absolute independence of the material has no truth. Active possession, viewed as an external activity, by which the universal right of appropriating natural things becomes actualized, is allied to physical strength, cunning, skill, all the means, in short, by which one is able to take hold corporeally of a thing. Owing to the qualitative differences of natural objects, the mastery over and possession of them has an infinitely diversified meaning, and a corresponding limitation and contingency. Moreover, no one kind of matter, such as an element, can be wholly possessed by any number of separate persons. In order to become a possible object of possession, it must be taken in separate parts, as a breath of air or draught of water. The impossibility of owning one kind of matter, or an element, depends finally, not upon external physical incapacity, but upon the fact that the person, as will, is not only individual, but directly individual, and that the external exists for him, therefore, only as a collection of particulars. (§13, *note* to §43.)

The process, by which we become master and external owner, is in a sense infinite, and must remain more or less undetermined and incomplete. None the less, however, has the material an essential form, because of which alone it is anything. The more I appropriate this form, so much the more do I come into real possession of the object. The consumption of food is a through-and-through change of its quality. The cultivation of skill in my body, and the education of my mind, are also more or less an active possession by means of thorough-going modification. Mind or spirit is above all that which I can make my own. But this possession is different from property. Property is completed in its relation to the free will. In the external relation of active possession something of externality remains as a residue, but with regard to the free will the owned object has reserved nothing. A matter without qualities, a something which in property is supposed to remain outside of me, and to belong wholly to the object, is an empty abstraction, which thought must expose and defeat.

Addition.—Fichte has raised the question, whether, if I have fashioned an object, its material is also mine. According to his view, if I have made a cup out of gold, any one may take the gold, provided that he does no injury to my handiwork. Though we may imagine that form and substance are separable in that way, the distinction is an empty subtlety. If I take possession of a field, and plough it, not only is the furrow mine, but also the ground which belongs to it. It is my will to take possession of the material, even the whole object. Hence the material is not masterless; it is not its own. Even if the material remains outside of the form which I give the object, the form is a sign that the object is to be mine. Hence the thing does not stay outside of my will or purpose. There is consequently nothing in it which can be taken hold of by another.

53. Property has its more direct phases in the relation of the will to the object. This relation is (α) direct and active taking of possession, in so far as the will is embodied in the object as in something positive. (β) In so

far as this object is negative towards the will, the will is visibly embodied in it as something to be negated. This is use. (γ) The return of the will into itself out of the object; this is relinquishment. These three phases are the positive, negative, and infinite judgments of the will concerning the object.

A. The Act of Possession

54. Taking possession is partly the simple bodily grasp, partly the forming and partly the marking or designating of the object.

Addition.—These modes of taking possession exhibit the progress from the category of particularity to that of universality. Bodily seizure can be made only of particular objects, while marking an object is done by a kind of picture-thinking. In marking I keep before me a representation, by which I intend that the object shall be mine in its totality, and not merely the part which I can hold in my hand.

55. (α) Corporeal possession, in which I am present directly, and my will is directly visible, appeals at once to the senses, and from that standpoint is the most complete kind of possession. But it is after all only subjective, temporary and greatly limited as well by surroundings as by the qualities of the object. But if I can connect an object with anything I have already, or if the two become connected accidentally, the sphere of direct physical prehension is to some extent enlarged.

Note.—Mechanical forces, weapons, instruments extend the compass of my power. If my ground is washed by the sea or a river, or lies adjacent to a bit of good hunting country or a pasturage, if it contains stone or other minerals, if there is any treasure in it or upon it, in each of these ways possession may be enlarged. It is the same if the enlargement occurs after I have possession and accidentally, as is the case with so-called natural accretions, such as alluvial deposits, and with objects that are stranded. Everything that is born is also an extension of my wealth, *fœtura* as they are called; but as they involve an organic relation, and are not external additions to an object already in my possession, they are different from the other accessories. All these adjuncts, some of them mutually exclusive, are possibilities by which one owner rather than another may the more easily take a piece of land into possession, or work it up; they may also be viewed as mere accidental accompaniments of the object to which they are added. They are in fact external concomitants which do not include any conception or living union. Hence it devolves upon the understanding to bring forward and weigh reasons for or against their being mine, and to apply the positive edicts of the law, so that a decision may be reached in accordance with the relative closeness of the connection between the object and its accessory.

Addition.—The act of possession assumes a separation of parts in the object. I take no more into my possession than I can touch with my body. But, secondly, external things have a wider range than I am able to cover physically. Something else stands in connection with what I own. Through the hand I exercise the act of ownership, but the compass of the hand can be enlarged. No animal has this noble member. What I grasp with it can itself become a means to further prehension. When I come into possession of a thing, the understanding goes at once over into it, and as a consequence not only what is directly laid hold upon is mine, but likewise what is connected with it. At this juncture positive law must introduce its prescripts, because nothing more than this can be deduced from the conception.

56. (β) When something that is mine is formed, it becomes independent of me, ceasing to be limited to my presence in this space or time, or to the presence of my consciousness and will.

Note.—The fashioning of a thing is the kind of active possession which is most adequate to the idea, because it unites the subjective and the objective. It varies infinitely according to the quality of the object and the purpose of the subject. To this head belongs likewise the formation or nurture of living things, in which my work does not remain something foreign, but is assimilated, as in the cultivation of the soil, the care of plants, and the taming, feeding, and tending of animals. It includes also any arrangement for the more efficient use of natural products or forces, as well as the effect of one material upon another, etc.

Addition.—This act of forming may in practice assume the greatest variety of aspects. The soil, which I till, is formed. The forming of the inorganic is sometimes indirect. When I, for instance, build a windmill, I have not formed the air, but I form something which will utilize the air. Yet, as I have not formed the air, I dare not call it mine. Moreover the sparing of a wild animal's life may be viewed as a forming, since my conduct is the preservation of the object. It is the same kind of act as the training of animals, only that training is more direct, and proceeds more largely from me.

57. In his direct life, before it is idealized by self-consciousness, man is merely a natural being, standing outside of his true conception. Only through the education of his body and mind, mainly by his becoming conscious of himself as free, does he take possession of himself, become his own property, and stand in opposition to others. This active possession of himself, conversely, is the giving of actuality to what he is in conception, in his possibilities, faculties, and disposition. By this process he is for the first time securely established as his own, becomes a tangible reality as distinguished from a simple consciousness of himself, and is capable of assuming the form of an object (§43, *note*).

Note.—We are now in a position to consider slavery. We may set aside the justification of slavery based upon the argument that it originates in superior physical force, the taking of prisoners in war, the saving and preserving of life, upbringing, education, or bestowal of kindnesses. These reasons all rest ultimately on the ground that man is to be taken as a merely natural being, living, or, it may even be, choosing a life which is not adequate to his conception. Upon the same footing stands the attempted justification of ownership as merely the status of masters, as also all views of the right to slaves founded on history. The assertion of the absolute injustice of slavery on the contrary, clinging to the conception that man, as spiritual, is free of himself, is also a one-sided idea, since it supposes man to be free by nature. In other words, it takes as the truth the conception in its direct and unreflective form rather than the idea. This antinomy, like all others, rests upon the external thinking, which keeps separate and independent each of two aspects of a single complete idea. In point of fact, neither aspect, if separated from the other, is able to measure the idea, and present it in its truth. It is the mark of the free spirit (§21) that it does not exist merely as conception or naturally, but that it supersedes its own formalism, transcending thereby its naked natural existence, and gives to itself an existence, which, being its own, is free.

Hence the side of the antinomy, which maintains the conception of freedom, is to be preferred, since it contains at least the necessary point of departure for the truth. The other side, holding to the existence, which is utterly at variance with the conception, has in it nothing reasonable or right at all. The standpoint of the free will, with which right and the science of right begin, is already beyond the wrong view that man is simply a natural being, who, as he cannot exist for himself, is fit only to be enslaved. This untrue phenomenon had its origin in the circumstance that the spirit had at that time just attained the level of consciousness. Hence through the dialectical movement of the conception arises the first inkling of the consciousness of freedom. There is thus by this movement brought to pass a struggle for recognition, and, as a necessary result, the relation of master and slave. But in order that the objective spirit, which gives substance to right, may not again be apprehended only on its subjective side, and that it may not again appear as a mere unsupported command, intimating that man in his real nature is not appointed to slavery, it must be seen that the idea of freedom is in truth nothing but the state.

Addition.—If we hold fast to the side that man is absolutely free, we condemn slavery. Still it depends on the person's own will, whether he shall be a slave or not, just as it depends upon the will of a people whether or not it is to be in subjection. Hence slavery is a wrong not simply on the part of those who enslave or subjugate, but of the slaves and subjects themselves. Slavery occurs in the passage from the natural condition of man to his true moral and social condition. It is found in a world where a wrong is still a right. Under such a circumstance the wrong has its value and finds a necessary place.

58. (γ) The kind of possession, which is not literal but only representative of my will, is a mark or symbol, whose meaning is that it is I who have put my will into the object. Owing to the variety of objects used as signs, this kind of possession is very indefinite in its meaning.

Addition.—Of all kinds of possession this by marking is the most complete, since the others have more or less the effect of a mark. When I seize or form an object, in each case the result is in the end a mark, indicating to others that I exclude them, and have set my will in the object. The conception of the mark is that the object stands not for what it is, but for what it signifies. The cockade, e.g., means citizenship in a certain state, although its colour has no connection with the nation, and represents not itself but the nation. In that man acquires possession through the use of a sign, he exhibits his mastery over things.

B. Use of the Object

59. The object taken into my possession receives the predicate "mine," and the will is related to it positively. Yet in this identity the object is established as something negative, and my will becomes particularized as a want or desire. But the particular want of one separate will is the positive, which satisfies itself; while the object is negative in itself, and exists only for my want and serves it. Use is the realization of my want through the change, destruction, or consumption of the object, which in this way reveals that it has no self, and fulfils its nature.

Note.—The view that use is the real nature and actuality of property floats before the mind of those who consider that property is dead and ownerless, if it is being put to no use. This they advance as reason for laying violent and unlawful hands upon property. But the will of an owner, by virtue of which a thing is his own, is the fundamental principle, of which use is only an external, special, and subordinate manifestation.

Addition.—In use is involved a wider relation than in possession by symbol, because the object, when used, is not recognized in its particular existence, but is by me negated. It is reduced to a means for the satisfaction of my wants. When the object and I come together, one of the two must lose its qualities, if we are to become identical. But I am a living thing who wills and truly affirms himself, while the object is only a natural thing. Therefore it must go to ground and I preserve myself. This constitutes the superiority and reason of the organic world.

60. Using an object in direct seizure is a single separate act. But when we have a recurring need, use repeatedly a product which replaces itself,

and seek to preserve its power to replace itself, a direct and single act of
seizure becomes a sign. It is universalized and denotes the possession of
the elemental or organic basis, the conditions of production.

61. A thing has in contrast with me, its possessor, no end of its own
(§42). Its substance as an independent thing is thus a purely external and
unsubstantial existence. As this externality when realized is the use, to
which I put it, so the total use or service of the object is the object itself
in its whole extent. When I am admitted to the complete use of a thing,
I am the owner of it. Apart from the entire range of use, nothing is left
over to be the possession of another.

Addition.—The relation of use to property is the same as that of substance to accident, of internal to external, of force to its manifestation.
But the force must be manifested; a farm is a farm only as it bears produce. He who has the use of a farm is the possessor of the whole, and to
suppose another ownership in addition is an empty abstraction.

62. Partial or temporary use, and partial or temporary possession, or
possibility of use, however, are to be distinguished from actual ownership.
The total use of a thing cannot be mine, while the abstract property is
somebody else's. The object would in that case contain a contradiction.
It would be wholly penetrated by my will and yet contain something im-
penetrable, namely, the empty will of another. The relation of my positive will to the thing would be objective and yet not objective.
Accordingly, possession is essentially free and complete.

Note.—The distinction between right to total use and abstract possession is due to the empty and formal understanding. To it the idea, which
in this case is the unity of possession or the personal will with the realization of this will, is not true. On the contrary, it holds as true these two
elements in their separation. This distinction of the understanding implies that an empty mastership of things is an actual relation. If we could
extend the term "aberration" beyond the mere imagination of the subject, and the reality, with which he is directly at variance, we might call
such a view of property an aberration of personality. How can what is
mine in one single object be without qualification my individual exclusive will, and also the individual exclusive will of someone else?

In the "Institut." libr. ii. tit. iv. it is said: "*Usufructus est jus alienis rebus
utendi, fruendi salva rerum substantia,*" and again: "*Ne tamen in universum in-
utiles essent proprietates, semper abscendente usufructu: placuit certis modis extin-
gui usumfructum et ad proprietatem reverti.*" "*Placuit*"—as though it were optional, whether or not to give sense to the formal distinction of the understanding. A *proprietas semper abscendente usufructu* would not only be *in-
utiles,* but no longer a *proprietas.* Many distinctions regarding property,
such as that into *res mancipi* and *nec mancipi,* and that into *dominium
Quiritarium* and *Bonitarium,* are merely historical dainties and do not be-

long to this place, because they have no relation to the conception of property. But the relation of the *dominium directum* to the *dominium utile,* and that of the contract which gives heritable right in another's land, and also the various ways of dealing with estates in fee, with their ground rents and other rents and impositions, have a clear bearing upon the distinction now under discussion. When these charges are irredeemably imposed, this formal distinction is indeed present, but it is again transcended when by the association of certain charges with the *dominium utile,* the *dominium utile* and the *dominium directum* become the same. If these relations contained no more that the formal distinction of the understanding, there would be opposed to each other not two masters (*domini*), but an owner and an empty master. But by virtue of the charges or taxes it is two owners, who stand in relation to each other, though they are not related by a common possession. In this relation is to be found the transition from property to use, a transition already operating when ownership, which was formerly reckoned as the more honourable, is given a secondary place, while the *utile* or produce of a *dominium directum* is regarded as the essential and rational.

It is fully fifteen hundred years since through the influence of Christianity the freedom of the person began to flourish, and at least in a small section of the human race take rank as a universal principle. But the recognition here and there of the principle of the freedom of property is, as it were, a thing of yesterday. This is a good illustration from world-history, of the length of time needed by the spirit to reach self-consciousness, and is a rebuke also to the impatience of opinion.

63. In use the object is a single one, definite in quality and quantity, and answers to a special need. But its special usefulness, when fixed quantitatively, can be compared with other objects capable of being put to the same use, and a special want, served by the object, and indeed any want may be compared with other wants; and their corresponding objects may be also compared. This universal characteristic, which proceeds from the particular object and yet abstracts from its special qualities is the value. Value is the true essence or substance of the object, and the object by possessing value becomes an object for consciousness. As complete owner of the object, I am owner of its value as well as of its use.

Note.—The feudal tenant is the owner of use only, not of the value.

Addition.—Quality here becomes quantity. Want is a term common to the greatest variety of things, and enables me to compare them. Thought in its progress starts from the special quality of an object, passes through indifference with regard to the quality, and finally reaches quantity. So in mathematics the circle, ellipse and parabola are specifically different, and yet the distinction of one curve from another is merely quantitative, being reduced to a mere quantitative difference in the largeness of their coefficients. In property the quantitative aspect, which issues from the qualitative, is value. The qualitative determines the quantum, however, and is therefore quite as much retained as superseded. When we consider the conception of value, the object is regarded only as a sign, counting not for what it is but for what it is worth. A letter of credit, *e.g.*, is not a kind of paper, but a sign of another universal, namely, its face value. The specific value of an object varies according to the want, but in order to express abstract worth, we use money. Money represents things, but since it does not represent want itself, but is only a sign of it, it is again governed by the specific value, which it merely stands for. One can be owner of an object without being master of its value. A family, which can neither sell nor pawn its goods, is not master of their value. But since the restrictions characterizing this form of property, such as fiefs, property conveyed in trust, etc., are not adequate to the conception of it, they are largely disappearing.

64. The form of the object and the mark are themselves external circumstances, deprived of meaning and worth if taken apart from use, employment, or some such manifestation of the subjective will. The presence of the will, however, is in time, and its objective reality is continuance of the subjective manifestation. If the manifestation lapses, the object, abandoned by the real essence of the will and of possession, becomes ownerless. Hence I may lose or acquire property through prescription.

Note.—Prescription does not run counter to strict right and is not introduced into law merely to cut short the strife and confusion, which would naturally arise out of old claims. It is founded on the reality of property, in other words upon the necessity that the will, in order to keep a thing, must manifest itself in it.—Public monuments are property of the nation, or rather they, like all works of art intended for use, are living and self-sufficient ends because of their indwelling soul of remembrance and honour. Deprived of this soul they are, so far as the nation is concerned, without a master, and become casually a private possession, as has happened with the Greek and Egyptian works of art in Turkey.—The private right of an author's family to his works is prescribed for similar reasons. These works become in a sense masterless, since they, like the monuments, though in an opposite way, become first common property, and then through various channels, private property. To set apart land for a cemetery and then not use it, or to set apart land never to be used, contains an empty unreal caprice. As to traverse this action does no injury, respect for it cannot be guaranteed.

Addition.—Prescription rests upon the supposition that I have ceased to look upon the object as mine. If a thing is to remain mine, there must be a continuous act of will, and this act reveals itself through use or preservation.—The decline in the value of public monuments was frequently illustrated during the Reformation in institutions founded for the saying of masses. The spirit of the old confession and therefore of these buildings had fled, and the buildings could be taken as private property.

C. Relinquishment of Property

65. I may relinquish property, since it is mine only by virtue of my having put my will into it. I may let a thing go unowned by me or pass it over to the will and possession of another; but this is possible only so far as the object is in its nature something external.

Addition.—Prescription is relinquishment without direct declaration of will. True relinquishment is a declaration that I will no longer regard the object as mine. The process in all its phases may be taken to be a true taking of possession. First there is the direct prehension; then by use property is thoroughly acquired; and the third step is the unity of both these elements, possession through relinquishment.

66. Some goods, or rather substantive phases of life are inalienable, and the right to them does not perish through lapse of time. These comprise my inner personality and the universal essence of my consciousness of myself, and are personality in general, freedom of will in the broadest sense, social life and religion.

Note.—What the spirit is in conception, or implicitly, it should also be in actuality; it should be a person, that is to say, be able to possess property, have sociality and religion. This idea is itself the conception of spirit. As *causa sui*, or free cause, it is that, *cujus natura non potest concipi nisi existens* (Spinoza, "Eth." Def. 1). In this very conception, namely, that spirit shall be what it is only through itself and by the infinite return into itself out of its natural and direct reality, lies the possibility of opposition between what it is only implicitly (§57), and what it is only explicitly. In the will this opposition is the possibility of evil, but in general it is the possibility of the alienation of personality and substantive being; and this alienation may occur either unconsciously or intentionally.—Examples of the disposal of personality are slavery, vassalage, inability to own property or lack of complete control over it. Relinquishment of reason, sociality, morality or religion occurs in superstition; it occurs also if I delegate to others the authority to prescribe for me what kind of acts I shall commit, as when one sells himself for robbery, murder, or the possibility of any other crime; it occurs when I permit others to determine what for me shall be duty or religious truth.

The right to nothing that is inalienable can be forfeited through lapse of time. The act by which I take possession of my personality and real being, and establish myself as having rights, responsibilities, and moral and religious obligations, deprives these attributes of that externality, which alone gives them the capacity of being possessed by another. Along with the departure of this externality goes the reference to time or to any previous consent or complaisance. This return of myself into myself, being the process by which I establish myself as idea or complete legal and moral person, does away with the old relation. It removes the violence which I and others had done to my own conception and reason, the wrong of having treated the infinite existence of self-consciousness as something merely extraneous, and of having suffered others to do the same. This return into myself reveals the contradiction implied in my having given into the keeping of others my right, morality or religion. I gave them what I did not myself possess, what, so soon as I do possess it, exists in essence only as mine, and not as something external.

Addition.—It lies in the nature of the matter that the slave has an absolute right to make himself free, or that, when anyone has hired out his morality for robbery and murder, the transaction is absolutely void. Anyone possesses the competency to annul such an agreement. It is the same with the letting of religiosity by a priest, who is my confessor. The inner religious condition every one must adjust by himself. A religiosity, part of which is handed over to some one else is not genuine, for the spirit is only one, and must dwell within me. To me it must belong to unite the act of worship with religious aspiration.

67. The use of single products of my particular physical endowments or mental capacities I may hand over to others for a limited time, since, when a time limit is recognized, these products may be said to have an external relation to my genuine and total being. If I were to dispose of my whole time, made concrete in work, and all my activity, I would be giving up the essence of my productions. My whole activity and reality, in short, my personality, would be the property of another.

Note.—This is the same relation as that (§61) between the substance of an object and its use. As it is only by limiting use that we can distinguish it from the object, so the use of my powers is to be distinguished from these powers themselves, only in so far as it has a quantitative limit. The total number of manifestations of a faculty is the faculty; the accidents are the substance; the particulars, the universal.

Addition.—The distinction, here analyzed, is that between a slave and a servant or day-labourer in our own time. The Athenian slave had possibly lighter occupation and higher kind of mental work than is the rule with our workmen. But he was a slave notwithstanding, since the whole circle of his activity was controlled by his master.

68. What is peculiar to a mental product can be externalized and directly converted into an object, which it is possible for others to produce. When another person has acquired the object, he may make the thought or, it may be, the mechanical genius in it, his own; a possibility which in

the case of literary works constitutes the reason and special value of acquisition. But, over and above this, the new owner comes at the same time into possession of the general power to express himself in the same way, and so of making any number of objects of the same kind.

Note.—In works of art the form, which images the thought in an external material, is so conspicuously the possession of the artist, that an imitation of it is really a product of the imitator's mental and mechanical skill. But in the case of literature or an invention of some technical contrivance, the form in which it is externalized is of a mechanical sort. In a book the thought is presented in a row of particular abstract signs; in an invention the thought has a wholly mechanical content. The way to reproduce such things, as mere things, is a matter of ordinary skilled labour. Between the two extremes, on the one side a work of art, and on the other a product of manual labour, there are all stages of production, some of which incline to one of the extremes, some to the other.

69. Since the purchaser of such a product of mental skill possesses the full use and value of his single copy, he is complete and free owner of that one copy, although the author of the work or the inventor of the apparatus remains owner of the general method of multiplying such products. The author or inventor has not disposed directly of the general method, but may reserve it for his private utterance.

Note.—The justification of the right of the author or inventor cannot be sought in his arbitrarily making it a condition, when he disposes of a copy, that the possibility of bringing out other copies shall not belong to the purchaser, but shall remain in his own hands. The first question is whether the separation of the object from the power to reproduce, which goes with the object, is allowable in thought, and does not destroy full and free possession (§62). Does it depend upon the arbitrary choice of the first producer to reserve to himself the power to reproduce or dispose of the product of his mind? Or, on the other hand, may he count it of no value, and give it freely with each separate copy? Now there is this peculiarity about this power, that through it the object becomes not merely a possession, but a means of wealth (see §170, and fol.). This new feature is a special kind of external use, and is different and separate from the use to which the object was directly appointed. It is not, as it is called, an *accessio naturalis* as are *fœtura*. Hence as the distinction occurs in the sphere of external use, which is naturally capable of being divided, the reservation of one part, while another is being disposed of, is not the retention of an ownership without *utile*.

The primary and most important claim of trade and commerce is to give them surety against highway robbery. In the same way the primary though merely negative demand of the sciences and arts is to insure the workers in these fields against larceny, and give their property protection.

But in the case of a mental product the intention is that others should comprehend it, and make its imagination, memory, and thought their own. Learning is not merely the treasuring up of words in the memory; it is through thinking that the thoughts of others are seized, and this after-thinking is real learning. Now that which is learned becomes in turn something which can be disposed of; and the external expression of this material may easily assume a form different from the form into which the original thinker threw his work. Thus those who have worked over the material a second time may regard as their own possession whatever money they may be able to extract from their work, and may contend that they have a right to reproduce it. In the transmission of the sciences in general, and especially in teaching positive science, church doctrine, or jurisprudence, are found the adoption and repetition of thoughts which are already established and expressed. This is largely the case with writings composed for the same purpose. It is not possible to state accurately, and establish explicitly by law and right, just how far the new form, which accrues through repeated expression, should transmute the scientific treasure or the thoughts of others, who are still in external possession, into a special mental possession of the person who re-constructs them; how far, in other words, a repetition of an author's work should be called a plagiarism. Hence plagiarism must be a question of honour, and should be refrained from on that score.

Laws against reprinting protect the property of author and publisher in a very definite but, indeed, limited measure. The ease with which one can intentionally alter the form or insert slight modifications into a large work on science or a comprehensive theory which is the work of another, and further, the great difficulty, when discoursing on what one has received, of abiding by the letter of the author, introduce, in addition to the special purposes requiring such a repetition, an endless variety of changes, which stamp upon the foreign article the more or less superficial impression of something which is one's own. The hundreds of compendiums, abridgments, compilations, arithmetics, geometries, religious tracts, every venture of a critical journal, an annual, or a cyclopædia, keep on repeating under the same or an altered title, although each may be maintained to be something new and unique. Yet the profit which the work promised the author or inventor in the first place may be wiped out, or the purpose of both author and imitator may be defeated, or one may be ruined.

It is noteworthy that the term plagiarism, or scholar's larceny is no longer heard. It may be that the principle of honour has dislodged it, or that the feeling of honour has vanished or ceased to be directed against plagiarism, or that a small compilation or slight change of form is ranked as an original and independent production, and so highly esteemed as to banish all thought of plagiarism.

70. Since personality is something directly present, the comprehensive totality of one's outer activity, the life, is not external to it. Thus the disposal or sacrifice of life is not the manifestation of one's personality so much as the very opposite. Hence I have no right to relinquish my life. Only a moral and social ideal, which submerges the direct, simple and separate personality, and constitutes its real power, has a right to life. Life, as such, being direct and unreflected, and death the direct negation of it, death must come from without as a result of natural causes, or must be received in the service of the idea from a foreign hand.

Addition.—The particular person is really a subordinate, who must devote his life to the service of the ethical fabric; when the state demands his life, he must yield it up. But should the man take his own life? Suicide may at first glance be looked upon as bravery, although it be the poor bravery of tailors and maid-servants. Or it may be regarded as a misfortune, caused by a broken heart. But the point is, Have I any right to kill myself? The answer is that I, as this individual am not lord over my life, since the comprehensive totality of one's activity, the life, falls within the direct and present personality. To speak of the right of a person over his life is a contradiction, since it implies a right of a person over himself. But no one can stand above and execute himself. When Hercules burnt himself, and Brutus fell upon his sword, this action against their personality was doubtless of an heroic type; but yet the simple right to commit suicide must be denied even to heroes.

Transition from Property to Contract

71. Outward and visible existence, as definite, is essentially existence for another thing (see *note* to §48). Thus property, as a visible external thing, is determined by its relations to other external things, these relations being both necessary and accidental. But property is also a manifestation of will, and the other, for which it exists, is the will of another person. This reference of will to will is the true and peculiar ground on which freedom is realized. The means by which I hold property, not by virtue of the relation of an object to my subjective will, but by virtue of another will, and hence share in a common will, is contract.

Note.—It is just as much a necessity of reason that men make contracts, exchange, and trade, as that they should have property (§45, *note*). In their consciousness it is some want, benevolence, or advantage, which occasions the contract, but really it is reason, or the idea as it is embodied in the realized will of a free person. It is taken for granted that contracting parties recognize one another as persons and owners. Recognition is contained and presupposed in the fact that contract is a relation of the objective spirit (§35, *note* to §57).

Addition.—In contract I hold property through a common will. It is the interest of reason that the subjective will become universal, and exalt itself to this level of realization. In contract the particular will remains, although it is now in conjunction with another will. The universal will assumes here no higher form than co-operation.

SECOND SECTION
Contract

72. In contract property is no longer viewed on the side of its external reality, as a mere thing, but rather as containing the elements of will, another's as well as my own. Contract is the process which presents and occasions the contradiction by which I, existing for myself and excluding another will, am and remain an owner only in so far as I identify myself with the will of another, and cease to be an owner.

73. Guided by the conception I must relinquish my property not merely as an external thing (§65), but as property, if my will is to become a genuine factor in reality. But by virtue of this procedure my will, when relinquished, is another will. The necessary nature of the conception is thus realized in a unity of different wills, which, nevertheless, give up their differences and peculiarities. But this identity implies not that one will is identical with the other, but rather that each at this stage remains an independent and private will.

74. For two absolutely distinct and separate owners there is now formed one will. While each of them ceases to be an owner through his own distinct will, the one will remains. Each will gives up a particular property, and receives the particular property of another, adopting only that conclusion with which the other coincides.

75. Since the two contracting parties appear as directly independent persons (α) contract proceeds from arbitrary choice; (β) the one will formed by the contract is the work merely of the two interested persons, and is thus a common, but not an absolutely universal will; (γ) the object of the contract is a single external thing, because only such a thing is subject to relinquishment at their mere option (§65 and fol.).

Note.—Marriage does not come under the conception of contract. This view is, we must say it, in all its shamelessness, propounded by Kant ("Metaph. Anf. der Rechtslehre," p. 106). Just as little does the nature of the state conform to contract, whether the contract be regarded as a compact of all with all, or of all with the prince or government.—The introduction of the relations of contract and private property into the functions of the state has produced the greatest confusion both in the law and in real life. In earlier times civil rights and duties were thought and maintained to be a directly private possession of particular individuals in opposition to the rights of prince and state. In more recent years, also, the rights of prince and state have been treated as objects of covenant. They are said to be based on contract, or the mere general consent of those who wish to form a state. Different as these two views of the state are, they agree in taking the phases of private property into another and a higher region. This will be referred to again when we come to speak of ethical observances and the state.

Addition.—It is a popular view in modern times that the state is a contract of all with all. All conclude, so the doctrine runs, a compact with the prince, and he in turn with the subjects. According to this superficial view, there is in contract only one unity of different wills; but in fact there are two identical wills, both of which are persons, and wish to remain possessors. Contract, besides, arises out of the spontaneous choice of the persons. Marriage, indeed, has that point in common with contract, but with the state it is different. An individual cannot enter or leave the social condition at his option, since every one is by his very nature a citizen of a state. The characteristic of man as rational is to live in a state; if there is no state, reason claims that one should be founded. A state, it is true, must grant permission either to enter or to leave it; but this permission is not given in deference to the arbitrary choice of the individual, nor is the state founded upon a contract which presupposes this choice. It is false to say that it rests with the arbitrary will of all to establish a state; rather is it absolutely necessary for every one to be in a state. The great progress of the modern state is due to the fact that it has and keeps an absolute end, and no man is now at liberty to make private arrangements in connection with this end, as they did in the middle ages.

76. Contract is formal when the two elements through which the common will arises, the negative disposal of the thing and the positive reception of it, are so divided, that one of the contracting parties makes one side of the agreement, and the other, the other. This is gift. Contract is real when each of the contractors performs both sides of the double agreement, and is and remains an owner. This is exchange.

Addition.—Contract involves two agreements to two things; I both give up and acquire a property. Real contract occurs, when each yields up and acquires possession; in giving up he remains an owner. Formal contract occurs when a person only gives up or acquires.

77. In real contract every one both keeps the same property as he had when he undertook the contract, and also yields up his property. Hence it is necessary to distinguish the property, which in contract remains permanently mine, from the external objects which change hands. The universal and self-identical element in exchange, that with regard to which the objects to be exchanged are equal, is the value (§63).

Note.—By the very conception of contract a *læsio enormis* annuls the agreement, since the contractor, in disposing of his goods, must remain in possession of a quantitative equivalent. An injury may fairly be called enormous, if it exceeds half of the value; but it is infinite, when a contract or any stipulation is entered into to dispose of an inalienable good (§66). A stipulation is only one single part or side of the whole contract, or a merely formal settlement, of which more hereafter. It contains only the formal phase of contract, the consent of one party to perform something, and the consent of the other party to accept the performance. It must, therefore, be classed amongst the so-called one-sided contracts. The division of contracts into one-sided and two-sided, and many other divisions of the same kind in Roman law, are superficial combinations, arising from some particular and external consideration, as, for instance, the way in which they are made. They may also introduce attributes which do not concern the nature of contract, such as those which have meaning only in reference to the administration of justice (*actiones*), and to the legal consequences of positive laws, or such as may arise out of wholly external circumstances and injure the conception of right.

78. The distinction between property and possession, between the substantive and the external side (§45), assumes in contract the form of a distinction between the common will or agreement and the realization of this will in performance. The agreement, taken by itself in its difference from performance, is something imagined or symbolic, appearing in reality as a visible sign. ("Encyclopædia of the Philosophical Sciences".) In stipulation it may be manifested by gesture or other symbolic act, but usually in an express declaration through speech, which is the most worthy vehicle of thought.

Note.—Stipulation, thus interpreted, is the form in which the content of a concluded contract is outwardly symbolized. But this symbol is only the form. By this is not meant that the content is still merely subjective, merely a desideratum, but that the conclusion of the actual arrangement is made by the will.

Addition.—As in property we had the distinction between property and possession, the substantive and the external, so in contract we have the difference between the common will as agreement and the particular will as performance. It is in the nature of contract that both the common and the particular wills should be manifested, because it is the relation of will to will. In civilized communities agreement, manifested by a sign, is separated from performance, although with ruder peoples they may concur. There is in the forests of Ceylon a tribe, which in trading puts down its property and waits patiently for the arrival of those who will place their property over against it; the dumb declaration of the will is not separated from performance.

79. As stipulation involves the will, it contains, from the standpoint of right, the substance of contract. In contrast with this substantive contract

the possession, which remains till the contract is fully carried out, has no reality outside of the agreement. I have given up a possession and my private control over it, and it has already become the property of another. I am legally bound to carry out the stipulation.

Note.—Mere promise is different from contract. What I promise to do, give or perform, is future and a mere subjective qualification of my will. I am at liberty to change my promise. But stipulation is already the embodiment of my volition. I have disposed of my property; it has ceased to be mine, and I recognize it as already belonging to another. The Roman distinction between *pactum* and *contractus* is not sound.

Fichte once laid it down that the obligation to hold to the contract began for me only when the other party began to do his share. Before performance I am supposed to be doubtful whether the other had been really in earnest. The obligation before performance is, therefore, said to be moral and not legal. The trouble is that stipulation is not merely external, but involves a common will, which has already done away with mere intention and change of mind. The other party may of course change his mind after the engagement, but has he any right to do so? For plainly I may choose to do what is wrong, although the other person begins to perform his side of the contract. Fichte's view is worthless, since it bases the legal side of contract upon the bad infinite, that is, an infinite series, or the infinite divisibility of time, material and action. The embodiment of the will in gesture or a definite form of words is its complete intellectual embodiment, of which the performance is the merely mechanical result.

It does not alter the case that positive law distinguishes between so-called real contracts and consensual contracts, real contracts being complete only when the actual performance (*res, traditio rei*) is added to consent. Sometimes in these real contracts the surrender to me of the object enables me to carry out my part of the engagement, and my obligation to act refers to the object only in so far as I have received it into my hands. This occurs in loan, interest, deposit, and sometimes in exchange also. These cases do not concern the relation of stipulation to performance, but merely the manner of performance. It is also optional in the case of contract to bargain that on one side the obligation shall not arise until the other party fulfils his share of the engagement.

80. The classification or rational treatment of contracts is deduced not from external circumstances, but from distinctions which are involved in the very nature of contract. These distinctions are those between formal and real contract, between property and possession or use, and between value and the specific thing. The subjoined classification agrees in the main with the Kantian ("Metaphysical Principles of the Theory of Right," p. 120). It is surprising that the old method of classification of

contracts into real and consensual, named and unnamed, has not long ago given way before something that is more reasonable.

A. Gift.

(1) Gift of an object or gift proper.

(2) Loan of an object—the gift of a portion of it or of a partial use or enjoyment of it, the lender remaining owner; (*mutuum* and *commodatum* without interest). The object is specific, or it may be regarded as universal, or it is, as in the case of money, actually universal.

(3) Gift of service, as for example the mere storage of a property (*depositum*). The gift of an object on the special condition that the receiver shall be owner on the giver's death, when the giver can no longer be owner, is bequest, and does not come under the conception of contract. It presupposes the civic community and positive legislation.

B. Exchange.

(1) Exchange as such.

(α) Exchange of objects, *i.e.* of one specific thing for another of the same kind.

(β) Purchase or sale (*emtio, venditio*). The exchange of a specific object, for a general object, which has the phase of value but not of use, namely money.

(2) Rent (*locatio, conductio*), relinquishment of the temporary use of a property for rent or interest,

(α) Renting of a specific thing, renting proper.

(β) Renting of a universal thing, so that the lessor remains owner only of the universal or the value. This is loan, *mutuum* and *commodatum* with interest. Whether the object be a flat, furniture, house, a *res fungibilis* or *non fungibilis,* this question gives rise, here also as in the second kind of gift, to particular qualifications that are unimportant.

(3) Contract for wages (*locatio operæ*)—relinquishment, limited in time or otherwise, of my labour or services, in so far as they are disposable (§67).

Akin to this is the brief and other such contracts, in which the performance depends upon character, confidence, or special talents. Here the service cannot be measured by its money value, which is not called wages, but an honorarium or fee.

C. Completion of a contract (*cautio*) through a security.

In contracts where I dispose of the use of a thing, as in rent, I am no longer in possession of it, but am still the owner. In exchange, purchase, or gift, I may have become owner, without being as yet in actual possession. Indeed, in every contract, except such as are directly on a cash basis, this separation is to be found. Security or pledge is concerned with an object which I give up, or an object which is to be mine. It either keeps or puts me in actual possession of the value, although in neither case am I in possession of the specific thing. The thing which I have either given up, or expect to receive, is my property only as regards its value; but as a specific thing it is the property of the holder of the pledge, who owns also whatever surplus value the object may have. Pledge is not itself a contract, but only a stipulation (§77), which completes contract on the side of possession of property.—Mortgage and surety are special forms of the pledge.

Addition.—In contract it was said that by means of an agreement a property becomes mine, although I have not possession as yet and shall have possession only by performing my part. If I am out-and-out owner of the object, the intention of a pledge is to place me at once in possession of its value; thus already in the engagement the possession is guaranteed. Surety is a special kind of pledge, some one offering his promise or credit as warrant for my performance. Here a person does, what in a pledge is done by a thing.

81. When persons are viewed as direct and incomplete, their wills are still particular, however identical they may be implicitly, and however much they may, in contract, be subordinated to the common will. So long as they are direct and incomplete, it is a matter of accident whether their particular wills accord with the general will, which has existence only by means of them. When the particular will is actually different from the universal, it is led by caprice, random insight and desire, and is opposed to general right. This is wrong.

Note.—It is from the standpoint of logic a higher necessity which brings about the transition to wrong. The two phases of the conception of right are (*a*), intrinsic right or the general will, and (*b*) right as it exists, or the particular will. It inheres in the abstract reality of the conception that these two phases should be opposed and given independence.— The particular, independent will is caprice and erratic choice, which I, in exchange, have yielded up with regard to only one single thing, but not altogether.

Addition.—In contract the two wills give rise to a common will. This common will is only relatively universal, and thus still in opposition to the particular will. Exchange or covenant, it is true, implies the right to demand performance. But the particular will may act in opposition to the general abstract right. Hence arises the negation, which was already implicit in the general will. This negation is wrong. The general procedure is this, to purify the will of its abstract simplicity, and thus to summon out of the common will the particular will, which in turn takes the field against the common will, the participants, in contract, still preserve their particular wills. Contract is not, therefore, beyond arbitrary caprice, and remains exposed to wrong.

THIRD SECTION
Wrong

82. Contract establishes general right, whose inner or relative universality is merely a generality based on the caprice of the particular will. In this external manifestation of right, right and its essential embodiment in the particular will are directly or accidentally in accord. In wrong this external manifestation becomes an empty appearance. This seeming reality consists in the opposition of abstract right to the particular will, involving a particular right. But this seeming reality is in truth a mere nullity, since right by negating this negation of itself restores itself. By turning back to itself out of its negation right becomes actual and valid, whereas at first it was only a contingent possibility.

Addition.—When intrinsic right or the general will is determined in its nature by the particular will, it is in relation with a non-essential. This is the relation of essence or reality to outward manifestation. Though the manifestation is in one aspect adequate to the essence, it is in another aspect inadequate; as a manifestation is contingency, essence is in relation with the unessential. Now in wrong this manifestation has the form of a seeming reality, which is to be interpreted as an outward reality inadequate to the essence. It deprives essence of reality, and sets up the empty abstraction as real. It is consequently untrue. It vanishes when it tries to exist alone. By its departure the essence is in possession of itself as its reality, and becomes master over mere semblance. It has thus negated the negation of itself, and become strengthened in the process. Wrong is this mere seeming reality, and, when wrong vanishes, right receives an added fixity and value. What we call essence or reality is the intrinsically universal will, as against which the particular will reveals itself as untrue, and does away with itself. The general will had in the first instance only an immediate being; but now it is something actual, because it has returned out of its negation. Actuality is active and finds itself in its opposite, while the implicit is to its negation passive.

83. Right, as particular and in its diverse shapes, is opposed to its own intrinsic universality and simplicity, and then has the form of a mere semblance. It is a mere seeming reality partly of itself and directly; partly is it so by means of the subject; partly is it established as a pure nullity. There arise therefore (*a*) unpremeditated or civic wrong, (*b*) fraud, and (*c*) crime.

Addition.—Wrong is the mere outer appearance of essence, giving itself forth as independent. If this semblance has a merely implicit and not an explicit existence, that is to say, if the wrong is in my eyes a right, the wrong is unpremeditated. The mere semblance is such for right but not for me. The second form of wrong is fraud. Here the wrong is not such for general right, but by it I delude another person; for me the right is a mere semblance. In the first case wrong was for right only a semblance or seeming wrong; in the second case right is for me, the wrong-doer, only a semblance or pretence. The third kind of wrong is crime. This is both of itself and also for me a wrong. I in this case desire the wrong, and make no use of the pretence of right. The other party, against whom the crime is done, is quite well aware that this unqualified wrong is not a right. The distinction between fraud and crime lies in this, that a fraudulent act is not yet recognized as a wrong, but in crime the wrong is openly seen.

A. Unpremeditated Wrong

84. Since the will is in itself universal, possession (§54) and contract, in themselves and in their different kinds, and also all the various manifestations of my will imply a reference to other rights at law. Since these rights are so external and varied, several different persons may have a right to one and the same object, each basing his claim to ownership on his right at law. Thus arise collisions.

85. A collision, in which the object is claimed on legal grounds, occurs in the region of civil law, and recognizes the law as the universal arbiter. The thing is admitted to belong to him who has the right to it. The legal contest merely finds whether a thing is mine or another's. This is a purely negative judgment, in which the predicate "mine" negates only the particular.

86. In law-suits the recognition of right is bound up with some private interest or view opposed to right. Against this mere appearance, intrinsic right, which is in fact implied in it (§85), comes on the scene as a reality purposed and demanded. This right, however, is demanded only abstractly, because the will as particular is not freed from direct contact with its private interest, and does not aim at the universal. Still, the law is here a recognized reality, as against which the contending parties must renounce their private views and interests.

Addition.—That which is intrinsically right has a definite ground, and I defend my wrong, which I maintain to be right, also on some ground. It is the nature of the finite and particular to make room for accidents. Collisions must occur, since we are at the stage of the finite. The first form of wrong negates only the particular will; but pays respect to the general right; it is thus the slightest of all forms of wrong. When I say that a rose is not red, I still admit that the object has colour. I thus do not deny the species, colour, but only the particular colour, red. It is the same here with right. Everybody wills the right, and for him the right only shall take place; his wrong consists in his holding that what he wills is right.

B. Fraud

87. Since intrinsic right, in distinction from particular and concrete right, is demanded, it is essential; but just because it is only demanded and in that light merely subjective, it is non-essential, and becomes simply an appearance. When the universal is degraded from the particular will to the merely apparent will, when, *e.g.,* contract is regarded as only an external association of the will, we have fraud.

Addition.—In fraud universal right is abused, but the particular will is respected. The person on whom the fraud is committed, is imposed upon and made to believe that he gets his rights. The right, which is demanded, however, is merely subjective and unreal, and in that consists the fraud.

88. I acquire property by contract for the sake of the special qualities of the thing. But I acquire it, also, because of its inner universality which consists partly in its value, partly in its being the property of another. Now it is at the option of the other party to produce a false appearance in the case of contract. There may be the free consent of both parties to the exchange of the mere given object in its bare particularity, and so far the transaction is not unjust. Yet the object may fail to have any intrinsic universality. (The infinite judgment in its positive expression or identical meaning. See "Encyclopædia of the Philosophical Sciences.")

89. To guard against the acceptance of a thing in its bare particularity, and in order to be fortified against an arbitrary will, there is at this juncture only a demand that the objective or universal side of the thing should be recognizable, that the objective should be made good as right, and that the arbitrary will, offending against right, should be removed and superseded.

Addition.—No penalty is attached to mere unpremeditated or unintentional wrong, since in it I have willed nothing against right. But to fraud penalties are due, since right is violated.

C. Violence and Crime

90. Since in property my will is embodied in an external thing, it follows that just as far as my will is reflected in that object, I can be attacked in it and placed under external compulsion. Hence my will may be enforced. Violence is done to it, when force is employed in order to obtain some possession or object of desire.

Addition.—In crime, which is wrong in its proper sense, neither right in general nor my personal right is respected. Both the objective and the subjective aspects of right are set at defiance by crime.

91. As a living creature a man may be compelled to do a thing; his physical and other external powers may be brought under the force of another. But the free will cannot be absolutely compelled (§5), but only in so far as it does not withdraw (§7) out of the external, to which it is held fast, or out of the imaginative reproduction of the external. It can only be compelled when it allows itself to be compelled.

92. Since it is only in so far as the will has visible existence that it is the idea and so really free, and its realized existence is the embodiment of freedom, force or violence destroys itself forthwith in its very conception. It is a manifestation of will which cancels and supersedes a manifestation or visible expression of will. Force or violence, therefore, is, according to this abstract treatment of it, devoid of right.

93. Since it in its very conception destroys itself, its principle is that it must be cancelled by violence. Hence it is not only right but necessary that a second exercise of force should annul and supersede the first.

Note.—Violation of a contract through failure to carry out the agreement, or violation of the legal duties toward the family or the state, through action or neglect, is the first violence. It is an exercise of force, if I retain another's property, or neglect to do some duty. Force exercised by a teacher upon a pupil, or by any one against incivility and rudeness, seems to be the first act of violence, not caused by any previous display of force. But the merely natural will is of itself a violence to the universal idea of freedom; and against the inroads of the uncivilized will the idea of freedom ought to be protected and made good. Either there must be assumed within the family or state a moral and social atmosphere, against which a crude naturalness is an act of violence, or else there is at first everywhere present a natural condition or state of violence, over which the idea has the right of mastery.

Addition.—In the state there can be heroes no more. They appear only in uncivilized communities. The aim of the hero is right, necessary and in keeping with the state; but he carried it out, as if it was his own private affair. The heroes, who founded states, and introduced marriage and husbandry, did not in this realize a recognized right. These acts issue merely from their particular wills. Yet as they imply the higher right of the idea against a merely natural state of things, their violence is lawful. Little can be effected against the force of nature merely by goodness.

94. Abstract right is a right to use force. A wrong done to this right is a force exercised against my liberty realized in an external thing. The preservation of my realized freedom against force must be itself an external act, and therefore a second force, which removes the first and takes its place.

Note.—To define strict abstract right as the right to use compulsion is to apprehend it as a result, which enters first of all by the roundabout way of wrong.

Addition.—Here may well be observed the difference between right and morality. In morality or the sphere in which I turn back into myself there are also two sides, for in it goodness is for me an end, and in accordance with this idea I must direct my life. Goodness is embodied in my resolution, and I realize it in myself. Yet this resolution is wholly internal, and, as a consequence, is not subject to coercion. The civil laws do not seek to stretch their control over the disposition. In morality I am independent, and the application of external force has no meaning.

95. A first violence, exercised by a free man, and doing injury to the concrete embodiment of freedom, namely right as right, is crime. Crime is the negative-infinite judgment in its complete sense. It negates not only the particular object of my will, but also the universal or infinite, which is involved in the predicate 'mine,' the very capacity for possessing rights; nor does it even utilize my opinion, as in fraud (§88). Here we are in the realm of criminal law.

Note.—The right to injure which constitutes crime, has indeed so far only the features we have pointed out; and crime has a meaning determined in each case by these special features. But the substance of these forms of right is the universal which remains the same in all its subsequent developments and modifications. So also crime remains the same in accordance with its conception. Hence the phase, noticed in the next paragraph, refers to particular and definite contents, as, *e.g.,* perjury, treason, counterfeiting, forgery, etc.

96. The actualized will, which alone is subject to injury, has, of course, a concrete existence, and varies, therefore, both in quality and in quantity. This variation gives rise to differences in the objective side of crime, which may injure only one side or phase of the will, or again, its whole concrete character and range, as in murder, slavery, and religious persecution.

Note.—The Stoic theory that there is but one virtue and one vice, the Draconian statutes, which punished every crime with death, and the barbarity of the formal code of honour, which found in every injury an unpardonable insult, all in common cling to the abstract view of the free will and personality, and refuse to take them in that concrete and definite realization which they must have, if they are to realize the idea.— Robbery and theft differ in quality, because in robbery personal violence is done to me as an actually present consciousness and as this self-determined subject.—Many qualitative phases of crime, as, for instance, an act done against public safety, are determined by definite social relations, and may be deduced from the conception, although they are often made in a roundabout way to depend upon consequences. A crime against public peace is of itself in its own direct composition heavier or lighter according to its extent and quality. The subjective moral quality referring to the higher distinction, as to how far the act is done consciously, will be dealt with later.

Addition.—Thought itself cannot determine how every single crime is to be punished. In many cases the positive features of the act must be considered. By the progress of civilization the estimate of crime becomes milder, to-day the criminal being punished less severely than he was a hundred years ago. It is not exactly that the crime or the punishment has become different but the relation between the two.

97. An injury done to right as right is a positive external fact; yet it is a nullity. This nullity is exposed in the actual negation of the injury and in the realization of right. Right necessarily brings itself to pass by cancelling the injury and assuming its place.

Addition.—By crime something is altered, and exists as so altered. But this existence is the opposite of itself, and so far null. Nullity consists in the usurpation of the place of right. But right, as absolute, is precisely what refuses to be set aside. Hence it is the manifestation of the crime which is intrinsically null, and this nullity is the essential result of all crime. But what is null must manifest itself as such, and make itself known as that which violates itself. The criminal act is not the primary and positive, to which punishment comes as the negative. It is the negative, and punishment is only the negation of a negation. Actual right destroys and replaces injury, thus showing its validity and verifying itself as a necessary factor in reality.

98. Injury, confined merely to external reality or possession of some kind, is detriment or damage to property or wealth. The cancellation of the injury or damage takes, when possible, the form of civic satisfaction or compensation.

Note.—When damage consists in the destruction of something which cannot be restored, compensation must take the form not of a particular object but of the universal quality, namely, value.

99. The injury which befalls the intrinsic or general will, the will, that is, of the injurer, the injured and all others, has just as little positive existence in this general will as in the bare external result. The general will, *i.e.* right or law, is self-complete, has no external existence at all, and is inviolable. Injury is merely negative also for the particular wills of the injured and others. It exists positively, on the other hand, only as the particular will of the criminal, and to injure this will in its concrete existence is to supersede the crime, which would otherwise be positively established, and to restore right.

Note.—The theory of punishment is one of the matters, which in the modern positive science of right has fared worst. The attempt is made to base this theory upon the understanding, and not, as should be done, upon the conception. If crime and its removal, or, more definitely, punishment, are regarded merely as evil, it might indeed be thought unreasonable to will a second evil merely because one already existed. (Klein, "Grunds. des peinlichen Rechts," §9 fol.) In the different theories of punishment, that it is preventive, deterrent, reformatory, etc., this superficial notion is taken to be fundamental. In the same superficial way the result of punishment is set down as a good. But here we are not dealing with an evil, and this or that good, but with wrong and justice. In these superficial theories the consideration of justice is set aside, and the moral aspect, the subjective side of crime, is made the essential. Also with the moral view are mingled trivial psychological notions about temptation, and the strength of sensual impulses opposing reason, about psychological compulsion also, and the influences affecting the imagination; it being forgotten that the subjective may freely abase itself to something contingent and unreal. The treatment of punishment in its character as a phenomenon, of its relation to the particular consciousness, of the effect of threats upon the imagination, and of the possibility of reform is of great importance in its proper place, when the method of punishment is to be decided on. But such treatment must assume that punishment is absolutely just. Hence everything turns on the point that in crime it is not the production of evil but the injury of right as right, which must be set aside and overcome. We must ask what that is in crime, whose existence has to be removed. That is the only evil to be set aside, and the essential thing is to determine wherein that evil lies. So long as conceptions are not clear on this point, confusion must reign in the theory of punishment.

Addition.—Feuerbach, in his theory of punishment, considers punishment as a menace, and thinks that if any one disregards the threat and commits a crime, the punishment must follow, since it was already known to the criminal. But is it right to make threats? A threat assumes that a man is not free, and will compel him by vividly presenting a possible evil. Right and justice, however, must have their seat in freedom and in the will, and not in the restriction implied in menace. In this view of punishment it is much the same as when one raises a cane against a dog; a man is not treated in accordance with his dignity and honour, but as a dog. A menace may incite a man to rebellion in order that he may demonstrate his freedom, and therefore sets justice wholly aside. Psychological compulsion may refer to distinctions of quality or quantity in crime, but not to the very nature of crime. Books of law, written in accordance with the principle that punishment is a threat, lack their proper basis.

100. The injury which the criminal experiences is inherently just be-

cause it expresses his own inherent will, is a visible proof of his freedom and is his right. But more than that, the injury is a right of the criminal himself, and is implied in his realized will or act. In his act, the act of a rational being, is involved a universal element, which by the act is set up as a law. This law he has recognized in his act, and has consented to be placed under it as under his right.

Note.—Beccaria, as is well known, has denied to the state the right of exacting the death penalty, on the ground that the social contract cannot be supposed to contain the consent of the individual to his own death; rather, as he thought, must the opposite be assumed. To this it must be replied that the state is not a contract (§75), nor, moreover, are the protection and security of the life and property of individuals in their capacity as separate persons, the unconditioned object of the state's existence. On the contrary, the state is the higher existence, which lays claim to the life and property of the individual, and demands the sacrifice of them.

Not only has the conception of crime, the reasonable essence of it, to be upheld by the state, with or without the consent of the individual, but rationality on its formal side, the side of the individual will, is contained in the act of the criminal. The criminal is honoured as reasonable, because the punishment is regarded as containing his own right. The honour would not be shared by him, if the conception and measure of his punishment were not deduced from his very act. Just as little is he honoured when he is regarded as a hurtful animal, which must be made harmless, or as one who must be terrified or reformed.—Moreover, punishment is not the only embodiment of justice in the state, nor is the state merely the condition or possibility of justice.

Addition.—The desire of Beccaria that men should consent to their own punishment is reasonable, but the criminal has already yielded consent through his act. It is both in the nature of crime and in the criminal's own will, that the injury caused by him should be superseded. In spite of this Beccaria's efforts to abolish capital punishment have had good results. Although neither Joseph II. nor the French have ever been able to obtain complete abolition of the death-penalty, still we have begun to see what crimes deserve death and what do not. Capital punishment has thus become less frequent, as indeed should be the case with the extreme penalty of the law.

101. The doing away with crime is retribution, in so far as retribution is in its conception injury of an injury, implying that as crime has a definite qualitative and quantitative context, its negation should be similarly definite. This identity, involved in the very nature of the case, is not literal equality, but equality in the inherent nature of the injury, namely, its value.

Philosophy of Right

Note.—If we were to deduce our definition of punishment, as science usually does, from accepted opinions as to the psychological experiences of consciousness, we could prove that in nations and individuals there is and has been a universal feeling that crime deserves punishment, and that it should be done to the criminal according to his act. Yet the sciences, which have drawn their decisions from universal opinion, the very next moment adopt conclusions at variance with their so-called universal facts of consciousness.

The category of equality has introduced much difficulty into the general notion of retribution. The view that it is just to mete out punishment in proportion to the special context of the crime, of course arises later than the essential relation of punishment to crime. Although, in order to make this essential relation specific, we must look about for other principles than merely the general principle of punishment, yet this general principle remains as it is. And more, the conception itself must contain the basis for special applications of it. The conception, made thus specific, implies of necessity the judgment that crime, as the product of a negative will, carries with it its own negation or punishment. This inner identity is reproduced by the understanding in the sphere of actual reality as equality. The quantitative and qualitative context of crime and its removal belongs to the external region, in which no absolute rule can be laid down (compare §49). In the region of the finite this rule of equality is only a demand which, as it is important to note, the understanding must more and more hold in check. However it goes on *ad infinitum,* and permits only of a continual approximation.

If we fail to observe the nature of the finite, and cling to absolute equality in matters of detail, there arises first of all the insuperable difficulty of fixing the kind of punishment. To do this satisfactorily psychology would have to reckon with the magnitude of the sensual motives, and also with whatever accompanies them as, *e.g.,* the greater strength of the evil will, or the weakness of the will, or its limited freedom. But that is not the sole difficulty. To adhere obstinately to the equalization of punishment and crime in every case would reduce retribution to an absurdity. It would be necessary to institute a theft in return for theft, robbery for robbery, and to demand an eye for an eye and a tooth for a tooth, although the criminal, as we can easily fancy, might have only one eye or be toothless. For these absurdities, however, the conception is not responsible. They are due to the attempt to equate crime and punishment throughout their minute details. Value, as the inner identity of things specifically different, has already been made use of in connection with contract, and occurs again in the civil prosecution of crime (§95). By it the imagination is transferred from the direct attributes of the object to its universal nature. Since the essential character of crime lies in its infinitude, *i.e.,* in the breach of its own right, mere external details vanish. Equality becomes only a general rule for determining the essential, namely, a man's real desert, not for deciding the special external penalty. Only when we limit ourselves to equality in the external details are theft and robbery unequal to fine and imprisonment. But from the standpoint of their value and their general capacity to be injuries, they can be equated. To approach as nearly as possible to this equality in value is, as has been remarked, the task of the understanding. If we ignore the relation of crime to its cancellation, and neglect the idea of value, and the possibility of comparing these two in terms of their value, we can see in punishment nothing more than the arbitrary attachment of an evil to an act not permitted (Klein, "Grunds. des peinlichen Rechts," §9).

Addition.—Retribution is the inner connection and identity of two things which in outward appearance and in external reality are different. Requital seems to be something foreign, and not of right to belong to the criminal. But punishment is only the manifestation of crime, the other half which is necessarily presupposed in the first. Retribution looks like something immoral, like revenge, and may therefore seem to be something personal. But it is the conception, not the personal element, which carries out retribution. Revenge is mine, says God in the Bible, and, when some find in the word retribution the idea of a special pleasure for the subjective will, it must be replied that it signifies only the turning back of crime against itself. The Eumenides sleep, but crime wakes them. So it is the criminal's own deed which judges itself. Although in requital we cannot venture upon equality of details, the case is different with murder, to which death is necessarily due. Life is the total context of one's existence, and cannot be measured by value. Its punishment, therefore, cannot be measured by value, but must consist in the taking of another life.

102. In the sphere of direct right the suppression of crime takes, in the first instance, the form of revenge. This in its content is just, so far as it is retribution; but in its form it is the act of a subjective will, which may put into any injury an infinite or unpardonable wrong. Hence its justice is a matter of accident, and for others means only private satisfaction. As revenge is only the positive act of a particular will, it is a new injury. Through this contradiction it becomes an infinite process, the insult being inherited without end from generation to generation.

Note.—Wherever crime is punished not as *crimina publica* but as *privata,* it still has attached to it a remnant of revenge. This is the state of affairs with the Jews, with the Romans in theft and robbery, and with the English in some special instances. Differing from private revenge is the exercise of revenge by heroes, adventurous knights, and others, all of whom appear when the state is in its infancy.

Addition.—In that condition of society where there are no judges and no laws, punishment always takes the form of revenge. This is defective, as it is the act of a subjective will, and has an inadequate content. Judges are persons, it is true, but they will the universal meaning of the law, and insert into punishment nothing which is not found in the nature of the act. But the injured person, on the other hand, may view the wrong act not in its necessary limits of quality and quantity, but simply as a wrong, and may in requital do what would lead to a new wrong. Amongst uncivilized peoples revenge is undying, as with the Arabs, amongst whom it can be suppressed only by a superior force or by impossibility. In several of our present regulations a trace of revenge survives, as when it is at the option of individuals to bring an injury to trial at court.

103. That the contradiction involved in this way of abolishing crime, and the contradictions found in other cases of wrong (§§86, 89), should be solved, is a demand made by a justice which is freed at once from all subjective interests and limits and from the arbitrariness of power. Justice, therefore, does not revenge but punishes. Here we have in the first instance the demand of a will, which, while particular and subjective, wills the universal as such. But the conception of morality is not simply demanded, but is in the process created.

Transition from Right to Morality

104. Crime and revenging justice represent the visible outer form of the development of the will as occurring, first of all, in the distinction between the universal will and the individual will, which exists independently in opposition to the universal. Next, by rising above the opposition, the universal will is turned back into itself and has become an independent reality. Thus right, when maintained against the independent private will, has validity, being realized through its own necessity.

This result is also arrived at by the development of the conception of will on the side of its inner character. The actualization of the will according to its conception proceeds in this way. Its first form is the abstract and simple phase it assumes in abstract right. This first form must be in the next place set aside and passed beyond (§21) in order that the will may become involved in the opposition of the abstract universal will and the independent particular will. Then by the removal of this opposition, *i.e.,* by the negation of a negation, it becomes an actualized will, free not only abstractly and potentially, but actually, as is necessary in a negativity which is able to refer itself to itself. Whereas in abstract right the will was itself mere personality, it now has its personality as its object. The subjectivity which is its own object is infinite, and freedom in its infinite subjectivity constitutes the principle of morality.

Note.—Let us for the sake of a closer inspection turn back to the elements, through which the conception of freedom progresses from the first abstract phase of the will to that phase, in which it refers itself to itself, the phase of the self-determining subject. Thus property being an external object, we have in it the phase of the abstract "mine;" in exchange we have the common "mine," the "mine" brought into existence by two wills; in wrong the will which belongs to the province of right, the will in its abstract, direct, and intrinsic existence, is made contingent by means of the particular will which is itself contingent. In morality this whole phase of will is so far transcended that its contingency is turned back into itself and made one with itself, and thus becomes a self-referring, infinite contingency of the will, or in a word subjectivity.

Addition.—To truth it belongs that the conception should exist, and that its reality should correspond to the conception. In right the will exists in an external object. But as it must have its existence in itself, in an internal thing, it must become its own object; it must pass into subjectivity and have itself over against itself. This relation to itself is affirmative, a relation brought about by the will only through the transcendence of its direct existence. When its firsthand existence is transcended in crime, the way is open, through punishment, the negation of a negation, to affirmation, that is, to morality.

SECOND PART
MORALITY

105. The moral standpoint is the standpoint of the will, not in its abstract or implicit existence, but in its existence for itself, an existence which is infinite (§104). This turning back of the will upon itself, or its actual self-identity, with its associated phases stands in contrast to its abstract implicit existence, and converts person into subject.

106. Subjectivity is the conception made definite, differing therefore from the abstract, general will. Further, the will of the subject, though it still retains traces of self-involved simplicity, is the will of an individual, who is an object for himself. Hence subjectivity is the realization of the conception.—This gives freedom a higher ground. Now at last there appears in the idea the side of its real existence, the subjectivity of the will. It is only in the will as subjective that freedom, or the potentially existing will, can be actualized.

Note.—Morality, the second sphere, gives an outline of the real side of the conception of freedom. Observe the process through which morality passes. As the will has now withdrawn into itself, it appears at the outset as existing independently, having merely a potential identity with the intrinsic or universal will. Then this abstract self-dependence is superseded; and, finally, the will is made really and consciously identical with the intrinsic or universal will. Now in this movement, as I have said, is illustrated the conception of freedom. Freedom or subjectivity is at first abstract and distinct from the conception of it. Then by means of this movement the soil of freedom is so worked up, that for the conception, and necessarily also for the idea, it receives its true realization. The process ends, therefore, when the subjective will has become an objective and truly concrete will.

Addition.—In right, taken strictly, nothing depends upon my purpose or intention. The question of the self-determination, impulse, or purpose of the will arises for the first time in morality. Since a man is to be judged according to the direction he has given himself, he is in this act free, let

the external features of the act be what they may. As no one can successfully assail a man's inner conviction, and no force can reach it, the
moral will is inaccessible. A man's worth is estimated by his inner act.
Hence the moral standpoint implies the realization of freedom.

107. As self-determination of will is at the same time a factor of the
will's conception, subjectivity is not merely the outward reality of will,
but its inner being (§104). This free and independent will, having now
become the will of a subject, and assuming in the first instance the form
of the conception, has itself a visible realization; otherwise it could not
attain to the idea. The moral standpoint is in its realized form the right
of the subjective will. In accordance with this right the will recognizes
and is a thing, only in so far as the thing is the will's own, and the will in
it is itself and subjective.

Note.—The process of the moral standpoint (Note to preceding paragraph) also appears as the development of the right of the subjective will,
or of the way in which the subjective will is realized. Thus the will ac-
counts what in its object it recognizes to be its own as its true conception, its objective or universal reality.

Addition.—Subjectivity of will, as a complete phase, is in its turn a
whole which, by its very nature, must also have objectivity. Freedom can
at first realize itself only in the subject, as it is the true material for this
realization. But this concrete manifestation of will, which we have called
subjectivity, is different from absolute will. From this new one-sidedness
of subjectivity must the will free itself, in order that it may become absolute will. In morality the interest peculiar to man is in question, and the
high value of this interest consists in man's knowing himself to be absolute, and determining himself. Uncivilized man is controlled by the
forces and occurrences of nature. Children have no moral will, but are
guided by their parents. Civilized man is determined from within, and
wills that he shall be in all he does.

108. The subjective will, in so far as it is directly its own object and
distinct from the general will (§106, note), is abstract, limited, and formal.
Subjectivity, however, is not formal merely, but, since it is the infinite self-
direction of the will, is the will itself taken formally. Since this formal
character, as it appears first of all in the particular will, is not as yet identical with the conception of will, the moral standpoint is the standpoint
of relation, of obligation or requirement.—Since, too, subjectivity involves difference, that is to say, opposition to objectivity as to a mere external existence, there arises here also the standpoint of consciousness
(§8), the standpoint of difference in general, of the finite and phenomenal phase of the will.

Note.—The moral is not at once opposed to the immoral, just as right
is not directly opposed to wrong. The general standpoint of both the

moral and the immoral depends upon the subjectivity of the will.

Addition.—In morality self-determination is to be construed as a restless activity, which cannot be satisfied with anything that is. Only in the region of established ethical principles is the will identical with the conception of it, and has only this conception for its content. In morality the will is as yet related to what is potential. This is the standpoint of difference, and the process of this standpoint is the identification of the subjective will with the conception of will. The imperative or ought, which, therefore, still is in morality, is fulfilled only in the ethical sphere. This sphere, to which the subjective will is related, has a twofold nature. It is the substance of the conception, and also external reality. If the good were established in the subjective will, it would not yet be realized.

109. The formal will, by its own determining character, contains at the outset the opposition of subjectivity and objectivity, and the appropriate activity (§8). Of this will we have these further phases. Concrete realization and determinate character are in the conception identical. The conception of the subjective will is first to make these two phases separate and independent, and then to establish them as identical. Determinate character in the self-determined will (α) is brought about in itself by itself, the opposition which it creates within itself being a self-bestowed content. This is the first negation, whose formal limit consists in its being fixed as merely subjective. (β) Since the will returns into itself and is infinite, this limit exists for it, and it wills to transcend the limitation. Hence it strives to convert its content out of subjectivity into objectivity, *i.e.,* some kind of directly given reality. (γ) The simple identity of the will with itself in this opposition is the content, which maintains itself amid these oppositions, and is indifferent to formal distinctions. This content is the end.

110. As at the moral standpoint, freedom or self-identity of will is for the will (§105), the simple identity of the content or end receives a further characteristic peculiar to itself.

(*a*) This content becomes mine in such a way that it in its identity is not only my inner end, but also, so far as it is externally realized, contains for me my subjectivity.

Addition.—The content of the subjective or moral will has a special character. Although it has attained the form of objectivity, it is yet always to contain my subjectivity. An act shall be counted mine only so far as it is on its inner side issued by me, and was my own proposition and intention. I do not recognize as mine anything in the outward act except what lay in my subjective will, and in the outer act I desire to see my subjective consciousness repeated.

111. (*b*) The content, though it contains something particular, from

whatever source it comes, is yet the content of a self-referring will, which is also self-identical and universal. Thus it has these two features (α) It aims to be in itself adequate to the universal will, or to have the objectivity of the conception; (β) yet, since the subjective will exists for itself, and is therefore independent and formal (§108), its aim is only an ought and is possibly not adequate to the conception.

112. (c) Though I preserve my subjectivity in accomplishing my ends (§110), yet in the objectification of these ends I pass beyond the simple and elementary subjectivity which is merely my own. This new external subjectivity, which is identical with me, is the will of others (§73). The sphere for the existence of the will is subjectivity (§106), and the will of others is the existence, which, though other than I, I yet give to my purpose. Hence the accomplishment of my purpose contains the identity of my will and that of others, and has to the will of others a relation which is positive.

Note.—The objectivity of the realized end has three senses, or rather contains in union the three following phases. (α) It is external direct reality (§109). (β) It is adequate to the conception (§112). (γ) It is universal subjectivity. The subjectivity which preserves itself in this objectivity implies (α) that the objective end shall be my own, so that in it I preserve myself as a particular individual (§110). The two phases (β) and (γ) of subjectivity concur with the phases (β) and (γ) of objectivity. At the moral standpoint these various phases are distinguished or joined merely in a contradiction. This is the superficial and finite nature of the moral sphere (§108). The development of the standpoint consists in the development of these contradictions and their solution, an achievement which at the present point of view is incomplete or merely relative.

Addition.—It was said that formal right contained only prohibitions, and that from the strict standpoint of legal right an act had only a negative reference to the will of others. In morals, on the contrary, the relation of my will to that of others is positive; that, which the subjective will realizes, contains the universal will. In this is present the production or alteration of some visible reality, and this has a bearing upon the will of others. The conception of morality is the internal relation of the will to itself. But there is here more than one will, since the objectification of the will implies the transcendence of the one-sidedness of the separate will, and the substitution of two wills having a positive relation one to the other. In right my will is realized in property, and there is no room for any reference of the will of others to my will. But morality treats of the well-being of others also. At this point this positive relation to others first makes its appearance.

113. The expression of the subjective or moral will is action. Of action it may be said that (α) I know its external fulfillment to be mine, (β)

it is essentially related to the conception in its phase as the ought or imperative, and (γ) it is essentially connected with the will of others.

Note.—Firstly, the expression of the moral will is action. The embodiment achieved by the will in formal right is a mere object. This realization is direct, and has in the first instance no actual express reference to the conception. Not having as yet come into conflict with the subjective will, the conception is not yet distinguished from it, and has no positive relation to the will of others. The commands of right are, hence, fundamentally prohibitions (§38). In contract and wrong, indeed, there begins to be seen a relation to the will of others, but the agreement, found at this point, is based upon arbitrary choice, while the essential reference to the will of others is in right merely the negative proposal to keep my property or the worth of it, and to let others keep theirs. Crime does in a way issue from the subjective will. But the content of a crime is fixed by written instructions and is not directly imputable to me. Hence as the legal act contains only some elements of a distinctively moral act, the two kinds of action are different.

114. The right of the moral will has three factors:

(*a*) The abstract or formal right. The act, as directly realized, is to be in its essential content mine, and embody the purpose of the subjective will.

(*b*) The specific side of an act or its inner content. (α) This is intention, which is for me, whose general character is fixed, the value and inner substance of the act, (β) and well-being, or the content taken as the particular end of my particular, subjective reality.

(*c*) The good, or the content taken as universal and exalted to universality and absolute objectivity. This is the absolute end of the will. As this is the sphere of reflection, we have the opposition of the universality, which is subjective, and hence involves in one aspect evil, and in another conscience.

Addition.—An act, to be moral, must in the first instance accord with my purpose, since the right of the moral will is to recognize as its realization nothing which is not found internally in the purpose. Purpose concerns the formal principle that the externalized will must also be internal to me. In the next place we ask after the intention, that is, the value of the act relatively to me. The third factor is not merely the relative, but the universal value of the act, the good. In the first phase of an act there is a breach between purpose and realization; in the second between what is given externally as universal will, and the particular internal character, which I give it; the third and last phase is the claim of my intention to be the universal content. The good is the intention exalted to the conception of the will.

Purpose and Responsibility

115. In the direct or immediate act the subjective will is finite, since it has to do with both an external object and its varied surroundings, all presupposed. An accomplished act makes a change in this ready-to-hand material, and the will is responsible, in so far as the changed material can be said to be mine.

Note.—An event or resultant condition is a concrete external reality, having an indefinite number of circumstances associated with it. Every particular element, shown to be in any sense a condition, ground or cause of such an event, and, therefore, to have contributed its portion, may be regarded as responsible for it, or at least as sharing in the responsibility. Hence in the case of such a richly varied event as the French Revolution, the formal understanding has to select from an untold multitude of circumstances that one to which it will attribute responsibility.

Addition.—What is contained in my purpose can be laid at my door, and this is one of the main considerations in the case of crime. But in simple responsibility there is found only the quite external judgment as to whether I have or have not done this thing. Thus merely to be responsible does not mean that the whole thing is to be imputed to me.

116. It is not my deed, if things, which I own, cause injury to others through some of their many external connections; this may happen even with my body as a mechanical or living object. Yet I am not wholly free from responsibility in such a case, since these things are still mine, although by their very nature they are often only imperfectly subject to my attention and control.

117. When the self-directing will proposes to act upon a given material, it has a representation of the circumstances. Since the material is supplied, the will is finite, and the results of the act are for it accidental. Hence they may contain something very different from the representation. But the right of the will in acting is to recognize as its own deed only those results which were consciously in its end and were purposed. That responsibility shall extend to the will only so far as the results were known, is the right of knowledge.

Addition.—The will has before it an outer reality, upon which it operates. But to be able to do this, it must have a representation of this reality. True responsibility is mine only in so far as the outer reality was within my consciousness. The will, because this external matter is supplied to it, is finite; or rather because it is finite, the matter is supplied. When I think and will rationally, I am not at this standpoint of finitude, nor is the object I act upon something opposed to me. The finite always has limit and boundary. There stands opposed to me that which is other than I, something accidental and externally necessary; it may or may not fall into agreement with me. But I am only what relates to my freedom; and the act is the purport of my will only in so far as I am aware of it. Œdipus, who unwittingly slew his father, is not to be arraigned as a patricide. In the ancient laws, however, less value was attached to the subjective side of the act than is done to-day. Hence arose amongst the ancients asylums, where the fugitive from revenge might be received and protected.

118. An act, when it has become an external reality, and is connected with a varied outer necessity, has manifold consequences. These consequences, being the visible shape, whose soul is the end of action, belong to the act. But at the same time the inner act, when realized as an end in the external world, is handed over to external forces, which attach to it something quite different from what it is in itself, and thus carry it away into strange and distant consequences. It is the right of the will to adopt only the first consequences, since they alone lie in the purpose.

Note.—The division of consequences into necessary and accidental is not accurate, because the inner necessity, involved in the finite, is realized as a necessity which is external, a necessity, that is to say, implying a relation of separate things, which are independent, indifferent to one another, and only externally connected. The principle "In acting neglect the consequences," and the principle "Judge an act by its consequences, and make them the standard of what is right and good," belong both alike to the abstract understanding. The consequences are the native form of the act, simply manifest its nature, and are nothing but the act itself. The act cannot scorn and disown them. Yet amongst the consequences is included that which is only externally attached to them and has no fellowship with the act itself.

The development of the contradiction involved in the necessary nature of the finite is in external reality the conversion of necessity into contingency and *vice versâ*. An overt act must therefore conform to this law. This law it is which stands the criminal in such good stead, if his act has had but few consequences; so also must the good act be contented to have few or no consequences. But when the consequences of crime have fully developed themselves, they add to the severity of the punishment.

The self-consciousness of the heroic age, painted in the tragedy of "Œdipus," for instance, had not risen out of its simplicity, or reflectively appreciated the difference between realized deed and inner act, between the outer occurrence and the purpose and knowledge of surroundings. Nor did it distinguish between one consequence and another, but spread responsibility over the whole area of the deed.

Addition.—In the fact that I recognize as mine only what was in my representation is to be found the transition from purpose to intention.

Only what I knew of the surroundings can be imputed to me. But there are necessary results attached to even the simplest act, and they are its universal element. The consequences, which may be prevented from taking effect, I cannot indeed foresee, but I ought to know the universal nature of each separate concrete deed. The thing which I ought to know is the essential whole, which refers not to special details of an act, but to its real nature. The transition from purpose to intention consists in my being aware not merely of my separate act, but of the universal bound up with it. This universal, when willed by me, is my intention.

SECOND SECTION
Intention and Well-being

119. The external embodiment of an act is composed of many parts, and may be regarded as capable of being divided into an infinite number of particulars. An act may be looked on as in the first instance coming into contact with only one of these particulars. But the truth of the particular is the universal. A definite act is not confined in its content to one isolated point of the varied external world, but is universal, including these varied relations within itself. The purpose, which is the product of thought and embraces not the particular only but also the universal side, is intention.

Note.—Intention (in German, "a looking away from") implies, according to its etymology, an abstraction, which has in part the form of universality, and partly is the extraction of a particular side of the concrete thing. The attempt to justify oneself by the intention consists, in general, in asserting that one special isolated phase is the subjective essence of the act.—To pass judgment upon an act simply as an external deed, without qualifying it as right or wrong, imparts to it a universal predicate; it is killing, arson, etc.—When the parts of external reality are taken one by one, their connection must naturally be external. Reality may be, in the first instance, touched at only a single point. Arson, *e.g.,* may be directly concerned with only a small piece of wood, a statement which is merely a proposition, but not a judgment. But this single point has a universal nature, which involves the extension of it. In life the separate part is not a mere part, but directly an organ, in which the universal is really present. Hence in murder it is not a separate piece of flesh, but the life itself which is destroyed. On one side subjective reflection, in its ignorance of the logical nature of the particular and the universal, permits of a dissection into mere particulars and their consequences. On the other side, the act in its finite and casual character naturally breaks up into separate parts.—The invention of the *dolus indirectus* is due to this way of thinking.

Addition.—Manifestly more or fewer circumstances may be included in an act. In the case of arson, *e.g.,* the fire may not take effect, or it may spread farther than the agent intended. Yet in neither case is the result due to good or bad fortune, since man in acting must deal with externality. An old proverb rightly enough says, "A stone flung from the hand is the devil's." In acting I must expose myself to misfortune; that also has a right to me, and is the manifestation of my own will.

120. The right of intention is that the universal quality of the act should not only be implicitly present, but should be known by the agent, and be part and parcel of his subjective will. Conversely the right of objectivity of action, as it may be called, is to maintain that it be known and willed by a subject in his character as thinking.

Note.—This right to this insight involves that children, imbeciles, and lunatics are completely, or almost completely, irresponsible for their actions. Just as actions on the side of their external reality include accidental results, so also the subjective reality contains an indeterminate element, which depends upon the strength of self-consciousness and prudence. But this uncertain element needs to be reckoned with only in the case of imbecility, lunacy, or childhood. These are the only conditions of mind which supersede thought and free will, and permit us to take an agent otherwise than in accordance with his dignity as free and rational.

121. The universal quality of action is in general the manifold content reduced to the simple form of universality. But the subject turned back into himself is particular, in opposition to the particulars of the objective world. He has in his end his own particular content, which constitutes the essential soul of his act. In the execution of this particular content of the act consists his subjective freedom in its concrete character. This is the subject's right to find in the act his satisfaction.

Addition.—I, as independent and self-referred, am particular, and opposed to the external side of the act. Its content is decided by my end. Murder and arson, *e.g.,* are quite general and not the positive content of me, a subject. When anyone has committed a crime, we ask why he has done it. Murder is not done for the sake of murder. There must be besides a particular positive end. If delight in murder were the motive of the crime, it would be the positive content of the subject as such, and the deed would be the satisfaction of his desire. The motive of a deed contains the moral element, which has the twofold signification of the universal in purpose and of the particular in intention. In modern times we are at pains to ask after the motive. Formerly the question was merely, Is this man just? Does he do his duty? Now we scrutinize the heart, and fix a gulf between the objective side of conduct and the internal subjective side, or motive. No doubt the subject's own determination must be considered. What he wills has its ground within him; he wills to satisfy a pleasure or gratify a passion. But right and good are also precisely such a content, due, however, not to nature but to my reason. To make my own freedom the content of my will is a pure characteristic of my freedom itself. Hence the higher moral phase is to find satisfaction in the act, not to harp upon a breech between the objectivity of the deed, and the self-consciousness of man. This defective mode of interpretation has its epochs as well in world-history as in the history of individuals.

122. By virtue of the particular element the act has for me subjective value or interest. In contrast with this end, whose content is the intention, the direct act in its wider content is reduced to a means. This end, as far as it is finite, can again be reduced to a means for a wider intention, and so on indefinitely.

123. The content of these ends is only (α) formal activity, that is, the subject's interest or aim is to be effected by his agency. Men desire to be themselves actively interested in whatever is or ought to be their own. (β) Further definite content is found for the still abstract and formal freedom of subjectivity only in its natural subjective embodiment, as inclinations, passions, opinions, whims, etc. The satisfaction of this content is well-being or happiness in its particular as also in its universal features. In this satisfaction consist the ends of finitude generally.

Note.—This is the standpoint of relation (§108). The subject at this stage emphasizes his distinctive and particular nature. Here enters the content of the natural will (§11). But the will is not in its simple and direct form, since the content belongs to a will which is turned back into itself, and raised to the level of a universal end, namely, well-being or happiness.

Addition.—In so far as the elements of happiness are externally provided, they are not the true elements of freedom. Freedom truly is itself only in an end constituted by itself, *i.e.,* the good. Here the question may be raised, Has man a right to set up for himself ends which are not free, and depend simply on his being a living thing? But life in man is not a mere accident, since it accords with reason. Man has so far a right to make his wants an end. There is nothing degrading in one's being alive. There is open to us no more spiritual region, in which we can exist, than that of life. Only through the exaltation of what is externally provided to the level of something self-created do we enter the higher altitude of the good. But this distinction implies no intolerance of either side of man's nature.

124. Since the subjective satisfaction of the individual, the recognition for example of oneself as honoured or famous, is involved in the realization of absolutely valid ends, the demand that only subjective satisfaction should appear as willed and attained, and also the view that in action subjective and objective ends exclude each other, are empty assertions of the abstract understanding. Nay, more, the argument becomes a positive evil

when it is held that, because subjective satisfaction is always found in every finished work, it must be the essential intention of the agent, the objective end being only a means to the attainment of this satisfaction. The subject is the series of his acts. If these are a series of worthless productions, the subjectivity of the will is also worthless; if the acts are substantial and sound, so likewise is the inner will of the individual.

Note.—The right of the subject's particular being to find himself satisfied, the right, in other words, of subjective freedom, constitutes the middle or turning-point between the ancient and the modern world. This right in its infinite nature is expressed in Christianity, and has been made the universal active principle of a new form of the world. The more definite manifestations of this principle are love, romance, the hope of the eternal salvation of the individual, morality also, and conscience. It includes, moreover, various other forms, which will be, in a measure, introduced in the sequel as the principle of the civic society, and as elements of the political constitution, but partly, however, appear in history generally, especially in the history of art, the sciences, and philosophy. This principle of particularity is now, indeed, one side of the contradiction, and, in the first resort, is at least quite as much identical with the universal as distinct from it. But abstract reflection fastens upon this element in its difference from and opposition to the universal, and propounds the view that morality must carry on a continued warfare against the satisfaction of oneself, demanding of us—

"Mit Abscheu zu thun was die Pflicht gebeut."[1]

The same abstract standpoint lies at the root of that psychological view of history, which seeks to disparage all great deeds and persons. It emphasizes the particular side, which it has already decreed to be evil, considers as the chief factor in the act the honour and glory, which may accrue to the agent, and transforms and converts the inclinations and passions, whose satisfaction was only one element of the total result, into the agent's main intention and active principle. This same abstract point of view asserts that because great acts, and the real result brought to pass by a series of them, have produced a great effect upon the world, and have naturally resulted to the agent in power, honour, and renown, therefore there belongs to the individual not the greatness, but merely these particular and external results. The reason assigned is that the particular consequence, since it was admittedly an end, must be the sole end. Such abstract thinking sees only the subjective side of great men, the side which constitutes its own essence. In its self-constituted vanity it overlooks their real nature. It takes the view of the "psychological valet for whom there

---

[1]"To do with aversion what duty requires."

are no heroes, not because there are no heroes, but because he is only a valet."

Addition.—The sentence, *In magnis voluisse sat est,* is right, if it means that one should will something great. But he should also carry it out, otherwise his volition is vain. The laurels of mere willing are dry leaves, which have never been green.

125. The subjective, whose concern is with the particular content of well-being, is, when it becomes infinite by being turned back into itself, at the same time brought into relation with implicit or general will. This new element, established, in the first instance, in particularity itself, is the well-being of others; in its complete but quite empty character it is the well-being of all. The well-being of many other particular persons is therefore an essential end or right of subjectivity. But since the absolute universal, which is distinguished from this particular content, is here defined simply as right, the ends of the particular will may or may not be in real accordance with the universal.

126. My own particularity, and likewise the particularity of others are, however, a right, only in so far as I am free. They cannot maintain themselves in opposition to their real basis. An intention to further my well-being or that of others, rightly called a moral intention, cannot justify a wrong act.

Note.—It is one of the most corrupt maxims of our day which, originating in the pre-Kantian period of the good heart, and furnishing the quintessence of some well-known touching dramas, undertakes in the case of wrong acts to excite interest in the so-called moral intention. It pictures bad persons as having hearts filled with good intentions and desires for their own well-being, and perhaps for that of others as well. A heightened form of this theory has been vamped up in our own time. Inner inspiration and feeling, the very soul of particularity, have been made the criterion of what is right, reasonable, and excellent. Crime has been pronounced right, reasonable, and excellent, as also have the thoughts which led to it, merely on the ground that they proceeded from inspiration and feeling, though they may have been in fact the most hollow and commonplace whims and most foolish opinions (§140, *note*).— Observe further that here under right and well-being we are considering the formal right and particular well-being of the individual. The so-called general welfare, the well-being of the state, the right of the real, concrete spirit is quite another region, in which formal right and the particular well-being or happiness of the individual are subordinate elements. It has already been remarked that it is one of the most frequent misconceptions of the abstract intellect to set up private right and private well-being as absolutely valid in opposition to the universal principle of the state.

Addition.—We may quote here the celebrated retort given to the libeller, who excused himself with the remark, "*Il faut donc que je vive.*" "*Je n'en vois pas la nécessité,*" was the reply. Life is not necessary against the higher fact of freedom. When the holy Crispinus steals leather to make boots for the poor, his act, though moral, is not right, and cannot be justified.

127. The particular interests of the natural will, viewed as a simple whole, constitute personal reality or the life. In the final resort, life, when in collision with another's rightful ownership, can claim the right of necessity, not on the ground of equity but of right. Observe that on the one side is placed the infinite destruction of our outer existence, and therefore the complete loss of rights; on the other side an injury to only a particular and limited embodiment of one's freedom. A slight injury to a particular possession does not violate the injured man's right, as such, or his capacity for right.

Note.—From this right of need flows the *benefit of competence* (*beneficium competentiæ*), by virtue of which there is allowed to the debtor some of his tools, implements, clothes, and means generally, all of which are of course the property of the creditor. The allowance covers so much as is deemed sufficient for the possible maintenance of one in the debtor's class.

Addition.—Life, or the totality of ends, has a right against abstract right. For instance, by the theft of a loaf of bread a property is doubtless injured. Still, if the act was the means of prolonging life, it would be wrong to consider it as ordinary theft. If the man whose life is in danger were not allowed to preserve himself, he would be without rights; and, since his life is refused him, his whole freedom is denied to him also. Many things, it is true, must go to secure life, especially if we regard the future. But to live now is all that is necessary; the future is not absolute, and remains exposed to accidents. Hence only the need of the immediate present can justify a wrong act. Yet the act is justified, because the agent, abstaining from it, would commit the highest wrong, namely, the total negation of his realized freedom. The *beneficium competentiæ* implies the right to ask that no man shall be wholly sacrificed to mere right.

128. Need reveals the finite and contingent character of both right and well-being, that is to say, of that abstract embodiment of freedom, which is not the existence of any particular person, and also of the sphere of the particular will, which excluded the universality of right. The one-sidedness or ideality of these phases is found in the conception itself. Right has already been embodied as the particular will (§106); and subjectivity, in the whole range of its particularity, is itself the embodiment of freedom (§127), and also, in its character as the infinite reference of the will to itself, is it implicitly the universal side of freedom. These two

elements in their truth and identity, although, in the first instance, only in relative reference to each other, are on the one hand the good, as the fulfilled and absolutely definite universal, and, on the other hand, conscience, or an infinite subjectivity, which is aware of itself, and determines in itself its content.

THIRD SECTION
The Good and Conscience

129. The good is the idea, or unity of the conception of the will with the particular will. Abstract right, well-being, the subjectivity of consciousness, and the contingency of external reality, are in their independent and separate existences superseded in this unity, although in their real essence they are contained in it and preserved. This unity is realized freedom, the absolute final cause of the world.

Addition.—Every stage is properly the idea, but the earlier steps contain the idea only in more abstract form. The I, as person, is already the idea, although in its most abstract guise. The good is the idea more completely determined; it is the unity of the conception of will with the particular will. It is not something abstractly right, but has a real content, whose substance constitutes both right and well-being.

130. In this idea well-being has value, not independently as the realization of the separate particular will, but only as universal well-being, as universal, that is, in its essence, intrinsically or in accordance with freedom. Hence, well-being is not a good, if separated from right; nor is right a good, if separated from well-being. *Fiat justitia* ought not to have *pereat mundus* as a consequence. The good, carrying a necessity to be actualized by the particular will, and comprising the vital essence of such a will, has absolute right over the mere abstract right of property and the particular ends of well-being. If either of these elements is distinguished from the good, it has validity only in so far as it accords with the good and subordinates itself to it.

131. The subjective will finds in the good the supremely essential, and has worth and merit only as its insight and intention accord with the good. In so far as the good in this place is still the abstract idea of the good, the subjective will is not yet carried up into it, and made one with it. It stands to the good in a relation of the following kind. As the good is for it what is real and substantial, it ought to make the good its end and realize it; and on the other hand it is only through the medium of the subjective will that the good can be realized.

Addition.—The good is the truth of the particular will. But the will is only that to which it sets itself. It is not inherently good, but becomes what it is only by its work. On the other side the good apart from the subjective will is only an abstraction having no reality. Reality first comes to the good through the private will. Thus the development of the good contains these three stages. (1) For me, as willing, the good should be particular will, and I should know it. (2) We should say what thing is good, and develop the particular phases of the good. (3) We determine the independent good, particularizing it as infinite and independent subjectivity. This inner determination is conscience.

132. It is the right of the subjective will that it should regard as good what it recognizes as authoritative. It is the individual's right, too, that an act, as the outer realization of an end, should be counted right or wrong, good or evil, lawful or unlawful, according to his knowledge of the worth it has when objectively realized.

Note.—The good is in general the essence of the will in its substantive and universal character, the will in its truth. It exists solely in and by means of thought. The doctrines that man cannot understand the truth but must deal with appearances only, and that thinking does harm to the good will, take away from spirit all its intellectual and ethical merit and value. The right to admit nothing, which I do not regard as reasonable, is the highest right of the subject. But because of its subjective character it is a formal right. So that on the opposite hand the right to the subject of the reasonable or objective remains.

Because of its formal nature insight may be either truth or mere opinion and error. Whether or not the individual attains to the right of his insight belongs, at least from the moral standpoint, to his particular subjective character. I can make it a claim upon myself, and regard it as a subjective right, that I should be convinced that the grounds of an obligation are good. I may even claim that I should know them in their conception and nature. But my demand for the satisfaction of my conviction as to what is good, what allowed and what not allowed, and also as to my responsibility, does not infringe upon the right of objectivity.

Right of insight into the good is different from right of insight (§117) with regard to action as such. The right of objectivity means that the act must be a change in the actual world, be recognized there, and in general be adequate to what has validity there. Whoso will act in this actual world has thereby submitted to its laws, and recognized the right of objectivity. Similarly in the state, which is the objectivity of the conception of reason, legal responsibility does not adapt itself to what any one person holds to be reasonable or unreasonable. It does not adhere to subjective insight into right or wrong, good or evil, or to the claims which an individual makes for the satisfaction of his conviction. In this objective field the right of insight is reckoned as insight into what is legal or illegal, or the actual law. It limits itself to its simplest meaning, namely, knowledge of or acquaintance with what is lawful and binding. Through the publicity of the laws and through general customs the state removes from the right of insight that which is for the subject its formal side. It removes also the element of chance, which at our present standpoint still clings to it.

The right of the subject to know the act as good or evil, legal or illegal, has the result of lessening or abolishing responsibility in the case of children, imbeciles, and lunatics, although the conditions of this responsibility cannot be definitely stated. But to take into consideration momentary fascination, the allurement of passion, drunkenness, or the strength of what are called sensual impulses generally, that impulse alone being excepted which forms the basis of the right of need (§120), to consider these things in estimating the character of a crime and its liability to punishment, or to suppose that these circumstances will remove the guilt of a criminal act, is to neglect right and the true dignity of manhood (§100, and §119, *note*). The nature of man is essentially universal. His consciousness does not exist as a mere abstract moment of time or in isolated parts. Just as the incendiary sets on fire not a separate piece of wood an inch long, which he touches with his match, but the universal involved in it, namely the house, so he does not exist merely in one single moment, or in one isolated passion for revenge. If so, he would be an animal, which, because of its dangerous and passionate nature would have to be killed. It is claimed that the criminal in the moment of his act must have presented clearly to himself the nature of the wrong he is doing and of his liability to punishment, if the act is to be counted to him for a crime. This claim seems to preserve to him the right of his moral subjectivity, but it really denies to him that indwelling intelligent nature, which in its active presence has no affinity with the clear images of purely animal psychology. Only in the case of lunacy is intelligence so distorted as to be separated from the consciousness of particular things and the doing of them. The sphere, in which circumstances are adduced as grounds for leniency, is not that of right but of mercy.

133. Since the good is the essence of the will of the particular subject, it is his obligation. As the good is distinct from particularity, and particularity occurs in the subjective will, the good has at the outset only the character of universal abstract essence. This abstract universal is duty. Hence duty, as is required by its character, must be done for duty's sake.

Addition.—The essence of the will is for me duty. Yet if I know no more than that the good is my duty, it is for me still abstract. Duty should be done for duty's sake, and it is my objective nature in the truest sense which I realize in duty; in doing it I am self-centred and free. It is the signal merit of the standpoint of the Kantian philosophy of action that it has made prominent this signification of duty.

134. Since an act requires its own special content and definite end, and duty in the abstract contains no such end, there arises the question, What

is duty? No answer is at once forthcoming, except "To do right, and to consider one's own well-being, and the general well-being, the well-being of others" (§119).

Addition.—Precisely the same question was proposed to Jesus, when it was asked of him, "What should be done to obtain eternal life?" The universal good cannot, if abstractly taken, be realized. If it is to be realized, it must be given a particular content.

135. The two points of this answer, being each of them conditioned and limited, are not in fact contained in duty itself, but effect the transition into the higher sphere of the unconditioned, or duty. In so far as duty is the universal or essence of the moral consciousness, and merely refers itself to itself within itself, it is only an abstract universality, and has for its characteristic an identity without content, an abstract positive, an absence of definite character.

Note.—It is important to be clear that the pure unconditioned self-direction of the will is the root of duty. This doctrine of volition attained to a firm basis and starting-point first of all in the Kantian philosophy through the thought of the infinite autonomy of the will (§133). Yet if this merely moral standpoint does not pass into the conception of the ethical system, this philosophical acquisition is reduced to empty formalism, and moral science is converted into mere rhetoric about duty for duty's sake. From such a position can be derived no inherent doctrine of duties. Materials, it is true, may be introduced from without, and in this way specific duties may be secured; but from duty, whose characteristic is an absence of contradiction or formal concord with itself, a characteristic which is no more than the establishment of abstract indefiniteness, no specific duties can be deduced. Nor, further, if any specific content of action comes up for consideration, is there in this principle any way of judging whether it is a duty or not. On the contrary, all manner of wrong and immoral acts may be by such a method justified.

The more detailed Kantian statement, the suitability of an act to be presented as a universal rule, implies indeed the more concrete notion of a condition, but really contains no other principle than absence of contradiction, or formal identity. The rule that there should be no private property contains of itself no contradiction, nor does the proposition that this or that particular nation or family should not exist, or that no one should live at all. Only if it is really fixed and assumed that private property and human life should exist and be respected, is it a contradiction to commit theft or murder. There can be no contradiction except of something that exists or of a content, which is assumed to be a fixed principle. Only such a content can an act agree with or contradict. But duty which must be willed only as such, and not for the sake of a content, is a formal identity excluding all content and specific character.

Other antinomies and developments of the Kantian position, in which is shown how the moral standpoint of relation wanders aimlessly around without being able to find a way of escape from the mere abstract imperative, I have given in the "Phänomenologie des Geistes."

Addition.—Although we exalted the standpoint of the Kantian philosophy, in so far as it nobly insists that duty should accord with reason, yet its weakness is that it lacks all organic filling. The proposition, "Consider if thy maxim can be set up as a universal rule" would be all right, if we already had definite rules concerning what should be done. A principle that is suitable for universal legislation already presupposes a content. If the content is present, the application of the law is an easy matter. But in the Kantian theory the rule is not to hand, and the criterion that there should be no contradiction produces nothing. Where there is nothing, there can be no contradiction.

136. Owing to the abstract nature of the good, the other side of the idea, *i.e.,* particularity in general, falls within subjectivity. This subjectivity, universalized by being turned back into itself, is absolute certitude[2] of itself within itself. In this character it establishes particularity, it determines and judges. This is conscience.[3]

Addition.—We may speak in a lofty strain of duty, and this way of speaking elevates mankind, and widens the heart. Yet if nothing definite comes of it, it at last grows tedious. Spirit demands and is entitled to a particular content. But conscience is the deepest internal solitude, from which both limit and the external have wholly disappeared. It is a thorough-going retreat into itself. Man in his conscience is no longer bound by the ends of particularity. This is a higher standpoint, the standpoint of the modern world. We have now arrived at the stage of consciousness, which involves a recoil upon itself. Earlier ages were more sensuous, and had before them something external and given, whether it was religion or law. But conscience is aware of itself as thought, and knows that my thought is for me the only thing that is binding.

137. True conscience is the disposition to desire what is absolutely good. It has therefore fixed rules, which are for it independently objective phases and duties. Distinguished from this, which is its content or truth, conscience is only the formal side of the activity of the will, and the will as particular has no content peculiarly its own. The objective system of rules and duties and the union of them with the subjective consciousness appear first in the sphere of ethical observance. But at the formal standpoint of morality, conscience is devoid of objective content. It is merely an infinite certitude of itself and is formal

---

[2]Gewissheit.
[3]Gewissen.

and abstract. It is the certitude of a particular subject.

Note.—Conscience expresses the absolute claim of the subjective self-consciousness to know in itself and from itself what right and duty are, and to recognize nothing except what it thus knows to be good. It asserts also that what it so knows and wills is right and duty in very truth. Conscience, as the unity of the subject's will with the absolute, is a holy place which it would be sacrilege to assault. But whether the conscience of a certain individual is proportionate to this idea of conscience, in other words, whether what the individual conscience holds and gives out to be good is really good, can be ascertained only by an examination of the contents of the intended good. Right and duty, viewed as absolutely reasonable phases of will, are not in essence the particular property of an individual. Nor do they assume the form of perception or any other phase of mere individual sensuous consciousness. They are the universal products of thought, and exist in the form of laws and principles. Conscience is therefore subject to the judgment whether it is true or not, and its appeal merely to itself is directly opposed to what it wills to be, the rule, that is, of a reasonable absolutely valid way of acting. For this reason the state cannot recognize conscience in its peculiar form as subjective consciousness, just as subjective opinion, or the dogmatic appeal to a subjective opinion, can be of no avail in science.

The elements which are united in true conscience can be separated. The determining subjectivity of consciousness and will may separate itself from the true content, proceed to establish itself, and reduce the true content to a form and unreality. Thus the term conscience is ambiguous. On the one hand it is presupposed in the identity of subjective consciousness and will with the true good, and is therefore maintained and recognized to be a holy thing. On the other hand it is the mere subjective return of consciousness into itself, claiming the authority which conscience in its first form possesses solely because of its absolutely valid and rational content. Now, at the moral standpoint, distinguished as it is in this treatise from ethical observance, there occurs only the formal conscience. The true conscience is mentioned here only to emphasize the difference between the two and to remove the possibility of supposing that here, where the formal conscience alone is considered, the argument is concerned with the true. But to repeat, the true conscience looms up only in the sequel, and has to do with the properly social disposition. The religious conscience, however, does not belong to this sphere at all.

Addition.—When we speak of conscience, it may easily be supposed that because of its abstract inner form, it is already the absolutely true conscience. But conscience as true wills absolute good and absolute duty. As we must here deal with the abstract good, conscience is so far devoid of this objective content, and is at first only the infinite certitude of itself.

138. Subjectivity, as abstract self-determination and pure certitude only of itself, dissolves within itself all definite realization of right and duty. It passes judgment within itself, determines solely out of itself what is good, and makes this self-produced good its content. It bestows reality upon a good which is at first only presented and intended.

Note.—The self-consciousness, which has reached absolute return into itself, is conscious of itself as something over which nothing that exists or is given to it can or ought to have any power. This tendency to look within, and know and decide from oneself what is right and good, assumes a more general form in history, appearing at epochs such as that of Socrates, the Stoics, etc., when the accepted ethical principles could not satisfy the better will. When the visible world has become untrue to freedom, the will no longer finds itself in the established morality, and is forced to seek the harmony, which the actual world has lost, in the inner ideal life. Since the right, which self-consciousness acquires in this way, is formal, everything depends upon the nature of the content, which it gives itself.

Addition.—In the simple conception of conscience all definite phases of will are dissolved, and must proceed out of it again. Everything that is recognized as right or duty can in the first instance be proved by thought to be worthless, limited, and merely relative. But subjectivity, though it dissolves all content, must develop it again out of itself. Everything which comes to pass in ethical observance, is to be produced by this activity of spirit. But, on the other side, this standpoint is defective, because it is merely abstract. When I am conscious of my freedom as inner substantive reality, I do no act; yet if I do act and seek principles, I must try to obtain definite characters for my act. The demand is then made that this definite context shall be deduced from the conception of the free will. Hence, if it is right to absorb right and duty into subjectivity, it is on the other hand wrong if this abstract basis of action is not again evolved. Only in times when reality is a hollow, unspiritual, and shadowy existence, can a retreat be permitted out of the actual into an inner life. Socrates appeared at the time of the decay of the Athenian democracy. He dissolved what was established, and fled back into himself, to seek there what was right and good. In our own time also it occurs more or less frequently that reverence for the established is wanting, and that man holds his own will as for himself valid and authoritative.

139. Self-consciousness, affirming to be vanity all otherwise valid marks of action, and itself consisting of pure inwardness of will, may possibly convert the absolute universal into mere caprice. It may make a principle out of what is peculiar to particularity, placing it over the universal and realizing it in action. This is evil.

Note.—If conscience is taken as formal subjectivity, it is on the verge of being transformed into evil. In a self-certitude, which exists for itself, knows and decides for itself, both morality and evil have their common root.

The origin of evil in general lies in the mystery, *i.e.,* the speculative process, of freedom, in the necessity of freedom to rise out of its natural state, and find itself within itself in opposition to the natural. In this opposition the natural will is contradictory of itself and incompatible with itself, and comes in this divided state into existence. Hence the particularity of the will itself receives the further mark of evil. Particularity has a twofold character, exhibited here in the opposition of the natural to the inner will. Through this opposition the inner phase of will gets only a relative and formal existence, and therefore has to create its content out of the elements of the natural will, such as desire, impulse, and inclination. These desires and impulses may be either good or evil. But again, owing to their mere naturalness, they are contingent, and the will, as at present constituted, takes them in their contingent character as its content and brings them under the form of particularity. It thus becomes opposed to universality, the inner objective reality or the good, which, since it involves the return of the will into itself and a consciousness aware of itself, stands at the other extreme from the direct objectivity of what is merely natural. Thus also is this inner condition of the will evil. Man is consequently evil at once by nature or of himself and through his reflection within himself. Evil is not limited solely either to nature as such, unless it were the natural condition of a will which confines itself to its particular content, or to the reflection which goes into itself and includes cognition, unless it were to adhere to an antagonism to the good.

Along with the phase, that evil of necessity is, goes inseparably the phase that evil of necessity shall not be. In other words, evil is that which is to be superseded. Nevertheless, evil from the first standpoint of disruption must make its appearance, since it constitutes the division between the unreasoning beast and man. We must not, however, remain at this standpoint, or cling to the particular as though it in contrast with the universal were essential, but must overcome it, and set it aside as null and void. Further, as to this necessity of evil, it is subjectivity, or the infinity constituted by the reflex action of consciousness, which has this opposition before itself and exists in it. If it remains there, *i.e.,* if it is evil, it exists simply for itself, counts itself as independent, and is mere caprice. Hence the individual subject as such has the guilt of his evil.

Addition.—Abstract certitude, which is aware of itself as the basis of everything, involves the possibility of willing the universality of the conception, but also the possibility of making a principle out of a particular content and realizing it. This second possibility is evil. To evil always belongs the abstraction implied in self-certitude, and man alone, just in so far as he can be evil, is good. Good and evil are inseparable, their unity lying in this, that the conception becomes objective to itself and forthwith, as an object, involves distinction. The evil will wills something that is opposed to the universality of will; but the good will is in accordance with its true conception.

The difficulty as to how the will can be evil is due usually to our thinking of the will as in only a positive relation to itself, and to our representing it as some definite thing existing for itself, *i.e.*, as the good. The question as to the origin of evil may be put better thus: How does the negative enter into the positive? If God in the creation of the world is supposed to be the absolutely positive, then, let man turn where he will, he cannot in the positive find the negative. The view that God permitted evil to exist, involving a passive relation of God to evil, offers no satisfactory solution of the problem. In the religious myth the origin of evil is not rationally conceived; the negative is not recognized to be in the positive. One is supposed to come after the other or to exist side by side with it, so that the negative comes to the positive from the outside. With this view thought cannot be satisfied. Thought desires a reason and a necessary relation, and insists that the negative and positive spring from the self-same root. The solution of the difficulty from the standing-ground of the conception is already contained in the conception. The conception, or, to speak more concretely, the idea, must in its very essence find distinctions in itself and establish itself as negative. To adhere to the positive merely, that is to say to the pure good, which shall be in its origin nothing but good, is an empty effort of the understanding, which creates difficulty by introducing one-sidedness and abstraction. But from the ground of the conception the positive phase is apprehended as an activity distinguishing itself from itself. Evil as well as good has its origin in the will, and the will in its conception is both good and evil. The natural will is, as it stands, a contradiction, implying a distinction of itself from itself, in order that it may be consciously for itself, and attain its inward nature.

The proposition, that owing to the nature of evil man is evil, in so far as his will is natural, is opposed to a current idea that it is precisely the natural will which is innocent and good. But the natural will is opposed to the content of freedom. The child, or uneducated man, possessing only the natural will, is not fully responsible. When we speak of man, we mean not children but self-conscious men. When we speak of good, we include a knowledge of it. Now, the natural or the ingenuous is of itself neither good nor evil, but when related to will, as freedom and knowledge of freedom, it is not free, and hence evil. When the natural is willed by man, it is no longer simply the natural, but the negative of the good, or the negative of the conception of the will.

If we were to say that, since evil lies in the conception, and exists of necessity, men are no longer responsible when they adopt it, it must be replied that their decision is their own deed, the act of their freedom, and therefore to be laid at their door. In religious fable it is said that man is like God in his having a knowledge of good and evil. The resemblance to God is a fact so far as the necessity is not a necessity of nature, but rather a decision transcending the state in which good and evil are involved alike. Since both good and evil confront me, I may choose either, resolve upon either, and take up either into my subjectivity. It is the nature of evil that man may will it, although he is not forced by necessity to do so.

140. As every end belongs to the purpose of actual concrete action, it necessarily has a positive side (§130), which self-consciousness knows on occasion how to bring forward. But as self-consciousness implies a turning back into oneself, and is aware of the universal of the will, an act has also a negative side. The positive side of an act, whose negative content stands in open contrast with the universal, may be looked on as a duty and an excellent motive, and be maintained by self-consciousness to be good for others as well as for itself. To hold it good for others is hypocrisy; and to hold it good for itself is a still higher summit of the subjectivity, which maintains itself to be the absolute.

Note.—The final most abstruse form of evil, that in which evil is turned into good and good into evil, in which, too, consciousness knows itself as the transforming power, and therefore as absolute, is the very summit of subjectivity from the moral standpoint. It is the form to which evil has risen in our time, and that, too, through philosophy, or rather a shallowness of thought, which has contorted a deep conception, and presumes to give itself the name of philosophy, just as it presumes to give to evil the name of good. In this note I shall mention briefly the chief forms of this subjectivity, which are in vogue.

(*a*) Dissimulation, or hypocrisy. In it are contained the following elements: (α) knowledge of the true universal, whether it be in the form of the feeling of right and duty, or in the form of a thorough knowledge of them; (β) the willing of the particular, which is in open strife with the universal; and (γ) explicit comparison of the universal and particular, so that, for the willing consciousness itself, its particular will is understood to be evil. These three elements comprise the act done with evil conscience, but are not yet hypocrisy as such.—It was at one time a very important question whether an act is evil only in as far as it is done with an evil conscience, *i.e.*, with a developed consciousness of the elements involved in the act. Pascal ("Les Provinc." 4e lettre) well draws out the consequences of an affirmative answer to this question. He says, "Ils seront tous damnés ces demi pécheurs, qui ont quelque amour pour la vertu.

Mais pour ces francs-pécheurs, pécheurs endurcis, pécheurs sans mélange, pleins et achevés, l'enfer ne les tient pas: ils ont trompé le diable à force de s'y abandonner."[4]

The subjective right of self-consciousness, to know whether the act falls under the category of good or evil, must not be thought of as colliding with the absolute right of the objectivity of this category. At least, the two are not to be represented as separable, indifferent to each other, and related only casually. And yet this is just the view which lay at the basis of the old-time question about saving grace.[5] Evil on its formal side is that which is most peculiarly the individual's own, since it is his subjectivity setting itself up as wholly and purely its own. For it he is, therefore, responsible (§139 and *note*). On the objective side, man in his conception as spirit is rational, and has solely in himself a universality, which is aware of itself. Hence we fail to treat him in accordance with the dignity of his conception, when we separate from him either the goodness of a good act or the evil of an evil act, and refuse to impute it to him as good or evil. How definite may be the consciousness of these two distinguishable sides in man, with what degree of clearness or obscurity this consciousness may become knowledge, or how far in an evil act conscience may be formal, are questions with which we are not much concerned. They belong to the empirical side of the subject-matter.

(*b*) But evil and to act with evil conscience are not yet hypocrisy. We must add the formal phase of untruth, in which evil is maintained to be good and good for others. The agent represents as good, conscientious, and pious an act, which is merely an artifice for the betrayal of others. But by means of what is otherwise good and pious, namely, by good reasons generally, an evil man may find a justification of his evil, transforming evil into something good for himself. The possibility of such a transformation is found in the abstract and negative subjectivity, which is conscious that all phases must submit to and spring from it.

[4]Pascal quotes also in the same place the prayer of Christ on the cross for his enemies, "Father, forgive them, for they know not what they do." He calls it a superfluous request, if the circumstance that they were not conscious of what they had done deprived the act of its taint of evil, since in that case it would not need to be forgiven. In the same way he quotes the view of Aristotle ("Nicomach." Eth. III. 2), who draws a distinction between the agent who is οὐκ εἰδὼς and one who is ἀγνοῶν. In the first case the agent acts involuntarily, the lack of knowledge having to do with external circumstances (§117), and is thus not responsible for the act. But with regard to the other case, Aristotle says, "No bad man really knows what should be done and left undone, and it is this lack (ἁμαρτία) which makes him unjust and evil. Ignorance of the choice between good and evil does not make an act involuntary or the agent irresponsible, but only makes the act bad." Aristotle has indeed a deeper insight into the connection of knowing and willing than is in vogue in the superficial philosophy, which teaches that ignorance, feeling, and inspiration are the truest principles of ethical conduct.

[5]Wirksame Gnade.

(*c*) Allied to the foregoing is what is known as probability. Its principle is that if consciousness can trump up one good reason, be it only the authority of a single theologian, whose judgment, it may be, is disapproved by others, the act is permissible, and conscience may be at ease. Such a reason or authority, it is acknowledged, gives at best only probability, but that is supposed to be enough to confirm the conscience. It is admitted also that a good reason does not exclude others, which may be quite as good. Further, in this form of subjectivity there is a touch of the objective in the concession that conduct should be based on a ground or reason. But to the many good reasons and authorities, which might be adduced in favour of a certain line of action, may be opposed just as many good reasons for an opposite course. Hence the decision is intrusted not to the objectivity of the thing, but to subjectivity; liking and caprice are made the discerners between good and evil, and ethical observance and religion are undermined. But since it is given out that some reason, and not private subjectivity, is the basis of decision, probability is so far a form of hypocrisy.

(*d*) The next higher stage is the assertion that the good will shall consist in willing the good; the willing of the abstract good shall be the sole requisite for a good act. Since the act, as a definite volition, has a content, while the abstract good determines nothing, it devolves upon the private individual to give the good filling and definiteness. In probability there must be obtained from some *Révérend Père* authority to bring a definite content under the general category of the good. But here every subject, simply as he stands, is invested with the dignity of giving a content to the abstract good, or, what is the same thing, of bringing a content under the universal. But this content is only one of several sides of a concrete act, which may, on another of its sides, be bad or criminal. And yet my subjective estimate of the good is the good as known by me in the act; it is my good intention (§111). Thus arises an opposition between different phases, in accordance with one of which the act is good, but in accordance with another, criminal. Here, too, would seem to come up the question, if, in the actual act, the intention is really good. But at this standpoint, at which abstract good is the determining motive, the good not only may but must be the real intention. And, however bad and criminal they may be in other directions, the results of an act, which completes a good intention, are also good. We seem forced to ask which of these sides is essential. But this objective question cannot here be put; or rather the only objective is the decision of the subjective consciousness itself. Besides, at this standpoint the terms essential and good have the same meaning. Both are abstractions. Good is that which in regard to the will is essential; and the essential in regard to the will is that an act shall be for me good. But here one may place any pleasurable content he likes under the abstract good, because this good, having no content of its own, is reduced to mean merely a bare positive, something, that is, which may have value from some point of view, and also in its direct phase may be made to count as an essential end. Such a positive action might be, *e.g.,* to do good to the poor, or to provide for myself, my life, or my family. Further, as the good is abstract, the bad also must be without content, and must receive definiteness from my subjectivity. Hence arises the moral end to hate and root out the bad.

Theft, cowardice, murder, as acts of a subjective will, imply at the very outset the satisfaction of this will, and are therefore something positive. Now, that the act may be good, I simply need to know this positive side of it as my intention. Hence the act is at once decided to be good, because to know it as good is involved in my intention. Theft for the benefit of the poor, theft or flight from battle, in order to fulfil the duty of caring for one's life or one's family, which may be poor, murder through hate and revenge, *i.e.,* to satisfy a sense of right, or of my right, or of the wickedness of another, or to satisfy a sense of the wrong done by him to me or others, or the world, or people generally, by extirpating him as thoroughly bad, and thus contributing something to the extermination of evil,—all these acts are on their positive side good in intention and so good in act. There is needed a superlatively small effort of the understanding to discover, as did the learned divines aforesaid, for every act a positive side, and a good reason or intention.—Hence it has been said that there are no evil men, because no one wills evil for evil's sake, an act which would be purely negative. He always wills something positive, and therefore, from this point of vision, good. In this abstract good the distinction between good and evil, and all real duties also, have disappeared. Accordingly, merely to will the good, merely to have a good intention when we act, is evil because the willed good is an abstraction, and the ascertainment of what is good is left to the caprice of the subject.

To this place belongs the famous sentence, "The end justifies the means." This expression, as it stands, is trivial, because one could as vaguely reply that a just end justifies the means, but an unjust end does not. The expression would then be tautological, since the means, if they are real means, are nothing of themselves but are only for the sake of something else, from which they derive their worth.—But this saying is not meant in a merely formal and indefinite sense. It justifies the use for a good end of something not strictly a means at all. It justifies and inculcates as a duty even crime and the violation of what is of itself just, as means for effecting a good end. In this saying there floats a general consciousness of the dialectic of the positive element, alluded to above, as it bears upon right and ethics, and upon such indefinite propositions as "Thou shalt not kill," "Thou shalt care for thy own well-being and that of thy family." In law and war, to kill is not only a right but a duty; but in these cases there is an accurate description of the circumstances under which, and also of the kind of men whom it is permitted or enjoined to kill. In the same way my well-being and the well-being of my family must yield to higher ends, and be reduced to means. But a crime is not an indistinct generality, which has to undergo a process of dialectic, but something definitely and objectively limited. Yet the end which is to oppose this crime and deprive it of its nature, the holy and just end, is only the subjective opinion of what is good or better. Thus, here again the will holds to the abstract good; and every absolutely valid mark of the good and bad, of right and wrong, is superseded by and handed over to the feeling, opinion, and liking of the individual.

(*e*) Subjective opinion is openly pronounced to be the rule of right and duty, when the conviction that a thing is right is declared to be the criterion of the ethical character of an act. As the good, which is here willed, is still without content, the principle of conviction implies that it is simply for the subject to decide whether the act is good or not. Thus here also all semblance of ethical objectivity has vanished. Such a theory has direct affinity with the so-called philosophy, already repeatedly alluded to, which denies the possibility of knowing the truth, and, in so doing, denies also the moral laws, which are the truth and reason of spirit as will. Such philosophizing, as it proclaims a knowledge of the truth to be vanity, and the circle of knowledge to be mere appearance, must obviously make appearance the principle of action also. Thus ethical principles are decided by the individual's peculiar view of life and his private conviction. This degradation of philosophy appears, indeed, to outsiders as of supremely small importance, and to be confined merely to the idle talk of the school. But the view necessarily makes its way into ethics, which is an essential part of philosophy. The real world sees the meaning of these views only when they have become a reality.

By the spread of the view that subjective conviction alone decides the ethical value of an act, it has come to pass that hypocrisy, formerly much discussed, is now hardly spoken of at all. To mark hypocrisy as evil is to believe that certain acts are beyond all question trespasses, vices, and crimes; that also, he who commits them must know what they are, knowing and recognizing, as he does, the principles and outward acts of piety and right, even in the false guise under which he misuses them. Or, perhaps, with regard to evil, it was assumed that it is a duty to know the good and to distinguish it from evil. In any case it was unconditionally claimed that men should do nothing vicious or criminal, and that if they did, they must, just so far as they are men, not cattle, be held responsible. But when the good heart, good intentions, and subjective conviction are said to decide the value of action, there is no longer any hypocrisy, or, for that matter, evil at all. Since whatever an individual does he can convert into good by the reflective intervention of good intentions and motives; and by virtue of his conviction his act is good.[6] There is no longer any absolute vice or crime. Instead of frank and free, hardened and untroubled transgression[7] appears the consciousness of complete justification through intention and conviction; my good intention and my conviction that the act is good make it good. To pass sentence upon an act is merely to judge of the intention, conviction, or faith of the agent. Faith is not used here in the sense in which Christ demands faith in objective truth. In that sense, if a man has a bad faith, *i.e.*, a conviction which is in its content evil, he must accordingly be condemned. But faith here means simply fidelity to conviction. When we ask if a man has remained true to his conviction, we refer to the merely formal subjective faith, which is supposed of itself to contain his duty.

Because the principle of conviction is subjective, there is forced upon us the thought of the possibility of error, and in this thought is the implication of an absolute law. But a law does not act; it is only a real human being who acts. If we are to estimate the worth of his acts according to this subjective principle, we can ask merely how far he has embodied the law in his conviction. Thus, if the acts are not to be judged and measured according to the law, it is not easy to perceive what purpose the law subserves. It is degraded to a mere external letter or empty word; and inevitably, since it is made a binding law and obligation only by my conviction.

Such a law may have the authority of God, of the state, and of centuries, in which it united men and gave substance to their acts and destiny. It may thus include the convictions of an untold number of individuals. And yet to it I oppose the authority of my private conviction—a conviction which has no other footing than authority. This, to all appearance, stupendous presumption is ignored by the principle which makes subjective conviction to be the rule.

Although reason and conscience, never wholly driven away by shallow science and sophistry, with bad logic but a higher insight concede the possibility of error, they yet reduce crime and evil to a minimum by call-

---

[6]"That he feels fully convinced I do not in the least doubt. Yet many commit the worst outrages from just such a conviction. Besides, if that reason could avail everywhere as an excuse, there would no longer be any rational judgment upon good and evil, honourable and mean conduct. Lunacy would have the same rights as reason, or rather reason would no longer have any right or esteem. Its voice would be a thing of naught. Who does not doubt is in the truth! I tremble at the results of such a toleration, which would be exclusively to the advantage of unreason." Fr. H. Jacobi to Count Holmer. Eutin 5th Aug., 1800, Concerning Count Stolberg's Conversion (Brennus, Berlin, Aug., 1802).

[7]Alluded to by Pascal above.

ing them errors. To err is human. Who has not often erred with regard to one thing and another, whether yesterday at dinner he had fresh or pickled cabbage, and in numberless other things of greater or less importance? And yet the distinction between important and unimportant vanishes, if we cling obstinately to mere subjective conviction. But the natural, though illogical, admission of the possibility of error, when it allows that a bad conviction is only an error, is turned into another defect of logic, that, namely, of dishonesty. At one time it is said that upon subjective conviction rests the ethical structure and the highest worth of man, and this conviction is declared to be most high and holy. At another time we are dealing with a mere error, and my conviction has become trivial, contingent, and accidental. In point of fact my conviction is of trifling moment if I cannot know the truth. In such a case it is also a matter of indifference how I think, and there remains for my thought merely that empty good, which is an abstraction of the understanding.

The principle of justification on the ground of conviction bears also upon others in their treatment of my action. They are quite right to hold my acts to be crimes, if this is in accordance with their belief and conviction. Thus I not only cannot anticipate any favourable treatment, but, on the contrary, am reduced from a position of freedom and honour to one of dishonour and slavery. And this happens through that very justice which I have adopted as my own, by the exercise of which I experience only an alien subjective conviction, and the working of a merely external force.

(*f*) Finally, the highest form in which this subjectivity fully grasps and expresses itself, is that which we, borrowing the name from Plato, have called irony. But it is only the name which is taken from Plato, who, like Socrates, used it in personal conversation against the opinions of the ordinary and of the sophistic consciousness, in order to bring out the idea of truth and justice; but in treating the superficial consciousness in this way he expressly excepts the idea. Irony is employed by him in conversation, only against persons; otherwise the essential movement of his thought is dialectic. So far was Plato from supposing the conversational process to be complete in itself, or irony to be the idea or ultimate form of thought, that he, on the contrary, terminated the backward and forward motion of thought, which prevails in subjective opinion, by sinking it in the substantive idea.[8]

---

[8] My deceased colleague, Professor Solger, adopted the interpretation of irony which Fried. v. Schlegel had at an early period of his literary career worked up till it became in his hands that subjectivity, which is conscious of itself as the highest. But Solger's superior judgment and more philosophic insight seized and retained of this view only the phase of dialectic proper, the moving pulse of the speculative method. Perfectly clear, however,

The summit of the subjectivity, which apprehends itself as ultimate, consists in a consciousness of itself as judge of truth, right, and duty. It is aware, indeed, of the objective ethical principle, but does not forget or renounce itself, or make any earnest effort to sink itself in this principle and act from it. Although it is in relation to this principle, it holds itself free from it, and is conscious of itself as willing and deciding in a certain way, and as being able quite as well to will and decide otherwise.—You, let us suppose, honestly take a law to be something absolute; but, as for me, I too have a share in it, but a much grander one than you, for I have

---

he cannot be said to be, nor can I agree with the conceptions which he developed in his recent thoughtful and detailed criticism of Schlegel's lectures. ["Kritik über die Vorlesungen des Herrn August Wilhelm v. Schlegel über dramatische Kunst und Literatur" (Wiener Jahrb. Bd. vii. S. 90 ff.).]

"True irony," says Solger (p. 92), "proceeds from the view that man, so long as he lives in this present world, can do his highest appointed task only in this world. To believe ourselves to be transcending finite ends is a vain imagination;" also "the highest exists for our conduct only in limited, finite form." This is, rightly understood, Platonic, and very truly spoken against the striving to attain the abstract infinite. But to say that the highest presents itself in a limited and finite form, as in ethics, and that the ethical is essentially reality and action, is very different from saying that the ethical is only a finite end. The finite form deprives the ethical matter of none of its real substance and infinitude. He goes on: "And just for this reason the highest is for us as empty as the lowest, and necessarily collapses along with us and our vain understanding. For truly the highest exists only in God, and reveals itself as divine in our collapse. In the divine we have no share, unless its immediate presence be revealed in the disappearance of our reality. The disposition, to which this principle of life is clearly present, is tragic irony." The name irony may be arbitrarily used to describe any state of mind, but it is far from clear how the highest goes down with our nothingness, or how the divine is revealed only in the disappearance of our reality. This position is also maintained in a passage on p. 91, which runs: "We see heroes in error in both thought and feeling, with regard not only to the effects of the most noble and the most beautiful, but also to their source and value; yes, we are exalted in the destruction of the best itself." The righteous destruction of ranting villains and criminals, of whom the hero in a modern tragedy, "Die Schuld," is an example, has indeed an interest for criminal law, but none for true art. But the tragic destruction of highly moral personages may interest, exalt, and reconcile us to itself, when they contract guilt by becoming opposing champions of equally just ethical forces, which by some misfortune come into collision. Out of this antagonism proceed the right and wrong of each party. There appears also the true ethical idea, purified and triumphant over one-sidedness, and therefore reconciled with and in ourselves. Hence it is not the highest in us which is overwhelmed, nor is it when the best is submerged that we are exalted, but, on the contrary, when the truth triumphs. This, as I have explained, in the "Phänomenologie des Geistes," is the true and pure ethical interest of the ancient tragedy, although in the romantic drama this function of tragedy suffers a further modification. But, apart altogether from the misfortune of tragic collision, and the destruction of the individuals caught in this misfortune, the ethical idea has a real and present existence in the ethical world, and the ethical reality, namely, the state, has as its purpose and result that this highest shall not present itself in the real world as something valueless. This aim or object of the state the ethical consciousness possesses intuitively, and the thinking consciousness conceives.

gone through and beyond it, and can turn it as I please. It is not the subject-matter which is excellent, but I am the excellent thing, and am master of law and fact. I toy with them at my pleasure, and can enjoy myself only when I ironically know and permit the highest to be submerged. This form, indeed, makes vain the whole ethical content of right, duty, and law, being an evil and in itself a wholly universal evil. Yet to it we must add the subjective vanity of knowing itself as empty of all content, and yet of knowing this empty self as the absolute.

This absolute self-complacency may in some cases pass beyond a solitary worship of itself, and frame some kind of community, the bond and essence of which would be the mutual asseveration of conscientiousness, good intentions, and reciprocal delight in purity. The members of this union would disport themselves in the luxury of self-knowledge and self-utterance, and would cherish themselves to their heart's content. In those persons, who have been called beautiful souls, we find even a more sublime subjectivity, making void all that is objective and shining by the light of its own unreality. These and other phases, which are in some measure connected with the foregoing forms of subjectivity, I have treated in the "Phänomenologie des Geistes." In that work the whole section on Conscience, especially the paragraphs dealing under a different heading with the transition into a higher stage, may be compared with the present discussion.

Addition.—Imagination may go further and convert the evil will into the pretence of the good. Though it cannot alter the substance of evil, it can lend to it the outer form and semblance of good. Every act contains something positive, and the demonstration that a thing is good, as opposed to evil, is effected by eliminating all but this positive. Thus I can maintain an act to be good in respect of my intention. Moreover, not only in consciousness, but also on the positive practical side of action, evil is connected with good. If self-consciousness gives out that the act is good only for others, it assumes the form of hypocrisy. But if it ventures to maintain that the act is good for itself, it rises to the still higher summit of a subjectivity, which is conscious of itself as absolute. For it good and evil, as they are in and of themselves, have wholly disappeared, and it can, therefore, give itself out for what it pleases. This is the standpoint of absolute sophistry, which itself assumes the style of lawgiver, and refers the distinction between good and evil to caprice. Most pronounced in hypocrisy are the religious dissemblers, the Tartüffes, who perform all kinds of ceremonies, and are in their own eyes pious, although doing what they please. To-day we seldom speak of hypocrites, partly because the accusation seems too strong, but also because hypocrisy in its direct form has disappeared. Direct falsehood and complete cloaking of the good have become too transparent. Nor is the total severance of good and evil any longer so simple and available, since their limits have been made uncertain by growing culture.

The more subtle form of hypocrisy now is that of probability, by which one seeks to represent a transgression as something good for his own conscience. This occurs only where morals and the good are fixed by authority, so that the reasons for maintaining the evil to be the good are as numerous as the authorities. Casuistic theologians, especially Jesuits, have worked up these cases of conscience, and multiplied them *ad infinitum*. Owing to this over-subtlety, good and evil come into collision, and are subject to such fluctuations that they seem to the individual to run into each other. The chief desideratum is only what is probable, an approximate good, for which a single reason or authority can be secured. Another peculiarity of this standpoint is that it contains only what is abstract, while the concrete filling is represented as unessential, or rather is left to mere opinion. Thus anyone may have committed a crime and yet willed the good. When, for instance, a wicked person is murdered, the positive side of the act may be asserted to be a desire to oppose and diminish evil.

The next stage of probability is reached when the subject depends not upon the authority and assertion of another, but upon himself. He relies upon his own conviction, and his belief that only through his conviction can a thing be good. The defect of this attitude is the determination to refer to nothing but the conviction itself, involving a rejection of the substance of absolute right, and a retention of the mere form. It is, of course, not a matter of indifference whether I do something through use and wont, or through the force of its truth. Yet objective truth is different from my conviction. Conviction holds no distinction at all between good and evil, for it is always only conviction; the bad would be only that of which I am not convinced. This highest standpoint, in extinguishing good and evil, is admittedly exposed to error, and is cast down from its high estate to mere contingency and disregard. This is irony, the consciousness that the highest criterion, the principle of conviction, is ruled by caprice, and is, therefore, ineffective. For this view the philosophy of Fichte is chiefly responsible, as it claims that the I is absolute. At least it maintains that absolute certitude marks the general condition of the I, which by a further development passes into objectivity. Of Fichte, however, it cannot properly be said that in the practical realm he has made the caprice of the subject a principle. But after him the particular, interpreted as the condition of the individual subject, and applied by Friedrich v. Schlegel to the good and beautiful, has been set up as God. Hence the objective good is only an image formed by my conviction, receiving its substance only through me, and appearing and vanishing at the pleasure of me, its lord and master. The objective, to which I am related, is brought to naught, and thus I hover over a dim and monstrous space, calling up phantoms and dispersing them at will. This last extreme of subjectivity arises only at a time of high culture, where serious faith has crumbled away, and all things have become vanity.

Transition from Morality to Ethical System

141. In behalf of conscience, or the mere abstract principle of determination, it is demanded that its phases shall be universal and objective. In the same way in behalf of the good which, though it is the essential universal of freedom, is still abstract, are also required definite phases; and for these phases is further demanded a principle which must, however, be identical with the good. The good and conscience, when each is raised into a separate totality, are void of all definiteness, and yet claim to be made definite. Still, the construction of these two relative totalities into an absolute identity is already accomplished in germ, since even the subjectivity or pure self-certitude, which vanishes by degrees in its own vacuity, is identical with the abstract universality of the good. But the concrete identity of the good and the subjective will, the truth of these two, is completed only in the ethical system.

Note.—A more detailed account of the transition of the conception is to be found in the "Logic." Here it is enough to say that the limited and finite by its very nature contains the opposite in itself. Such a finite thing is either the abstract good, which is as yet unrealized, or the abstract subjectivity, which is good only in intention. Abstract good implicitly contains its opposite, *i.e.,* its realization, and abstract subjectivity, or the element in which the ethical is realized, implicitly contains its opposite, *i.e.,* the good. Thus, when either of these two is taken in a one-sided way, it has not yet positively realized all that it is capable of being. The good, apart from all subjectivity and definite character, and the determining subjectivity, apart from anything that it may become, arrive at a higher actuality by a negative process. Each clings at first to its one-sided form, and resolves not to accept what it possesses potentially, thus constituting itself an abstract whole. Then it annuls itself in that capacity, and thereby reduces itself to the level of one element in a whole. Each of them becomes one element of the conception. The conception, in turn, is manifested as their unity, and, having received reality through the establishment of its elements, now exists as idea. The idea is the conception, when it has fashioned its elements into reality, and at the same time exists in their identity as their dynamic essence.

The simplest realization of freedom is right. When self-consciousness is turned back upon itself, freedom is realized as the good. The third stage, which is here in its transition exhibited as the truth of the good and of subjectivity, is likewise quite as much the truth of right. The ethical is subjective disposition, and yet contains right implicitly. But that this idea is the truth of the conception of freedom must not be an assumption derived from such a source as feeling, but must in philosophy be demonstrated. This demonstration is made only when right and the moral self-consciousness are proved to exhibit of themselves the tendency to run back into this idea as their result. Those who believe that proof and demonstration can be dispensed with in philosophy, show that they are still a long distance from the first thought of what philosophy is. They may speak of other things indeed, but they have no right to discuss philosophy, if they have not understood the conception.

Addition.—The two principles which we have so far considered, both the abstract good and conscience, are as yet without their opposing principles. The abstract good is etherealized into something wholly devoid of power, something into which I can introduce any content at all. And the subjectivity of spirit is equally without content, since it has no objective significance. Hence there may arise a longing after objectivity. Man would debase himself to the complete dependence of a serf, in order to escape the torment of sheer inanity and negativity. Many Protestants recently passed over to the Catholic church, simply because they found no substance in their own inner life. They were willing to accept any fixed and tangible authority, even though it had not the security which comes from thought. The social order is the unity, and according to the conception the reconciliation also of the subjective good with the objective absolute good. Morality is the general form of the will as subjective; but the ethical order is not simply the subjective form and the self-determination of the will, but contains their conception, namely, freedom. Neither right nor morality can exist independently, but must have the ethical as its pillar and support. In right is wanting the element of subjectivity, and in morality is wanting the objective, so that neither by itself has any actuality.

Only the infinite, the idea is actual. Right exists only as a branch of a whole, or as a vine twining itself about a firmly rooted tree.

THIRD PART
THE ETHICAL SYSTEM

142. The ethical system is the idea of freedom. It is the living good, which has in self-consciousness its knowing and willing, and through the action of self-consciousness its actuality. Self-consciousness, on the other hand, finds in the ethical system its absolute basis and motive. The ethical system is thus the conception of freedom developed into a present world, and also into the nature of self-consciousness.

143. The conception of the will, when united with the realization of the will, or the particular will, is knowing. Hence arises the consciousness of the distinction between these two phases of the idea. But the consciousness is now present in such a way that each phase is separately the totality of the idea, and has the idea as its content and foundation.

144. The objective ethical principle which takes the place of the abstract good is in its substance concrete through the presence in it of subjectivity as its infinite form. Hence it makes differences which are within itself, and therefore are due to the conception. By means of these differences, it obtains a sure content, which is independent and necessary, and reaches a standing ground raised above subjective opinion and liking. This content is the self-originated and self-referring laws and regulations.

Addition.—In the ethical principle as a whole occur both the objective and the subjective elements; but of this principle each is only a form. Here the good is substance, or the filling of the objective with subjectivity. If we contemplate the social order from the objective standpoint, we can say that man, as ethical, is unconscious of himself. In this sense Antigone proclaims that no one knows whence the laws come; they are everlasting, that is, they exist absolutely, and flow from the nature of things. None the less has this substantive existence a consciousness also, which, however, is only one element of the whole.

145. The ethical material is rational, because it is the system of these phases of the idea. Thus freedom, the absolute will, the objective, and the circle of necessity, are all one principle, whose elements are the ethical forces. They rule the lives of individuals, and in individuals as their

modes have their shape, manifestation, and actuality.

Addition.—Since the phases of the ethical system are the conception of freedom, they are the substance or universal essence of individuals. In relation to it, individuals are merely accidental. Whether the individual exists or not is a matter of indifference to the objective ethical order, which alone is steadfast. It is the power by which the life of individuals is ruled. It has been represented by nations as eternal justice, or as deities who are absolute, in contrast with whom the striving of individuals is an empty game, like the tossing of the sea.

146. (β) This ethical reality in its actual self-consciousness knows itself, and is therefore an object of knowledge. It, with its laws and forces, has for the subject a real existence, and is in the fullest sense self-dependent. It has an absolute authority or force, infinitely more sure than that of natural objects.

Note.—The sun, moon, mountains, rivers, and all objects of nature doubtless exist. They not only have for consciousness the authority of existence in general, but have also a particular nature. This nature consciousness regards as valid, and in its varied relation and commerce with objects and their use comports itself accordingly. But the authority of the social laws is infinitely higher, because natural things represent reason only in a quite external and particular way, and hide it under the guise of contingency.

147. On the other hand, the various social forces are not something foreign to the subject. His spirit bears witness to them as to his own being. In them he feels that he is himself, and in them, too, he lives as in an element indistinguishable from himself. This relation is more direct and intuitive than even faith or trust.

Note.—Faith and trust belong to the beginning of reflection, presupposing picture thought and such discernment as is implied in the judgment that to believe in a heathen religion is different from being a heathen. The relation, or rather identity without relation, in which the ethical principle is the actual life of self-consciousness, can indeed be transformed into a relation of faith and conviction. By further reflection, also, it may pass into an insight based on reasons, which originate in some particular end, interest, or regard, in fear or hope, or in historical presuppositions. But the adequate knowledge of these belongs to the conception arrived at through thought.

148. The individual may distinguish himself from these substantive ethical factors, regarding himself as subjective, as of himself undetermined, or as determined to some particular course of action. He stands to them as to his substantive reality, and they are duties binding upon his will.

Note.—The ethical theory of duties in their objective character is not comprised under the empty principle of moral subjectivity, in which, indeed, nothing is determined (§134), but is rightly taken up in the third part of our work, in which is found a systematic development of the sphere of ethical necessity. In this present method of treatment, as distinguished from a theory of duties, the ethical factors are deduced as necessary relations. It is, then, needless to add, with regard to each of them, the remark that it is thus for men a duty. A theory of duties, so far as it is not a philosophic science, simply takes its material out of the relations at hand, and shows how it is connected with personal ideas, with widely prevalent principles, and thoughts, with ends, impulses, and experiences. It may also adduce as reasons the consequences, which arise when each duty is referred to other ethical relations, as well as to general well-being and common opinion. But a theory of duties, which keeps to the logical settlement of its own inherent material, must be the development of the relations, which are made necessary through the idea of freedom, and are hence in their entire context actual. This is found only in the state.

149. A duty or obligation appears as a limitation merely of undetermined subjectivity and abstract freedom, or of the impulse of the natural will, or of the moral will which fixes upon its undetermined good capriciously. But in point of fact the individual finds in duty liberation. He is freed from subjection to mere natural impulse; he is freed from the dependence which he as subjective and particular felt towards moral permission and command; he is freed, also, from that indefinite subjectivity, which does not issue in the objective realization implied in action, but remains wrapped up in its own unreality. In duty the individual freely enters upon a liberty that is substantive.

Addition.—Duty limits only the caprice of subjectivity, and comes into collision only with abstract good, with which subjectivity is so firmly allied. When men say we will to be free, they have in mind simply that abstract liberty, of which every definite organization in the state is regarded as a limitation. But duty is not a limitation of freedom, but only of the abstraction of freedom, that is to say, of servitude. In duty we reach the real essence, and gain positive freedom.

150. The ethical, in so far as it is reflected simply in the natural character of the individual, is virtue. When it contains nothing more than conformity to the duties of the sphere to which the individual belongs, it is integrity.

Note.—What a man ought to do, or what duties he should fulfil in order to be virtuous, is in an ethical community not hard to say. He has to do nothing except what is presented, expressed and recognized in his established relations. Integrity is the universal trait, which should be found in his character, partly on legal, partly on ethical grounds. But from the standpoint of morals a man often looks upon integrity both for himself and others as secondary and unessential. The longing to be unique and peculiar is not satisfied with what is absolute and universal, but only with some situation that is exceptional.

The name "virtue" may quite as well be applied to the different aspects of integrity, because they, too, although they contain nothing belonging exclusively to the individual in contrast with others, are yet his possession. But discourse about the virtues easily passes into mere declamation, since its subject matter is abstract and indefinite, and its reasons and declarations are directed to the individual's caprice and subjective inclination. In any present ethical circumstance, whose relations are fully developed and actualized, virtue in the strict sense has place and reality only when these relations come into collision. But genuine collisions are rare, although moral reflection can, on the slightest provocation, create them. It can also provide itself with the consciousness that, in order to fulfil its special mission, it must make sacrifices. Hence, in undeveloped conditions of social life virtue as such occurs more frequently, because ethical principles and the realization of them are more a matter of private liking, belonging indeed to the nature of peculiarly gifted individuals. Thus, the ancients have attributed virtue in a special way to Hercules. So, too, in the ancient states, where ethical principles had not expanded into a system of free self-dependent development and objectivity, ethical defects had to be compensated for by the genius of the private individual. Thus the theory of the virtues, so far as it differs from a mere theory of duties, embraces the special features of character due to natural endowments, and thus becomes a spiritual history of the natural in man.

Since the virtues are the ethical reality applied to the particular, and are on this subjective side indefinite, there arises, in order to make them definite, a quantitative distinction of more and less. Hence the consideration of the virtues calls up the opposing vices as defects. Thus Aristotle defines a particular virtue, when rightly understood, as the mean between too much and too little.

The content, which receives the form of duties and also of virtues, is the same as that which has the form of appetites (§19, *note*). Besides, they all have the same content as their basis. But because the content of the appetites still belongs to unformed will and natural perception, and is not developed to an ethical order, the only object which they have in common with the content of duties and virtues is abstract. Since it in itself is indeterminate, it does not contain for the appetites the limits of good and evil. Thus appetites, if we consider their positive side, are good, if their negative side evil (§18).

Addition. If a man realizes this or that social project, he is not at once virtuous, though such, indeed, he is, when this way of behaving is a fixed element of his character. Virtue is not wholly objective; it is rather ethical virtuosity. To-day we do not speak of virtue as formerly, for the reason that ethical principles are not now so much a feature of a particular individual. The French speak most of virtue, because amongst them the individual is more his own peculiar property, and acts according to the dictates of nature. The Germans, on the other hand, are more reflective, and amongst them the same content attains the form of universality.

151. The ethical, when simply identical with the reality of individuals, appears as a generally adopted mode of action, or an observance. This is the custom, which as a second nature has been substituted for the original and merely natural will, and has become the very soul, meaning, and reality of one's daily life. It is the living spirit actualized as a world; by this actualization does the substance of spirit exist as spirit.

Addition.—As nature has its laws, as the animals, trees, the sun, fulfil their law, so observance belongs to the spirit of freedom. What right and morality are not as yet, the ethical principle is, namely, spirit. The particularity involved is not yet that of the conception, but only of the natural will. So, too, from the standpoint of morality, self-consciousness is not yet spiritual consciousness. It is occupied simply with the value of the subject in himself; the subject, who frames himself according to the good and against evil, has yet the form of caprice. But, here at the ethical point of view, will is the will of spirit, and has a correspondingly substantive content. Pedagogy is the art of making men ethical. It looks upon man as natural, and points out the way in which he is to be born again. His first nature must be converted into a second spiritual nature, in such a manner that the spiritual becomes in him a habit. In the spiritual disposition the opposition of the natural and subjective will disappears, and the struggle of the subject ceases. To this extent habit belongs to ethics. It belongs also to philosophic thought, which demands that the mind should be armed against sallies of caprice, rout and overcome them, in order that rational thought may have free course. It is true, on the other hand, that mere habit causes death, which ensues when one gets thoroughly used to life, and has become physically and mentally dulled. Then the opposition due to subjective consciousness and spiritual activity has disappeared. Man is active only in so far as he has not attained something which he desires to effect. When this is fully accomplished, activity and vitality vanish, and the lack of interest, which then pervades him, is mental or physical death.

152. Substantive ethical reality attains its right, and this right receives its due, when the individual in his private will and conscience drops his self-assertion and antagonism to the ethical. His character, moulded by ethical principles, takes as its motive the unmoved universal, which is open on all its sides to actual rationality. He recognizes that his worth and the stability of his private ends are grounded upon the universal, and de-

rive their reality from it. Subjectivity is the absolute form and the existing actuality of the substance. The difference between the subject and substance, as the object, end, and power of the subject, forthwith vanishes, like the difference between form and matter.

Note.—Subjectivity, which is the foundation for the real existence of the conception of freedom (§106), is at the moral standpoint still distinguished from the conception. In ethics it is adequate to the conception, whose existence it is.

153. In that individuals belong to the ethical and social fabric they have a right to determine themselves subjectively and freely. Assurance of their freedom has its truth in the objectivity of ethical observance, in which they realize their own peculiar being and inner universality (§147).

Note.—To a father seeking the best way to bring up his son, a Pythagorean, or some other thinker, replied, "Make him a citizen of a state which has good laws."

Addition.—The attempts of speculative educators to withdraw people from their present social life and bring them up in the country, a proposal made by Rousseau in "Emile," have been vain, because no one can succeed in alienating man from the laws of the world. Although the education of young men must take place in solitude, we cannot believe that the odour of the world of spirits does not in the end penetrate their seclusion, or that the power of the spirit of the world is too feeble to take possession of even the remotest corner. Only when the individual is a citizen of a good state, does he receive his right.

154. The right of individuals to their particularity is contained in the concrete ethical order, because it is in particularity that the social principle finds a visible outer manifestation.

155. Right and duty coincide in the identity of the universal and the particular wills. By virtue of the ethical fabric man has rights, so far as he has duties, and duties so far as he has rights. In abstract right, on the contrary, I have the right and another person the corresponding duty; and in morals I resolve to consider as an objective duty only the right of my own knowledge and will and of my own well-being.

Addition.—The slave can have no duties, but only the free man. If all rights were on one side and all duties on the other, the whole would be broken up. Identity is the only principle to which we must now adhere.

156. The ethical substance, as the union of self-consciousness with its conception, is the actual spirit of a family and a nation.

Addition.—The ethical framework is not abstract like the good, but in a special sense real. Spirit has actuality, and the accidents or modes of this actuality are individuals. Hence as to the ethical there are only two possible views. Either we start from the substantive social system, or we proceed atomically and work up from a basis of individuality. This latter method, because it leads to mere juxtaposition, is void of spirit, since mind or spirit is not something individual, but the unity of individual and universal.

157. The conception of this idea exists only as spirit, as active self-knowledge and reality, since it objectifies itself by passing through the form of its elements. Hence it is,

A. The direct or natural ethical spirit, the family. This reality, losing its unity, passes over into dismemberment, and assumes the nature of the relative. It thus becomes

B. The civic community, an association of members or independent individuals in a formal universality. Such an association is occasioned by needs, and is preserved by the law, which secures one's person and property, and by an external system for private and common interests.

C. This external state goes back to, and finds its central principle in, the end and actuality of the substantive universal, and of the public life dedicated to the maintenance of the universal. This is the state-constitution.

FIRST SECTION
The Family

158. The family is the direct substantive reality of spirit. The unity of the family is one of feeling, the feeling of love. The true disposition here is that which esteems the unity as absolutely essential, and within it places the consciousness of oneself as an individuality. Hence, in the family we are not independent persons but members.

Addition.—Love is in general the consciousness of the unity of myself with another. I am not separate and isolated, but win my self-consciousness only by renouncing my independent existence, and by knowing myself as unity of myself with another and of another with me. But love is feeling, that is to say, the ethical in the form of the natural. It has no longer a place in the state, where one knows the unity as law, where, too, the content must be rational, and I must know it. The first element in love is that I will to be no longer an independent self-sufficing person, and that, if I were such a person, I should feel myself lacking and incomplete. The second element is that I gain myself in another person, in whom I am recognized, as he again is in me. Hence love is the most tremendous contradiction, incapable of being solved by the understanding. Nothing is more obstinate than this scrupulosity of self-consciousness, which, though negated, I yet insist upon as something positive. Love is both the source and solution of this contradiction. As a solution it is an ethical union.

159. A right, which comes to the individual by reason of the family

and constitutes his life in it, does not appear in the form of a right, that is, the abstract element of a definite individuality, until the family is dissolved. Then those, who should be members, become in feeling and reality self-dependent persons. What was theirs by right of their position in the family, they now receive in separation in an external way, in the form of money, maintenance, or education.

Addition.—The family has this special right, that its substantive nature should have a sphere in actuality. This right is a right against external influences and against abandonment of the unity. But, on the other hand, love is subjective feeling, which, if it oppose the unity of the family, destroys it. If in such a case a unity is insisted on, it can comprehend only things that are external and independent of feeling.

160. The family when completed has the three following phases:

  (*a*) The form of its direct conception, marriage.
  (*b*) External reality, the family property and goods and the care of them.
  (*c*) Education of children and dissolution of the family.

A. Marriage

161. Marriage, as the elementary social relation, contains firstly the factor of natural life. As marriage is also a substantive fact, natural life must be viewed in its totality as the realization of the species, and the process which the realization involves. But, secondly, the merely inner, potential and, when actualized, external unity of the sexes is transformed in self-consciousness into the spiritual unity of self-conscious love.

Addition.—Marriage is essentially an ethical relation. Formerly, in the majority of what are called rights of nature, marriage was interpreted on its physical or natural side. It has thus been looked upon simply as a sexual relation, and as excluding all the other features of marriage. But such a view is no more crude than to conceive of marriage merely as civil contract, a view found in Kant. In accordance with this view, individuals form a compact through mere caprice, and marriage is degraded to a bargain for mutual use. A third doctrine, equally reprehensible, bases marriage on love only. Love, which is feeling, admits the accidental on every side, as the ethical cannot do. Hence, marriage is to be defined more exactly as legal ethical love. Out of marriage has disappeared the love, which is merely subjective.

162. As a subjective starting-point for marriage either the special inclination of two persons for each other may be the more observable, or else the provision and general arrangements of the parents. The objective point of departure, however, is the free consent of the two to become one person. They give up their natural and private personality to enter a unity, which may be regarded as a limitation, but, since in it they

attain to a substantive self-consciousness, is really their liberation.

Note.—That an individual may be objective, and so fulfil his ethical duty, he should marry. The circumstances attending the external starting-point are naturally a matter of chance, depending largely upon the state of reflective culture. In this there may be either of two extremes. Either well-meaning parents arrange beforehand for the marriage of two persons, who, when they have made each other's acquaintance as prospective husband and wife, are then expected to love each other. Or, on the other hand, inclination is supposed first to appear in the two persons, left absolutely to their private selves. The extreme, in which marriage is resolved on prior to inclination, and both resolution and inclination are then present in the actual marriage, is the more ethical. In the other extreme, it is the individual's private and unformed nature, which makes good its pretensions. This extreme is in close alliance with the subjective principle of the modern world (§124, *note*).

Modern dramas and other works of art produce an atmosphere of the chilliest indifference, by the way in which they represent the motive of sexual love. This feeling of indifference is due to the association in the drama of ardent passion with the most utter contingency, the whole interest being made to depend simply upon merely private persons. The event is, doubtless, of the very last importance to these persons, but not in itself.

Addition.—Amongst nations where women are held in slight esteem, parents arrange the marriage of their children, without ever consulting them. The children submit, because the particularity of feeling as yet makes no claim at all. The maiden is simply to have a husband, the man a wife. In other circumstances regard may be had to means, connections, political hopes. To make marriage the means for other ends may cause great hardship. But in modern times the subjective point of departure, *i.e.*, being in love, is thought to be the only thing of consequence. In this it is taken for granted that each one must wait till his hour has struck, and that he can bestow his love upon one and only one individual.

163. The ethical side of marriage consists in the consciousness that the union is a substantive end. Marriage thus rests upon love, confidence, and the socializing of the whole individual existence. In this social disposition and reality natural impulse is reduced to the mode of a merely natural element, which is extinguished in the moment of its satisfaction. On the other hand, the spiritual bond of union, when its right as a substantive fact is recognized, is raised above the chances of passion and of temporary particular inclination, and is of itself indissoluble.

Note.—It has already been remarked that there is no contract in connection with the essential character of marriage (§75). Marriage leaves behind and transcends the standpoint of contract, occupied by the person who is sufficient for himself. Substance is such as to be in essential relation to its accidents.[1] The union of personalities, whereby the family becomes one person, and its members its accidents, is the ethical spirit. The ethical spirit, stripped of the many external phases which it has in particular individuals and transitory interests, has been by picture-thought given independent form, and reverenced as the Penates, etc. In this attitude of mind is found that religious side of marriage and the family, which is called piety. It is a further abstraction, when the divine and substantive reality is separated from its physical embodiment. The result of this procedure is that feeling and the consciousness of spiritual unity become what is falsely called Platonic love. This separation is in keeping with the monastic doctrine, in which natural vitality is regarded simply as negative, and is given by this very separation an infinite importance.

Addition.—Marriage is distinguished from concubinage, since in con-cubinage the chief factor is the satisfaction of natural impulse, while in marriage this satisfaction is subordinate. Hence, in marriage one speaks without blushing of occurrences, which apart from the marriage relation cause a sense of shame. Therefore, also, is marriage to be esteemed as in itself indissoluble. The end of marriage is ethical, and therefore occupies so high a place that everything opposing it seems secondary and power-less. Marriage shall not be liable to dissolution through passion, since pas-sion is subject to it. But, after all, it is only in itself indissoluble, for, as Christ says, divorce is permitted, but only because of hardness of heart. Marriage, since it contains feeling, is not absolute, but open to fluctua-tions, and has in it the possibility of dissolution. Yet the laws must make the possibility as difficult as can be, and must retain intact the right of the ethical against inclination.

164. Just as in the case of contract it is the explicit stipulation, which constitutes the true transference of property (§79), so in the case of the ethical bond of marriage the public celebration of consent, and the cor-responding recognition and acceptance of it by the family and the com-munity, constitute its consummation and reality. The function of the church is a separate feature, which is not to be considered here. Thus the union is established and completed ethically, only when preceded by so-cial ceremony, the symbol of language being the most spiritual embodi-ment of the spiritual (§78). The sensual element pertaining to the nat-ural life has place in the ethical relation only as an after result and acci-dent belonging to the external reality of the ethical union. The union can be expressed fully only in mutual love and assistance.

Note.—When the question as to the chief end of marriage is asked with a view to enact or recast laws, it means: Which particular side of the

---

[1]See "Encyclopædia of the Philosophical Sciences."

reality of marriage must be accepted as the most essential? But no one separate phase of marriage comprises the whole range of its absolute ethical content; and one or other phase of its existence may be wanting without injury to its essence.—In the celebration of marriage the essence of the union is clearly understood to be an ethical principle, freed from the accidents of feeling and private inclination. If the solemnization be taken for an external formality, or a so-called mere civil requisition, the act loses all purpose except that of edification, or of an attestation to the civic regulation. Indeed, there may perhaps remain only the positive arbitrariness of a civil or ecclesiastical command. Now, not only is a command of this kind indifferent to the nature of marriage, but in so far as the two persons have because of it ascribed value to the formality, and counted it as a condition precedent to complete abandonment to each other, it is an alien thing, bringing discord into the disposition of love, and thwarting the inner nature of the union. The opinion that the marriage ceremony is a mere civic mandate professes to contain the loftiest conception of the freedom, intensity, and completeness of love; but in point of fact it denies the ethical side of it, which implies a limitation and repression of the mere natural tendency. Reserve is already found naturally in a sense of shame, and is by the more articulate spiritual consciousness raised to the higher form of modesty and chastity. In a word, the view of marriage just criticised rejects the ethical side, by virtue of which consciousness gathers itself out of its native and subjective condition, and attains to the thought of the substantive. Instead of always holding before itself the accidental character of sensual inclination, it casts off the fetters of this state and engages itself to what is substantive and binding, namely, the Penates. The sensual element is reduced and conditioned by the recognition of marriage as an ethical bond. Insolent is the view of the mere understanding, which is unable to apprehend marriage in its speculative nature. This substantive relation, however, is in harmony with the unsophisticated ethical sense, and with the laws of Christian nations.

Addition.—It is laid down by Friedrich v. Schlegel, in "Lucinde," and by a follower of his in the "Letters of an Unknown" (Lübeck and Leipzig, 1800), that the marriage-ceremony is a superfluous formality. They argue that by the form of marriage love, which is the substantive factor, loses its value; they represent that the abandonment to the sensual is necessary as proof of the freedom and inner reality of love. This style of argument is usual with seducers. Besides, as regards the relation of man to woman, it is woman who, in yielding to sense, gives up her dignity, whereas man has another field than the family for his ethical activity. The sphere of woman is essentially marriage. Her rightful claim is that love should assume the form of marriage, and that the different elements existing in love should be brought into a truly rational connection.

165. The natural office of the sexes receives, when rationalized, intellectual and social significance. This significance is determined by the distinction which the ethical substance, as conception, introduces by its own motion into itself, in order to win out of the distinction its own life or concrete unity.

166. In one sex the spiritual divides itself into two phases, independent, personal self-sufficiency, and knowing and willing of free universality. These two together are the self-consciousness of the conceiving thought, and the willing of the objective final cause. In the other sex the spiritual maintains itself in unity and concord. This sex knows and wills the substantive in the form of concrete individuality and feeling. In relation to what is without one sex exhibits power and mastery, while the other is subjective and passive. Hence the husband has his real essential life in the state, the sciences, and the like, in battle and in struggle with the outer world and with himself. Only by effort does he, out of this disruption of himself, reach self-sufficing concord. A peaceful sense of this concord, and an ethical existence, which is intuitive and subjective, he finds in the family. In the family the wife has her full substantive place, and in the feeling of family piety realizes her ethical disposition.

Note.—Hence piety is in the "Antigone" of Sophocles most superbly presented as the law of the woman, the law of the nature, which realizes itself subjectively and intuitively, the law of an inner life, which has not yet attained complete realization, the law of the ancient gods, and of the under-world, the eternal law, of whose origin no one knows, in opposition to the public law of the state. This opposition is in the highest sense ethical, and hence also tragic; it is individualized in the opposing natures of man and woman.

Addition.—Women can, of course, be educated, but their minds are not adapted to the higher sciences, philosophy, or certain of the arts. These demand a universal faculty. Women may have happy inspirations, taste, elegance, but they have not the ideal. The difference between man and woman is the same as that between animal and plant. The animal corresponds more closely to the character of the man, the plant to that of the woman. In woman there is a more peaceful unfolding of nature, a process, whose principle is the less clearly determined unity of feeling. If women were to control the government, the state would be in danger, for they do not act according to the dictates of universality, but are influenced by accidental inclinations and opinions. The education of woman goes on one hardly knows how, in the atmosphere of picture-thinking, as it were, more through life than through the acquisition of knowledge. Man attains his position only through stress of thought and much specialized effort.

167. Marriage in its essence is monogamy, because in this relation it is

the personality, the directly exclusive individuality which subsides and resigns itself. The true inner side of marriage, the subjective form of the real substantive institution, issues only out of such a mutual renunciation of personality as is shared in by no one else. Personality acquires the right of being conscious of itself in another, only in so far as the other appears in this identity as a person or atomic individuality.

Note.—Marriage, or monogamy, rather, is one of the principles on which the ethical life of a community depends most absolutely. Hence the institution of marriage is represented as one of the features of the divine or heroic founding of the state.

168. Since marriage proceeds out of the free resignation by both sexes of that personality which is infinitely peculiar to themselves, it must not occur within the bounds of natural identity, which involves great intimacy and unlimited familiarity. Within such a circle individuals have no exclusive personality. Marriage must rather take place in families that are unconnected, and between persons who are distinct in their origin. Between persons related by blood, therefore, marriage is contrary to the conception of it. It is an ethical act done in freedom, and not controlled by direct natural conditions and their impulses. Marriage within these limits is likewise contrary to true natural feeling.

Note.—To regard marriage as grounded not on a right of nature but on natural sexual impulse, to view it as a capricious contract, to give such an external reason for monogamy as the number of men in relation to the number of women, and to give only vague feelings as cause sufficient to prohibit marriage between blood connections, all such theories are due to the current idea of a state of nature, and to the opinion that such a state possesses rights. They are, however, devoid of the conception of rationality and freedom.

Addition.—Consanguineous marriages find opposition, in the first instance, in the sense of shame. This feeling of hesitation is justified by the conception. What is already united cannot be first of all united by marriage. As to the relation of mere nature, it is known that amongst animals copulation within one stock produces weaker offspring. What is to be joined ought to be at first distinct and separate. The power of production, both of spirit and body, is greater, the deeper are the oppositions out of which it restores itself. Familiarity, intimacy, habituation due to the same course of action, ought not to occur previous to marriage, but should be found for the first time in the married state. Their appearance after marriage has richer results and a higher value, the more numerous have been the points of difference.

169. The family, as person, has its external reality in property. If it is to furnish a basis for the substantive personality of the family, it must take the form of means.

B. The Family Means

170. It is not enough that the family has property, but, as a universal and lasting person, it needs a permanent and sure possession, or means. When property is treated abstractly, there occur at random the particular needs of the mere individual, and also the self-seeking of the appetites. These now take on an ethical aspect, and are changed into provision for a common interest.

Note.—In the wise sayings concerning the founding of states, the institution of a sure property makes its appearance in connection with the institution of marriage, or at least with the introduction of an orderly social life.—When we come to the civic community, we shall see in what family competence consists, and how it is to be secured.

171. The husband is the head of the family, and when it, as a legal person, collides with other families, he is its representative. It is expected of him, further, to go out and earn its living, care for its needs, and administer the family means. This means is a common possession, to which each member has a common but not a special right. This general right and the husband's right to dispose of the property may conflict, because the ethical sentiment (§158), which in the family is still in its simplest form, is subject to chance and violence.

172. Marriage establishes a new family, which has its own independent footing as against the stems or houses from which it has proceeded. The connection of the new family with these stems is consanguinity, but the principle of the new family is ethical love. Thus, the individual's property is essentially allied to his marriage, and less intimately to his original stock or house.

Note.—A marriage-settlement, which imposes a limit to the common possession of goods by the wedded couple, or any other arrangement by which the right of the wife is retained, is intended to be security against the dissolution of the marriage-tie by death or divorce. In such an event the different members of the family are by this arrangement apportioned their shares of the common possession.

Addition.—In many law codes the more extended range of the family circle is retained. It is looked upon as the real bond of union, while the tie of the single family is regarded as comparatively unimportant. Thus in the older Roman law the wife of the lax marriage is more closely allied to her relatives than to her husband and children. In feudal times, also, the necessity of preserving the *splendor familiæ* led to reckoning under the family only its male members. Thus the whole family connection was the chief object of concern, and the newly-formed family was placed in the background. Notwithstanding this, every new family is more essential than the wider circle bounded by the tie of consanguinity. A married couple with their children form a nucleus of their own in opposition to the more extended household. Hence the financial status of individuals must be more vitally connected with marriage than with the wider family union.

C. Education of the Children and Dissolution of the Family

173. The unity of marriage which, as substantive, exists only as an inner harmony and sentiment, but, so far as it exists actually, is separated in the two married persons, becomes in the children a unity, which has actual independent existence, and is an independent object. This new object the parents love as an embodiment of their love.—The presupposition of the direct presence of the two people as parents becomes, when taken on its merely natural side, a result. This process expands into an infinite series of generations, which beget and are presupposed. At this finite and natural standpoint the existence of the simple spirit of the Penates is represented as species or kind.

Addition.—Between husband and wife the relation of love is not yet objective. Though feeling is a substantive unity, it has as yet no footing in reality. This foothold parents attain only in their children, in whom the totality of their alliance is visibly embodied. In the child the mother loves her husband, and the father his wife. In the child both parents have their love before their eyes. Whereas in means the marriage tie exists only in an external object, in children it is present in a spiritual being, in whom the parents are loved, and whom they love.

174. Children have the right to be supported and educated out of the common family means. The right of parents to the service of their children, as service, is limited to and based upon family cares. The right of parents over the free choice of their children is just as clearly limited to correction and education. The purpose of chastisement is not mere justice; it has a subjective moral side, its object being to restrain a freedom, which is still bound to nature, and to instill the universal into the child's consciousness and will.

Addition.—Man does not possess by instinct what he is to be, but must first of all acquire it. Upon this is based the child's right to be educated. As it is with children, so is it with nations under paternal government; the people are supplied with food out of storehouses, and are not looked upon as self-dependent or of age. The services required of children must bear upon their education and promote their good. To ignore this good would destroy the ethical element of the relation, and make the child a slave. A prominent feature in the education of children is correction, intended to break their self-will, and eradicate what is merely sensual and natural. One must not expect to succeed here simply with goodness, because the direct volition of children is moved by immediate suggestions and likings, not by reasons and ideas. If we give children reasons, we leave it open to them whether to act upon them or not. In this way everything depends upon their pleasure. In the fact that parents constitute the universal and essential is included the necessity of obedience on the part of children. When no care is taken to cherish in children the feeling of subordination, a feeling begotten in them by the longing to be big, they become forward and impertinent.

175. Children are potentially free, and life is the direct embodiment of this potential freedom. Hence they are not things, and cannot be said to belong to any one, their parents or others. But their freedom is as yet only potential. The education of children has with regard to family life a twofold object. Its positive aim is to exalt the ethical nature of the child into a direct perception free from all opposition, and thus secure that state of mind, which forms the basis of ethical life. The child thus passes his earlier years in love, trust, and obedience. Its negative aim is to lift the child out of the natural simplicity, in which it at first is, into self-dependence and free personality, and thus make it able to leave the natural unity of the family.

Note.—That the children of Roman parents were slaves is one of the facts which most tarnishes the Roman law. This wounding of the ethical life in its most intimate quarter is an important element in forming an estimate of the world-historical character of the Romans, as well as of their tendency towards formal right.

The necessity for the education of children is found in their inherent dissatisfaction with what they are, in their impulse to belong to the world of adults, whom they reverence as higher beings, and in the wish to become big. The sportive method of teaching gives to children what is childish under the idea that it is in itself valuable. It makes not only itself ridiculous, but also all that is serious. It is scorned by children themselves. Since it strives to represent children as complete in their very incompleteness, of which they themselves are already sensible. Hoping to make them satisfied with their imperfect condition, it disturbs and taints their own truer and higher aspiration. The result is indifference to and want of interest in the substantive relations of the spiritual world, contempt of men, since they have posed before children in a childish and contemptible way, and vain conceit devoted to the contemplation of its own excellence.

Addition.—Man, as child, must have been included with his parents in the circle of love and mutual confidence, and the rational must appear in him as his own most private subjectivity. At the outset the education given by the mother is of greater importance, since social character must be planted in the child as feeling. It is noticeable that children as a rule love their parents less than the parents do their children. Children are on the way to meet independence and wax in strength; besides they have their parents in a sense behind them: but parents possess in their children the objective embodiment of their union.

176. Marriage is only the direct form of the ethical idea, and has its objective reality in the inwardness of subjective sentiment and feeling. In this is found its first exposure to accident. Just as no one may be forced to marry, so there must be no positive legal bond to hold together persons, between whom have arisen hostile thoughts and acts. A third authority must, however, intervene to hold intact the right of marriage and the right of the ethical fabric against the inroads of mere opinion, and the accidents of fleeting resolves. It must also distinguish between the effervescence of feeling and total alienation, and have proof of alienation before permitting divorce.

Addition.—As marriage rests only upon a subjective sentiment which is liable to change, it may be dissolved. The state, on the contrary, is not subject to division, since it rests upon the law. Marriage should be indissoluble, but this desirable state of things remains a mere moral command. Yet, since marriage is ethical, it cannot be dissolved at random, but only by a constituted ethical authority, be it the church or the law. If total alienation has taken place on account of adultery, for example, then the religious authority also must sanction divorce.

177. The ethical or social dismemberment of the family occurs when the children have grown to be free personalities. They are recognized as legal persons, when they have attained their majority. They are then capable both of possessing free property of their own and of founding their own families, sons as heads of the family, and daughters as wives. In the new family the founders have now their substantive office, in contrast with which the first family must occupy a subordinate place as mere basis and point of departure. The family stock is an abstraction which has no rights.

178. The natural disruption of the family by the death of the parents, especially of the husband, necessitates inheritance of the family means. Inheritance is the entering into peculiar possession of the store that is in itself common. The terms of inheritance depend on degree of relation and on the extent of the dispersion throughout the community of the individuals and families, who have broken away from the original family and become independent. Hence inheritance is indefinite in proportion to the loss of the sense of unity, since every marriage is the renunciation of former connections, and the founding of a new independent family.

Note.—It has been supposed that on the occasion of a death a fortune loses its owner, and falls to him who first gets possession of it. Actual possession, however, so the supposition runs, is generally made by relatives, since they are usually in the immediate neighbourhood of the deceased.

Hence what customarily happens, is, for the sake of order, raised by positive law into a rule. This theory is little more than a whim, and altogether overlooks the nature of the family relation.

179. Through the dismemberment of the family by death there is afforded free scope for the capricious fancy of the testator, who may bestow his means in accordance with his personal likings, opinions, and ends. He may leave his possessions to friends and acquaintances instead of to the family, adopting the legal mode of bequest by embodying his declaration in a will.

Note.—Into the formation of a circle of friends by a bequest, which is authorized by ethical observance, there enters, especially in the case of wills, so much of arbitrariness, wilfulness, and selfishness, that the ethical element becomes extremely shadowy. Indeed the legal permission to be arbitrary in drawing up a will is rather the cause of injury to ethical institutions and, also, of underhand exertions and servility. It occasions and justifies the absurd and even malign desire to link to so-called benefactions and bequests of property, which in any case ceases at death to be mine, conditions that are vain and vexatious.

180. The principle that the members of a family become independent legal persons (§177) allows something of capricious discrimination with regard to the natural heirs to enter inside even the family circle. But this discrimination is greatly limited in order not to injure the fundamental relation of the family.

Note.—The simple direct freedom of choice of the deceased cannot be construed as the principle at the basis of the right to make a will. More particularly is this the case, if this wilfulness is opposed to the substantive right of the family, whose love and esteem for the deceased would be the chief reason for carrying out after his death his wayward behest. Such a will contains nothing so worthy of respect as the family right. Formerly the validity of a last will and testament lay only in its arbitrary recognition of others. This validity can be conceded to a testamentary disposition only when the family relation, in which it would otherwise be absorbed, is weak and ineffective. But to ignore the province of the family relation, when it is real and present, is unethical; and it would also weaken its inherent ethical value to extend the boundaries of a testator's caprice.

The harsh and unethical Roman law makes unlimited caprice inside the family the chief principle of succession. In accordance with this law the son could be sold by the father, and would, if freed, again come under his father's power. Only after being freed from slavery the third time, was he really free. According to these laws the son did not *de jure* come of age, and was not a legal person. Only what he took in war, *peculium castrense,* was he entitled to possess. When he, on being three times sold and freed, passed out of his father's power, he did not inherit along with those, who had remained in family servitude, except by the insertion of a special clause in the will. Similarly, the wife, in so far as she had entered marriage not as a slave, *in manum conveniret, in mancipio esset,* but as a matron, did not so much belong to the family, which had by her marriage been established, and was actually hers, as to the family of her birth. Hence she was excluded from inheriting wealth, which belonged to what was really her own family. Though wife and mother she was disinherited.

It has already been observed (§3, *note*) that, as the feeling of rationality developed, efforts were made to escape from the unethical elements of these and other laws. The expression *bonorum possessio,* which, as every learned jurist knows, is to be distinguished from *possessio bonorum,* was drawn into service by the judges instead of *hereditas,* through the employment of a legal fiction, by means of which a *filia* was changed by a second baptism into a *filius.* It thus sometimes became the sad necessity of the judges slyly to smuggle in the reasonable as an offset to bad laws. Hence, the most important institutions became pitifully unstable, and evils arose, which necessitated in turn a tumultuous mass of counter legislation.

The unethical results, flowing from the right of free choice allowed by Roman law to testators, are well known from history and from the descriptions of Lucian and others. As to marriage it is a direct and simple ethical relation, and implies a mingling of what is substantive with natural contingency and inner caprice. By making children slaves, and by kindred regulations, conspicuously by ready and easy divorce, preference is openly conceded to wilfulness over the right of the substantive ethical fact. Thus Cicero himself, who, in his "Officiis" and other works has written many a fine thing about the *Honestum* and *Decorum,* devised the scheme of sending away his wife in order that he might with a second wife get a sufficient dowry to pay his debts. When such things occur, a way is paved by the law for the ruin of morals; or rather the laws are the necessary product of this ruin and decay.

The institution of heirs-at-law is introduced in order to preserve the glory of the family stock. It makes use of substitutions and family trusts by excluding from the inheritance the daughters in favour of the sons, or the rest of the family in favour of the eldest son, or by sanctioning some other inequality. By it injustice is done to the principle of freedom of property (§62). Besides, it rests upon an arbitrary will, which has absolutely no right to be recognized, since it aims to preserve a particular stock or house rather than a particular family. But the family, and not the stock or house is the idea, which has the right to be preserved. Moreover, the ethical fabric is as likely to be maintained by the free disposal of property and equality of succession, as family trees are to be preserved by an opposite course.

In institutions like the Roman the right of marriage (§172) is every-where misinterpreted. Marriage is the complete founding of a new and actual family, in contrast with which the family, as the *stirps* or *gens* is called, is an abstraction, becoming, as the generations pass by, ever more shadowy and unreal (§177). Love, the ethical element in marriage, is a feeling for real present individuals, and not for an abstraction. It is shown further on (§356) that the world-historical principle of the Roman empire is an abstraction of the understanding. It is also shown further on (§306) that the higher political sphere introduces a right of primogeni-ture and an inalienable family fortune, based, however, not on an arbi-trary act of will, but on the necessary idea of the state.

Addition.—Amongst the Romans in earlier times a father could disin-herit his children, and even put them to death. Afterwards neither of these acts was allowed. Efforts were made to bring both the unethical and also the illogical attempt to make it ethical into one system, the retention of which constitutes the difficulty and weakness of our law of inheri-tance. Wills may certainly be permitted, but in them should prevail the idea that the right of arbitrary decision grows only with the dispersion and separation of the members of the family. The so-called family of friendship, which bequest brings into existence, should appear only when there are no children or near relatives. Something offensive and dis-agreeable is associated with testamentary dispositions generally. In them I reveal those to whom I have inclination. But inclination is arbitrary, can be obtained surreptitiously, and is allied to whim and fancy. It may even be required in a will that an heir shall subject himself to the greatest in-dignities. In England, where they are given to riding all sorts of hobbies, an infinite number of absurdities are attached to wills.

Transition of the Family into the Civic Community

181. In a natural way and essentially through the principle of person-ality, the family separates into a number of families, which then exist as independent concrete persons, and are therefore related externally to one another. The elements bound up in the unity of the family, which is the social idea still in the form of the conception, must now be re-leased from the conception and given independent reality. This is the stage of difference. Here, at the outset, to use abstract expressions, we have the determination of particularity, which is nevertheless in relation to universality. The universal is, in fact, the basis, which is, however, as yet only internal, and therefore exists in the particular only formally, and in it is manifested externally. Hence in this relation occasioned by re-flection the ethical is, as it were, lost; or rather since it, as essence, of ne-

cessity appears or is manifested, it occurs in its phenomenal form. This is the civic community.

Note.—The extension of the family or the transition of it into another principle has in the actual world two phases. It is on one side the peaceful expansion of the family into a people or nation, whose component parts have a common natural origin. On the other side it is the collection of scattered groups of families by superior force, or it is their voluntary association, in order to satisfy by co-operation their common wants.

Addition.—Universality has here a point of outlet in the independence of particularity. At this point the ethical appears to be lost. Consciousness finds in the identity of the family what is properly its first divine and obligatory principle. But now there appears a relation, in which the particular is to be the prime factor in determining my conduct. Thus the ethical seems to be discarded and superseded. But in this view I am really in error, for, while I believe myself to be retaining the particular, the universal and also the necessity of social unity still remain for me fundamental and essential. Besides, I am at the stage of appearance, and although my particular nature remains for me the determining factor and end, I serve in this way the universal, which does not relax its own special hold of me.

SECOND SECTION
The Civic Community

182. The concrete person, who as particular is an end to himself, is a totality of wants and a mixture of necessity and caprice. As such he is one of the principles of the civic community. But the particular person is essentially connected with others. Hence each establishes and satisfies himself by means of others, and so must call in the assistance of the form of universality. This universality is the other principle of the civic community.

Addition.—The civic community is the realm of difference, intermediate between the family and the state, although its construction followed in point of time the construction of the state. It, as the difference, must presuppose the state. On the self-dependent state it must rely for its subsistence. Further, the creation of the civic community belongs to the modern world which alone has permitted every element of the idea to receive its due. When the state is represented as a union of different persons, that is, a unity which is merely a community, it is only the civic community which is meant. Many modern teachers of political science have not been able to develop any other view of the state. In this society every one is an end to himself; all others are for him nothing. And yet without coming into relation with others he cannot realize his ends.

Hence to each particular person others are a means to the attainment of his end. But the particular purpose gives itself through reference to others the form of universality, and in satisfying itself accomplishes at the same time the well-being of others. Since particularity is bound up with the conditioning universal, the joint whole is the ground of adjustment or mediation, upon which all individualities, all talents, all accidents of birth or fortune disport themselves. Here the fountains of all the passions are let loose, being merely governed by the sun of reason. Particularity limited by universality is the only standard to which the particular person conforms in promoting his well-being.

183. The self-seeking end is conditioned in its realization by the universal. Hence is formed a system of mutual dependence, a system which interweaves the subsistence, happiness, and rights of the individual with the subsistence, happiness, and right of all. The general right and well-being form the basis of the individual's right and well-being, which only by this connection receives actuality and security. This system we may in the first instance call the external state, the state which satisfies one's needs, and meets the requirements of the understanding.

184. When the idea is thus at variance with itself, it imparts to the phases of the peculiarly individual life, *i.e.,* to particularity, the right to develop and publish themselves on all sides, and to universality it concedes the right to evince itself as the foundation and necessary form, overruling power and final end of the particular. In this system the ethical order is lost in its own extremes. It is a system characterized by external appearance and constituted by the abstract side of the reality of the idea. In it the idea is found only as relative totality, and inner necessity.

Addition.—The direct unity of the family is here broken up into a multiplicity, and the ethical is lost in its extremes. Reality is at this stage externality, involving the dissolution of the conception, the liberation and independence of its realized elements. Although in the civic community particular and universal fall apart, they are none the less mutually connected and conditioned. While the one seems to be just the opposite of the other, and is supposed to be able to exist only by keeping the other at arm's length, each nevertheless has the other as a condition. Thus most people, for example, regard the payment of taxes as injuring their particularity, and as opposing and crippling their plans. True as this may seem to be, the particular purpose cannot be carried out apart from the universal. A land, in which no taxes were paid, would not be allowed to distinguish itself for the strength of its individuals. In the same way it might appear as if it would be better for the universal to draw to itself the resources of the individual, and become a society such as was delineated by Plato in his "Republic." But this, too, is only a mere appearance, since both elements exist only through and for each other, and are wrapped up in each other. When I promote my end, I promote the universal, and the universal in turn promotes my end.

185. When independent particularity gives free rein to the satisfaction of want, caprice, and subjective liking, it destroys in its extravagance both itself and its substantive conception. On the other hand the satisfaction whether of necessary or of contingent want is contingent, since it contains no inherent limit, and is wholly dependent on external chance, caprice, and the power of the universal. In these conflicts and complexities the civic community affords a spectacle of excess, misery, and physical and social corruption.

Note.—The independent development of particularity (compare §124, *note*), is the element which was revealed in the ancient states as an inflow of immorality causing ultimately their decay. These states, founded as they were partly upon a patriarchal and religious principle, partly upon a spiritual though simple ethical life, and originating in general in native intuitions, could not withstand the disunion and infinite reflection involved in self-consciousness. Hence, so soon as reflection arose, the state succumbed, first in sentiment and then in fact. Its as yet simple principle lacked the truly infinite power implied in a unity, which permits the opposition to reason to explode with all its force. In this way it would rise superior to the opposition, preserve itself in it, and take it into itself.

Plato in his "Republic" represents the substantive ethical life in its ideal beauty and truth. But with the principle of independent particularity, which broke in upon Greek ethical life at his time, he could do nothing except to oppose to it his "Republic," which is simply substantive. Hence he excluded even the earliest form of subjectivity, as it exists in private property (§46, *note*) and the family, and also in its more expanded form as private liberty and choice of profession. It is this defect, which prevents the large and substantive truth of the "Republic" from being understood, and gives rise to the generally accepted view that it is a mere dream of abstract thought, or what we are used to calling an ideal. In the merely substantive form of the actual spirit, as it appears in Plato, the principle of self-dependent and in itself infinite personality of the individual, the principle of subjective freedom does not receive its due. This principle on its inner side issues in the Christian religion, and on its outer side in the Roman world, where it was combined with abstract universality. It is historically later than the Greek world. So, too, the philosophic reflection, which fathoms the depth of this principle, is later than the substantive idea found in Greek thought.

Addition.—Particularity, taken abstractly, is measureless in its excess, and the forms of excess are likewise measureless. A man's appetites, which are not a closed circle like the instinct of the animal, are widened by picture-thought and reflection. He may carry appetite even to the spurious infinite. But on the other side privation and want are also measureless. The confusion, due to the collision of appetite and privation, can only be set to rights by the state. If the Platonic state excludes particularity, no hope can be held out to it, as it contradicts the infinite right of the idea to allow to particularity its freedom. In the Christian religion, the right of subjects and also the existence, which is self-referring and self-dependent, have received a marked expansion. And at the same time the whole is sufficiently strong to establish harmony between particularity and the ethical unity.

186. But the principle of particularity develops of its own accord into a totality, and thus goes over into universality. In this universality it has its truth and its right to positive realization. Since at the standpoint of dualism, which we now occupy (§184), the principles of particularity and universality are independent, their unity is not an ethical identity. It does not exist as freedom, but as a necessity. That is to say the particular has to raise itself to the form of universality, and in it it has to seek and find its subsistence.

187. Individuals in the civic community are private persons, who pursue their own interests. As these interests are occasioned by the universal, which appears as a means, they can be obtained only in so far as individuals in their desire, will, and conduct, conform to the universal, and become a link in the chain of the whole. The interest of the idea as such does not, it is true, lie in the consciousness of the citizens; yet it is not wholly wanting. It is found in the process, by means of which the individual, through necessity of nature and the caprice of his wants, seeks to raise his individual natural existence into formal freedom and the formal universality of knowing and willing. Thus, without departing from its particular nature, the individual's character is enlarged.

Note.—The view that civilization is an external and degenerate form of life is allied to the idea that the natural condition of uncivilized peoples is one of unsophisticated innocence. So also the view that civilization is a mere means for the satisfaction of one's needs, and for the enjoyment and comfort of one's particular life, takes for granted that these selfish ends are absolute. Both theories manifest ignorance of the nature of spirit and the end of reason. Spirit is real only when by its own motion it divides itself, gives itself limit and finitude in the natural needs and the region of external necessity, and then, by moulding and shaping itself in them, overcomes them, and secures for itself an objective embodiment. The rational end, therefore, is neither the simplicity of nature nor the enjoyments resulting from civilization through the development of particularity. It rather works away from the condition of simple nature, in which there is either no self or a crude state of consciousness and will, and transcends the naïve individuality, in which spirit is submerged. Its externality thus in the first instance receives the rationality, of which it is capable, namely, the form of universality characteristic of the understanding. Only in this way is spirit at home and with itself in this externality as such. Hence in it the freedom of spirit is realized. Spirit, becoming actualized in an element, which of itself was foreign to its free character, has to do only with what is produced by itself and bears its own impress.—In this way the form of universality comes into independent existence in thought, a form which is the only worthy element for the existence of the idea.

Culture or education is, as we may thus conclude, in its ultimate sense a liberation, and that of a high kind. Its task is to make possible the infinitely subjective substantiality of the ethical life. In the process we pass upwards from the direct and natural existence to what is spiritual and has the form of the universal.—In the individual agent this liberation involves a struggle against mere subjectivity, immediate desire, subjective vanity, and capricious liking. The hardness of the task is in part the cause of the disfavour under which it falls. None the less is it through the labour of education that the subjective will itself wins possession of the objectivity, in which alone it is able and worthy to be the embodiment of the idea.—At the same time the form of universality, into which particularity has moulded itself and worked itself up, gives rise to that general principle of the understanding, in accordance with which the particular passes upward into the true, independent existence of the individual. And since the particular gives to the universal its adequate content and unconditioned self-direction, it even in the ethical sphere is infinitely independent and free subjectivity. Education is thus proved to be an inherent element of the absolute, and is shown to have infinite value.

Addition.—We call those men educated or cultured, who can perform all that others do without exhibiting any oddities of behaviour. Uneducated men thrust their eccentricities upon your notice, and do not act according to the universal qualities of the object. It easily happens that the uneducated man wounds the feelings of others, since he lets himself go, and does not trouble himself about their sensibilities. Not that he desires to injure them at all, but his conduct is not in unison with his will. Education refines particularity, and enables it to conduct itself in harmony with the nature of the object. True originality, which creates its object, desires true culture, while untrue originality adopts insipidities, which are characteristic of a lack of culture.

188. The civic community contains three elements:

A. The recasting of want, and the satisfaction of the individual through his work, through the work of all others, and through the satisfaction of their wants. This is a system of wants.

B. Actualization of the general freedom required for this, *i.e.*, the protection of property by the administration of justice.

C. Provision against possible mischances, and care for the particular interest as a common interest, by means of police and the corporation.

A. The System of Wants

189. The particularity, which is in the first instance opposed to the universal will (§60), is subjective want. It gets objectivity, *i.e.*, is satisfied (α), through external objects, which are at this stage the property of others, and the product of their needs and wills, and (β) through active labour, as connecting link between subjective and objective. Labour has as its aim to satisfy subjective particularity. Yet by the introduction of the needs and free choice of others universality is realized. Hence rationality comes as an appearance into the sphere of the finite. This partial presence of rationality is the understanding, to which is assigned the function of reconciling the opposing elements of the finite sphere.

Note.—It is the task of political science, which originates at this point, to detect the laws governing the movement of the masses in the intricacy of their qualitative and quantitative relations. This science has sprung from the soil of modern times. Its development reveals the interesting process by which thought (see Smith, Say, Ricardo) examines the infinite multitude of particulars lying before it, and exposes their simple, active, regulating principles. These principles belong to the understanding. As on the one side the principle of reconciliation involves a recognition of the external presence or appearance in the sphere of want of the reason which is active in the object; so, on the exact contrary, is this also the sphere in which the understanding with its subjective aims and moral opinions lets loose its discontent and moral vexation.

Addition.—It depends altogether on accident how such universal wants, as those of food, drink, and clothing, are to be satisfied. The soil is more fertile in one place than another; years differ in their yield; one man is diligent, while another is lazy. But this swarm of arbitrary things begets universal features, and what appears to be pure abstraction and absence of thought becomes bound by a necessity, which enters of itself. To discover the element of necessity is the object of political science, a science which does honour to thought, because it finds laws in a mass of accidents. Interesting is it to witness the action and reaction of the different relations, how the special circles group themselves, influence others, and in turn receive from them help or hindrance. So remarkable is this interpretation of facts in a sphere, where everything seems to be postponed to the free will of the individual, that it almost passes belief. It resembles the planets, which though to the eye always complex and irregular in their movements, are yet governed by ascertained laws.

(a) *Want and its Satisfaction*

190. The animal has a limited range of ways and means for satisfying his limited wants. Man in his dependence proves his universality and his ability to become independent, firstly, by multiplying his wants and means, and, secondly, by dissecting the concrete want into parts. The parts then become other wants, and through being specialized are more abstract than the first.

Note.—The object is in right a person, in morals a subject, in the family a member, in the city generally a burgher (*bourgeois*); and here, at the standpoint of want (§123, note), he is the concrete product of picture-thought which we call man. Here, and properly only here, is it that we first speak of man in this sense.

Addition.—The animal is particular in its being, having instinct, and a strictly limited means of satisfaction. Some insects are confined to a certain kind of plant; other animals have a wider circle and can inhabit different climates, but still their range is limited in contrast with that of man. Man's need of shelter and clothing, his having to destroy the natural form of food, and adapt it by cooking to his changed taste, give him less aplomb than the animal. Indeed, as spirit, he ought to have less. The understanding, with its grasp of differences, brings multiplicity into wants: and, when taste and utility become criteria of judgment, they change even the wants themselves. It is in the end not the appetite, but the opinion which has to be satisfied. It is the province of education or culture to dissect the concrete need into its elements. When wants are multiplied, the mere appetites are restricted; for, when man uses many things, the propulsion to any one of them is not so strong, a sign that the force of physical need in general is diminished.

191. The means for satisfying the specialized wants are similarly divided and increased. These means become in their turn relative ends and abstract wants. Hence the multiplication expands into an infinite series of distinctions with regard to these phases, and of judgments concerning the suitability of the means to their ends. This is refinement.

Addition.—What the English call "comfortable" is something endless and inexhaustible. Every condition of comfort reveals in turn its discomfort, and these discoveries go on for ever. Hence the new want is not so much a want of those who have it directly, but is created by those who hope to make profit from it.

192. The satisfaction of want and the attainment of means thereto become a realized possibility for others, through whose wants and labour satisfaction is in turn conditioned. The abstraction, which becomes a quality of wants and means (§191), helps to determine the mutual relation of individuals. This general recognition of others is the element

which makes the isolated abstract wants and means concrete and social.

Addition.—Through the compulsion I am under to fashion myself according to others arises the form of universality. I acquire from others the means of satisfaction, and must accordingly fall in with their opinions. At the same time I am compelled to produce the means for the satisfaction of the wants of others. One plays into the other; and the two are interdependent. Everything particular becomes in this way social. In the matter of dress, time of eating, etc., we follow convention, because it is not worth while exercising our insight and judgment. He is the most prudent who does as others do.

193. The social element is a special instrument both of the simple acquisition of the means, and also of the reduplication of the ways by which want is satisfied. Further, it contains directly the claim of equality with others. Both the desire for equality, including the imitation of others, and also the desire of each person to be unique, become real sources of the multiplication and extension of wants.

194. Social want joins the direct or natural want with the spiritual want due to picture-thinking; but the spiritual or universal factor outweighs the other. The social element brings a liberation, by which the stringent necessity of nature is turned aside, and man is determined by his own universal opinion. He makes his own necessity. He has arbitrary choice, being in contact with a contingency which is not external but internal.

Note.—It has been held that man as to want is free in a so-called state of nature, in which he has only the so-called simple wants of nature, requiring for their satisfaction merely the means furnished directly and at random by nature. In this view no account is taken of the freedom which lies in work, of which more hereafter. Such a view is not true, because in natural want and its direct satisfaction the spiritual is submerged by mere nature. Hence, a state of nature is a state of savagery and slavery. Freedom is nowhere to be found except in the return of spirit and thought to itself, a process by which it distinguishes itself from the natural and turns back upon it.

195. This liberation is formal, since the particular side of the end remains the fundamental content. The tendency of the social condition indefinitely to increase and specialize wants, means, and enjoyments, and to distinguish natural from unrefined wants, has no limits. Hence arises luxury, in which the augmentation of dependence and distress is in its nature infinite. It operates upon an infinitely unyielding material, namely, an external means, which has the special quality of being the possession of the free will. Hence it meets with the most obdurate resistance.

Addition.—Diogenes in his completely cynical character is properly only a product of Athenian social life. That which gave birth to him was the public opinion, against which his behaviour was directed. His way of life was therefore not independent, but occasioned by his social surroundings. It was itself an ungainly product of luxury. Wherever luxury is extreme, there also prevail distress and depravity, and cynicism is produced in opposition to over-refinement.

(b) Labour

196. The instrument for preparing and acquiring specialized means adequate to specialized wants is labour. By labour the material, directly handed over by nature for these numerous ends, is specialized in a variety of ways. This fashioning of the material gives to the means value and purpose, so that in consumption it is chiefly human products and human effort that are used up.

Addition.—The direct material, which requires no working up, is small. Even air must be acquired, since it has to be made warm. Perhaps water is the only thing which man can use, simply as it is. Human sweat and toil win for men the means for satisfying their wants.

197. Training on its theoretical side is developed by the great variety of objects and interests, and consists not only in numberless picture-thoughts and items of knowledge, but also in mobility and quickness of imagination, a mental alertness in passing from one image, or idea, to another, and in the apprehension of intricate general relations. This is the training of the understanding, with which goes the development of language. Practical training, or training by labour, consists in habituation to an employment, which satisfies a self-caused want. Its action is limited partly by the nature of the material, but chiefly by the caprice of others. It involves an habitual use of skill acquired by practice and implying objective conditions.

Addition.—The barbarian is lazy, and is distinguished from the civilized man by his brooding stupidity. Practical training consists in habitual employment and the need of it. The unskilled workman always makes something different from what he intended, because he is not master of his own hands. A workman is skilled, who produces what he intended, whose subjective action readily accords with his purpose.

198. The universal and objective in work is to be found in the abstraction which, giving rise to the specialization of means and wants, causes the specialization also of production. This is the division of labour. By it the labour of the individual becomes more simple, his skill in his abstract work greater, and the amount he produces larger. The result of the abstraction of skill and means is that men's interdependence or mutual relation is completed. It becomes a thorough necessity. Moreover, the abstraction of production causes work to be continually more mechanical, until it is at last possible for man to step out and let the machine take his place.

(c) Wealth

199. Through the dependence and co-operation involved in labour, subjective self-seeking is converted into a contribution towards the satisfaction of the wants of all others. The universal so penetrates the particular by its dialectic movement, that the individual, while acquiring, producing, and enjoying for himself, at the same time produces and acquires for the enjoyment of others. This is a necessity, and in this necessity arising out of mutual dependence is contained the fact of a general and permanent wealth (§170). In it each person may share by means of his education and skill. Each, too, is by it assured of subsistence, while the results of his labour preserve and increase the general wealth.

200. But particular wealth, or the possibility of sharing in the general wealth, is based partly on skill, partly on something which is directly the individual's own, namely, capital. Skill in its turn depends on capital, and on many accidental circumstances. These also in their manifold variety make more pronounced the differences in the development of natural endowments, physical and mental, which were unequal to begin with. These differences are conspicuous everywhere in the sphere of particularity. They, along with other elements of chance and accident, necessarily produce inequalities of wealth and skill.

Note.—Nature is the element of inequality. Yet the objective right of particularity of spirit, contained in the idea itself, does not in the civic community supersede the inequality set up by nature. On the contrary, it produces inequality out of spirit and exalts it to an inequality of talents, wealth, and intellectual and moral education. To oppose to the objective right a demand for equality is a move of the empty understanding, which takes its own abstraction and mandate to be real and reasonable. In the sphere of particularity the universal images itself, forming with the particular merely a relative identity. The particular thus retains both the natural and the capricious particularity, and also a remnant of the state of nature. It is the reason immanent in the system of human wants and their activities, which fashions this system into an organic whole, of which the differences are members. (See next §.)

201. The infinitely varied means and their infinitely interlacing play of mutual production and exchange are gathered together by virtue of the universality inherent in their content, and become divided into general masses. The whole is thus formed into particular systems of wants, means, and labour, ways and methods of satisfaction, and theoretical and practical training. Amongst these systems the individuals are apportioned, and compose a cluster of classes or estates.

Addition.—The manner of sharing in the general wealth is left to each particular individual, but the general differences, found in the division of the civic community, are essential. The family is the first basis of the state, and classes or estates are the second. This second is of consequence because private persons, through self-seeking, are compelled to turn themselves out towards others. This is the link by which self-seeking is joined to the universal or the state, whose care it must be to keep the connection strong and steadfast.

202. Classes are, in terms of the conception, (a) the substantial or direct, (b) the reflecting or formal, and (c) the universal.

203. (a) The wealth of the substantial class is contained in natural products obtained by cultivation. The soil is capable of being an exclusive, private possession, and demands not merely the taking from it what it bears naturally, but an objective working up. Since the returns of labour depend on the seasons, and harvests are influenced by variable weather and other natural conditions, provision for wants must take account of the future. However, owing to the natural conditions, this way of life involves but little reflection, and is but slightly modified by subjective volition. It therefore embodies in substantive feeling an ethical life resting directly upon trust and the family relation.

Note.—States are rightly said to come into existence with the introduction of agriculture along with the introduction of marriage. The principle of agriculture involves the cultivation of the soil, and therefore, also, private ownership of property (compare §170, *note*). It takes the life of nomadic tribes back to the repose of private right and to the secure satisfaction of wants. Joined also to the agricultural life are the limitation of sexual love to marriage, the extension of this bond to an enduring universal relation, the extension of want to family maintenance and of possession to family wealth. Safety, protection by fortification, and uninterrupted satisfaction of wants are all commendable *prima facie* characteristics of these two fundamental ethical institutions. They are forms of universality, or ways by which reason or the absolute end seeks to realize itself. In this connection nothing can be more interesting than the ingenious and learned explanations which my much honoured friend, Mr. Creuzer, has given in the fourth volume of his "Mythologie und Symbolik" with regard to the agrarian festivals, images, and sanctuaries of the ancients. In these customs and rites the introduction of agriculture and kindred institutions was known and revered as a divine act.

From the side of private-right, especially the administration of justice, and from the side of instruction, culture, and also of religion, the substantive character of this class undergoes modifications. These modifications, however, are due to the development of reflection, and affect not the substantive content but the form.—They occur also in the other classes.

Addition.—In our time agriculture, losing some of its naturalness, is managed in a reflective way like a factory, and acquires the character of the second class. Yet it will always retain much of the substantive feeling, which pervades the patriarchal life. In it man accepts what is given with a simple mind, thanks God for it, and lives in the assurance that the goodness of God will continue. What he gets suffices him, and he uses it because it comes again. This is the simple disposition unaffected by the desire for wealth. It may be described as the type of the old nobility, who consumed simply what was there. In this class nature does the chief share of the work, and man's diligence is in comparison secondary. In the second class the understanding is the essential factor, and the natural products are regarded simply as furnishing material.

204. (b) The business of the industrial class is to alter the form of the products of nature. This class is indebted for its subsistence to its labour, to reflection, and also to the interposition of the wants and labours of others. For that which it produces and enjoys it has to thank mainly its own activity.—Its field of action is again divided into three parts:—(i.) Labour for individual wants of the more concrete kind, and at the request of particular persons. This is manual labour, or the work of single artisans. (ii.) The more abstract collective mass of labour, which is also for particular needs but due to a general demand. This is manufacture. (iii.) Business of exchange, by which one special means of subsistence is given for others, chiefly through money, the general medium of exchange, in which is realized the abstract value of all merchandise. This is commerce.

Addition.—The individual in the industrial class is referred to himself, and this self-reference is intimately connected with the demand for a legal status. Consequently the sense for freedom and order has mainly arisen in cities. The first class needs to think little about itself. What it acquires is the gift of a stranger, nature. With it the feeling of dependence is primary. With this feeling is easily associated a willingness to submit to whatever occurs. The first class is therefore more inclined to subjection, the second to freedom.

205 (c) The business of the universal class is with the universal interests of society. Hence it must be relieved of the direct task of providing for itself. It must possess private means, or receive an allowance from the state, which claims his activity. His private interest may thus find satisfaction in his labour for the universal.

206. A class is a particularity which has become objective, and the foregoing are the general divisions in accordance with the conception. Yet capacity, birth, and other circumstances have their influence in determining to what class an individual shall belong. But the final and essential factor in the case is subjective opinion and private freedom of choice. In this sphere free choice has its right, honour, and dignity. If a thing happens in this sphere according to internal necessity, it is *ipso facto*

occasioned by free arbitrary choice, and for the subjective consciousness bears the stamp of its will.

Note.—In reference to the principle of particularity or subjective caprice may be clearly discerned the difference between the political life of the East and that of the West, between the ancient and the modern world. In the ancient world the division of the whole into classes was produced objectively of itself, because it is implicitly rational. But the principle of subjectivity does not receive its due, since the separation of individuals into classes is either a function of the rulers, as in Plato's "Republic" (Rep. iii. 120), or else it rests upon mere birth, as in the caste system of India. Now subjective particularity is an essential element of communal life, and, when it is not taken up into the organization of the whole and reconciled in the whole, it must prove a hostile force and pave the way for the ruin of the social order (see §185, *note*). It either over-turns society, as was the case in the Greek states and the Roman repub-lic, or, when the existing order is able to preserve itself by force or by religious authority, it then manifests itself as internal corruption and complete degradation. This happened in a measure amongst the Lacedemonians, and now is completely the case with the inhabitants of India.

But when subjective particularity is welcomed by objective order, and given its rights and place, it becomes the animating principle of the civic community, stimulates thought and promotes merit and honour. The recognition of the claim that whatever in the civic community and the state is rationally necessary should occur through subjective free choice is a fuller definition of the popular idea of freedom (§121).

207. The particularity of the individual becomes definitely and actu-ally realized, only by his limiting himself exclusively to one of the par-ticular spheres of want. In this system the ethical sense is that of rectitude or class-honour. It involves the decision of the individual by means of his own native activity, diligence, and skill to make himself a member of one of these classes, preserve himself in it, and provide for himself only through the instrumentality of the universal. He should acknowledge this position, and also claim to have it recognized by others.—Morality has its peculiar place in this sphere, where the ruling factor is reflection upon one's action, or consideration of the end involved in particular wants and in well-being. Here also the element of chance in satisfying these ends makes random and individual assistance a duty.

Note.—Youth is specially apt to struggle against the proposal that it should decide upon a particular vocation, on the ground that any deci-sion is a limitation of its universal scope and a mere external necessity. This aloofness is a product of the abstract thinking, which clings to the universal and unreal. It fails to recognize that the conception must experience a division into conception and its reality, if it is to have a definite and particular realization (§7), and to win for itself reality and ethical objectivity.

Addition.—By the sentence that a man must be something we understand that he must belong to a definite class; for this something signifies a substantive reality. A human being without a vocation is a mere private person, who has no place in any real universal. Still, the individual in his exclusiveness may regard himself as the universal, and may fancy that when he takes a trade or profession, he is sinking to a lower plane. That is the false notion that a thing, when it attains the realization which properly belongs to it, limits itself and gives up its independence.

208. The principle of the system of wants, namely the particularity of knowing and willing, contains absolute universality, or the universality of freedom, only in the abstract form of right of property. But here right is no longer merely implicit, but is found in valid reality as protection of property through the administration of justice.

B. Administration of Justice

209. The relative principle of the mutual exchange of wants and labour for their satisfaction has in the first instance its return into itself in the infinite personality generally, *i.e.,* in abstract right. Yet it is the very sphere of the relative which in the form of education gives embodiment to right, by fixing it as something universally acknowledged, known, and willed. The relative also, through the interposition of knowledge and will, supplies right with validity and objective actuality.

Note.—It is the essence of education and of thought, which is the consciousness of the individual in universal form, that the I should be apprehended as a universal person, in whom all are identical. Man must be accounted a universal being, not because he is a Jew, Catholic, Protestant, German, or Italian, but because he is a man. This thinking or reflective consciousness, is of infinite importance. It is defective only when it plumes itself upon being cosmopolitan, in opposition to the concrete life of the citizen.

Addition.—From one point of view it is by means of the system of particularity that right becomes externally necessary as protection of individuals. Although right proceeds out of the conception, it enters into being only because it is serviceable for wants. To have the thought of right, one must be educated to the stage of thinking, and not linger in the region of the merely sensible. We must adapt the form of universality to the objects, and direct the will according to a universal principle. Only after man has found out for himself many wants, the acquisition of which is an inseparable element of his satisfaction, is he able to frame laws.

210. The objective actuality of right consists partly in existing for consciousness, or more generally in its being known, and partly in having, and being generally recognized as having, the validity and force of a reality.

(a) Right as Law

211. What is in essence right becomes in its objective concrete existence constituted,[2] that is, made definite for consciousness through thought. It, having right and validity, is so recognized, and becomes law.[3] Right in this characterization of it is positive right in general.

Note.—To constitute something as universal, *i.e.,* to bring it as universal to consciousness, is to think (§13, *note,* and §21, *note*). The content in thus being brought back to its simplest form is given its final mould. Only when what is right becomes law does it receive not merely the form of universality, but its own truest character. It is to select only one phase of law, if we consider it merely as a valid rule of conduct imposed upon all. Preceding this feature is the internal and essential element of law, namely, the recognition of the content in its definite universality. Even the rights of custom exist as thought and are known. Animals have law in the form of instinct; man alone has law in the form of custom. The difference between custom and law consists merely in this, that customs are known in a subjective and accidental way, and hence are in their actual form more indefinite than laws. In custom, the universality of thought is more obscured, and the knowledge of right is a partial and accidental possession of a few. The idea that customs rather than laws should pass over into life is a deception, because the valid laws of a nation, when written and collected, do not cease to be customs. People speak nowadays, indeed, most of all of life and of things passing over into life, when they are conversant with nothing but the deadest material and the deadest thoughts. When customs come to be collected and grouped, as takes place with every people which reaches a certain grade of civilization, there is formed a statute-book. It is somewhat different from a statute-book properly so-called. A collection is formless, indefinite, and fragmentary, whereas a real statute-book apprehends and expresses in terms of thought the principles of law in their universality. England's land-law or common law is, as is well known, made up both of statutes, having the forms of laws, and of so-called unwritten laws. However, this unwritten law is written with a vengeance, and a knowledge of it is possible only by reading the many quartos which it fills. The monstrous confusion which prevails in that country, both in the administration of

---

[2]Gesetzt.
[3]Gesetz.

justice and in the subject-matter of the law, is graphically portrayed by those who are acquainted with the facts. They specially notice that, since the unwritten law is contained in the decisions of law-courts and judges, the judges are continually the lawgivers. Further, the judges are both directed and not directed to the authority of their predecessors. They are so directed, because their predecessors are said to have done nothing but interpret the unwritten law. They are not so directed, because they are supposed to have in themselves the unwritten law, and hence have a right to determine whether previous decisions are in keeping with it or not.

To avoid a similar confusion, which would have arisen in the administration of justice at Rome, when in later times the views of all the celebrated lawyers were made authoritative, one of the emperors hit upon an ingenious expedient. He passed a law, by which was founded a kind of college consisting of the jurisconsults who were longest deceased. This body had a president, and came to decisions through a majority of votes (Mr. Hugo's "History of Roman Law," §354).—It is the task of a nation, or at least of its jurisconsults, not indeed to make a system of laws entirely new in content, but to recognize the existing content of laws in its definite universality. They should apprehend it in thought, while also making additions with regard to its application to special cases. To refuse to a people or its lawyers this right would be a flagrant insult.

Addition.—The sun and the planets have laws, but they do not know them. Barbarians are ruled by impulses, customs, feelings, but have no consciousness of them. When right is established as law and known, all random intuitions and opinions, revenge, compassion, and self-interest, fall away. Only then does right attain its true character and receive its due honour. In being apprehended right is purified from all mixture of chance elements, and thus becomes for the first time capable of universal application. Of course, in the administration of the laws collisions will necessarily occur, which must be settled by the understanding of the judge; otherwise, the execution of the law would be merely mechanical. But to do away with collisions by giving full scope to the judge's well-meant opinions would be the poorest solution of the difficulty. Collisions, in fact, belong to the nature of thought, the thinking consciousness and its dialectic, while the mere decision of a judge is arbitrary.

In favour of rights of custom it is usually adduced that they are living; but life, consisting in simple identity with the subject, does not constitute the essence of the matter. Right must be known in thought. It must be a system in itself, and only as a system can it be valid for civilized peoples. Very recently the vocation of making laws has been abolished. This is not only an affront, but also implies the absurdity that to no individual has been given the capacity to systematize the infinite multitude of existing laws, and expose the universal contained in them, when this task is precisely the most pressing need of the day. Similarly, it has been held that a digest of decisions, such as the *Corpus juris,* is preferable to a statute-book giving a detailed exhibition of the universal. A certain particularity and reminiscence of the historical is supposed to be contained in the decisions, and in a statute-book it is thought that these advantages would be wanting. But the mischievous nature of a mere collection is clearly manifest in the practice of the English law.

212. Through this identity of the abstract or implicit with what is actually constituted,[4] only that right is binding which has become law.[5] But since to constitute a thing is to give it outer reality, there may creep into the process a contingency due to self-will and other elements of particularity. Hence, the actual law may be different from what is in itself right.

Note.—Hence, in positive right that which is lawfully established is the source of the knowledge of what is right, or, more accurately, is the final resort in litigation. Positive jurisprudence is to that extent an historical science based on authority. Additions are a matter of the understanding, and concern outward arrangements, combinations, results, further applications, and the like. But when the understanding meddles with the essential substance of the matter, it may serve up singular theories, of which those regarding criminal law are an illustration.—It is not only the right but the necessary duty of positive science, it is true, to deduce out of its positive data the historic progress and also applications and ramifications. Yet it cannot be wondered at if it be regarded as a fair cross-question whether a specific finding is after all wholly in accordance with reason (compare on this point §3 *note*).

213. Right is realized in the first instance in the form of constituted law. But it must in its content have further realization. It must apply to the matter of the relations bearing on property and contract, complicated and ramified as these relations in the civic community become. It must apply also to the ethical relations of feeling, love, and confidence, but only in so far as they contain the phase of abstract right (§159). The moral commands, touching the will in its most private subjectivity and particularity, cannot be the object of positive legislation. But additional material for legislation is furnished by the rights and duties which flow from the administration of justice itself and from the state.

Addition.—Of the higher relations of marriage, love, religion, and the state, only those aspects can be objects of legislation, which are by their nature capable of having an external embodiment. Here the laws of different nations are very different. Amongst the Chinese, for example, it is a law of the state that the husband shall love his first wife more than any

---

[4]Gesetzt.
[5]Gesetz.

of the others. If he is convicted of the contrary, he is flogged. So, too, in the older laws may be found many prescripts concerning integrity and honour, things that are wholly internal and do not fall within the province of legislation. But as to the oath, where the matter is laid upon the conscience, integrity and honour must be viewed as in it outwardly substantive.

214. Besides applying to the particular as a whole, the constituted law applies to the special case. Here it enters the quantitative region left unoccupied by the conception. This is, of course, the abstract quantitative, which is found in exchange as value. The conception furnishes in this region only a general limit, inside of which there is room for considerable uncertainty. But fluctuations of opinion must be cut short, and a conclusion reached. Hence, inside of this limit a decision has the character of accident and caprice.

Note.—To whittle the universal down not only to the particular but to the individual case is the chief function of the purely positive in law. It cannot, for example, be determined by reason, or decided by any phase of the conception itself, whether forty lashes or thirty-nine, a fine of four dollars or three dollars and ninety-nine cents, imprisonment for a year or three hundred and sixty-four or three hundred and sixty-six days, be the just punishment for a crime. And yet a lash, a cent, or a day too much or too little is an injustice.

Reason itself recognizes that contingency, contradiction, and appearance have their sphere or right, limited though it is, and is not at pains to rectify these contradictions. Here the purpose is solely to reach actuality, that is, somehow or other within the given limit to get the matter settled. This settlement is the office of formal self-certitude or abstract subjectivity, which, observing the prescribed limit, may bring the matter to issue simply for settlement's sake. Or its reasons for its decision are, if it has any, of this kind, that it should use round numbers, or that the number should be forty less one.

It is of no real significance that the law does not make the final decision demanded by reality, but hands it over to the judge, limiting him merely by a maximum and minimum. The maximum and minimum are themselves round numbers, and do not do away with the requirement that the judge shall pronounce a finite purely positive sentence. On the contrary, this action devolves upon him necessarily.

Addition.—Undoubtedly the laws and the administration of justice contain in one of their aspects something contingent, since the law, though of a universal character, must nevertheless be applied to special cases. If we were to declare against this element of contingency, we would pronounce in favour of an abstraction. The exact quantity of punishment cannot be found in any factor of the conception; and whatever judgment may be made, it is to some extent arbitrary. But this contingency is itself necessary. If one were to argue from the presence of contingency that a code of laws was imperfect, he would overlook the fact that perfection of such a kind is not to be attained. Law must, hence, be taken as it stands.

(b) Law as Incorporated

215. Since the binding force of law rests upon the right of self-consciousness (§132 and *note*), the laws ought to be universally made known.

Note.—To hang up the laws, as did Dionysius the Tyrant, so high that no citizen could read them, is a wrong. To bury them in a cumbrous apparatus of learned books, collections of decisions and opinions of judges, who have deviated from the rule, and, to make matters worse, to write them in a foreign tongue, so that no one can attain a knowledge of them, unless he has made them a special subject of study, is the same wrong in another form.—The rulers, who have given their people a definite and systematized book of common law, or even an unshapely collection such as that of Justinian, should be thanked and lauded as public benefactors. Moreover, they have done a decisive act of justice.

Addition.—Jurists, who have a detailed knowledge of the law, often look on it as their monopoly. He who is not of their profession, they say, shall not be heard. The physicists treated Goethe's theory of colours harshly, because he was not of their vocation, and was a poet besides. But we do not need the services of a shoemaker to find out if the shoe fits, nor do we need to belong to a particular trade in order to have a knowledge of the objects which are of universal interest in it. Right concerns freedom, the worthiest and holiest thing in man, the thing which he must know in so far as he is answerable to it.

216. We are in the presence of an antinomy. Simple universal characteristics are needed in a public statute-book and yet the finite material by its nature gives rise to endless definition; the context of any law should be a rounded-off and complete whole, and yet there must continually be new legal findings. But the right to a completed statute-book remains unimpaired, since this antinomy does not occur in the case of fixed general principles, but only with their specialization. General principles can be apprehended and presented apart from special cases.

Note.—One chief source of complexity in legislation occurs in the case of any historic institution, which in its origin contains an injustice. In the course of time it is sought to infuse into this institution reason and absolute right. An illustration of this procedure was cited above from Roman law (§180, *note)*. It occurs also in the old feudal law and elsewhere. But it is essential to understand that, owing to the nature of finite material, any application to it of principles, absolutely reasonable and in themselves universal, must be an infinite process. To require of a statute-book that it should be absolutely finished, and incapable of any modification—a malady which is mainly German—and to base this demand upon the reason that, if the book cannot be completed, it cannot come up to the so-called imperfect and therefore falls short of reality, rest upon a twofold misunderstanding. This view implies a misconception of the nature of such finite objects as private right, whose so-called perfection consists simply in a perennial approximation. It implies, too, a misconception of the difference between the universal of the understanding and that of reason, and also of their application to the finite and particular material, which goes on to infinity. *Le plus grand ennemi du Bien c'est le Meilleur* is the expression of the truly sound human understanding in contrast with empty reasonings and reflections.

Addition.—If completeness means the complete collection of every individual thing or instance which belongs to a given sphere, no science can be complete. If we say that philosophy or any other science is incomplete, it seems like saying that we must wait till it is perfected, as the best thing may yet be lacking. In this way there is no getting on at all, neither in the seemingly completed science of geometry, in which, nevertheless, new elements are being introduced, nor in philosophy, which, though dealing with the universal idea, may be continually more and more specialized. The universal law cannot be forever merely the ten commandments. Yet it would be absurd to refuse to set up the law "Thou shalt not kill" on the ground that a statute-book cannot be made complete. Every statute-book can, of course, be better. It is patent to the most idle reflection that the most excellent, noble, and beautiful can be conceived of as still more excellent, noble, and beautiful. A large old tree branches more and more without becoming a new tree in the process; it would be folly, however, not to plant a new tree for the reason that it was destined in time to have new branches.

217. In the civic society what is intrinsically right becomes law. What was formerly the simple and abstract realization of my private will becomes, when recognized, a tangible factor of the existing general will and consciousness. Acquisition of property and other such transactions must therefore be settled in accordance with the form assigned to this realized right. Hence, property now depends upon contract, and, in general, upon those formalities, which furnish legal proof of possession.

Note.—The original or direct titles to property and methods of acquisition (§54 and fol.) disappear in the civic community, or occur in it only as separate accidents and limited elements.—Forms are rejected by feeling, which holds to the subjective, and by reflection, which clings to the abstract side of the necessary formality. On the other hand the dead understanding clings to formalities in opposition to the thing itself, and infinitely increases their number.—For the rest it is involved in the whole process of education to win oneself free by hard and long endeavour from the sensuous and direct form, and attain to the form of thought with its appropriate simple expression. It is only in the earliest stages of legal science that ceremony and formalities are significant. They are then esteemed as the thing itself rather than its outer symbol. In Roman law is found a host of details and expressions, which formerly belonged to religious ceremonies, and should in law have given place to phases of thought and their appropriate expression.

Addition.—In law what is in itself right is constituted. In property I possess something which was without an owner; this must now be recognized and constituted as mine. Hence, with regard to property arise in a community legal forms. We place boundary stones as a sign for others to take notice of; we have registers of mortgages and lists of properties. In the civic community property is generally obtained by contract, a legal process which is fixed and definite. Against forms the objection may be urged that they exist merely to bring money to the authorities. Or they may be held to be objectionable as indicating a lack of confidence. It may be said that the maxim "A man is his word" has lost its force. But the essential thing about the form is that what is really right should be constituted as right. My will is rational; it has validity; and this validity is to be recognized by others. Here my subjectivity and that of others must fall away, and the will must attain a certainty, assurance, and objectivity, which can be realized only through the form.

218. In the civic community property and personality have a legal recognition and validity. Hence, crime is injury done not merely to an infinite subject, but to a universal fact, which has firm and sure reality. Here occurs, therefore, the view that crime is a menace to society. On the one hand the magnitude of the crime is increased, but on the other hand the security, felt by society, lessens the external importance of the injury. As a result, crime is now often punished more lightly.

Note.—The fact that, when one member of a community suffers, all others suffer with him, alters the nature of crime, not indeed in its conception, but in its external existence. The injury now concerns the general thought and consciousness of the civic community, and not merely the existence of the person directly injured. In the heroic ages, portrayed in the tragedies of the ancients, the citizens did not regard themselves as injured by the crimes which the members of the royal houses committed against one another.—Crime, which in its inner nature is an infinite injury, must as a realized fact submit to a qualitative and quantitative measure (§96). This outward fact is conditioned by the general idea and consciousness of the validity of the laws. Hence, the danger to the civic community is one way of measuring the magnitude of a crime, or one of its attributes.—The quality or magnitude varies with the condition of a community. In the circumstances lies the justification of inflicting upon a theft of a few cents or a turnip the penalty of death, while it imposes a mild punishment upon a theft of a hundred or several hundred times the amount. Although the idea of danger to the civic community seems to aggravate the crime, it has really ameliorated the penalty. A penal code belongs to its time and to the condition in which the civic community at that time is.

Addition.—An offence seems to be aggravated, if it is perpetrated in a community, and yet in such a case it is treated with more leniency. This appears to be self-contradictory. But although a crime could not be allowed by the community to go unpunished, since it would then be constituted as right, yet, because a community is sure of itself, a crime is always merely a single, isolated act of hostility without any foothold. By means of the very steadfastness of the community crime becomes a mere subjective act, which appears to spring not so much out of deliberate will as out of natural impulse. Hence, a more lenient view is taken of crime, and punishment also is ameliorated. If the community is still unsettled, an example must be made by means of punishment, for punishment is itself an example against the example of crime. But in the sure and firm community the position of crime is so unstable, that a lesser measure of punishment is sufficient to supersede it. Severe punishments are not absolutely unjust, but are due to the condition of the time. A criminal code cannot apply to all times, and crimes are mere seeming existences, which draw after them a greater or less rejection of themselves.

(c) The Court of Justice

219. Right, having entered reality in the form of law, and having become an actual fact, stands in independent opposition to the particular will and opinion of right, and has to vindicate itself as a universal. The recognition and realization of right in each special case without the subjective instigation of private interests, is the office of a public power, the court of justice.

Note.—The office of judge and the court of justice may have originated historically in the patriarchal relation, in force, or in voluntary choice. This is for the conception of the object a matter of indifference. To regard the administration of justice by princes and rulers merely as a courtesy and favour, as does Herr von Haller in his "Restoration of Political Science," is to have no inkling of the fact that, when we speak of law and the state, we mean that its institutions are reasonable and absolutely necessary; and that, when we consider the reasonable basis of the laws, we have nothing to do with the form of their origin. The extreme opposite to this view is the crude idea that the administration of justice is club-law or despotism, which suppressed liberty by violence. But the administration of the law is to be looked upon as the duty quite as much as the right of the public authority. Whether to delegate the discharge of this office to some power or not is not at the option of any individual.

220. Revenge, or the right against crime (§102), is right only in itself. It is not right in the form of law, *i.e.,* it is not in its actual existence just. The place of the injured person is now taken by the injured universal, which is actualized in a special way in the court of justice. To pursue and punish crime is its function, which therefore ceases to be a mere subjective retaliation or revenge, and is in punishment transformed into a true reconciliation of right with itself. In the act of punishment, viewed objectively, right is reconciled to itself, and restores itself by superseding the crime and realizing its own inherent validity. In punishment, viewed subjectively, or from the standpoint of the criminal, the law, known by him and available for his protection, is atoned for. The execution of the law upon him, or the satisfaction of justice, he finds to be simply the completed act of his own law.

221. A member of the civic community has the right to bring a cause before the court of justice, and is also in duty bound to appear in the court, and accept from it the decision of the point in dispute.

Addition.—Every individual has the right to bring his case before the court. But he must know the laws, otherwise the privilege would be of no service to him. But it is also a duty for him to appear before the court. Under the feudal system the prince or noble defied the court, and refused to appear, regarding it as a wrong if the court summoned him before it. This condition of things is contradictory of the real function of the court. In more recent times the prince has in private affairs recognized the courts as superior to him, and in free states his cases are usually lost.

222. By the court it is required that a right be proved. The legal process gives the contending parties an opportunity to substantiate their claim by evidence, and put the judge in possession of a knowledge of the case. The necessary steps are themselves rights; their course must be legally fixed; and they form an essential part of theoretical jurisprudence.

Addition.—It may stir men to revolt if they have a right, which is refused to them on the score that it cannot be proved. But the right, which I have, must be at the same time constituted. I must be able to present and prove it, and only when that, which it really is, is constituted as law, is it of any avail to me in a community.

223. The stages of the legal process may be more and more minutely subdivided, and each stage has its right. As this subdivision has no inherent limit, the legal process, which is already of itself a means, may be

opposed to the end, and become something external. Though this extensive formality is meant for the two contending parties and belongs to them as their right, it may become an evil and an instrument of wrong. Therefore, in order that the two parties, and right itself as the substantive basis, may be protected against the legal process and its misuse, it is by way of law made a duty for them to submit themselves to a simple court, the civil court of arbitration, for a preliminary trial, before going to the higher court.

Note.—Equity includes a departure from formal right through moral and other regards, and refers directly to the content of the suit. A court of equity decides upon the particular case, without adhering to the formalities of the legal process. It is not confined to the objective evidence, as is formal law. It decides upon the interest peculiar to each particular suit. Its judgment is not meant to be applied generally.

224. As the public promulgation of the laws is one of the rights of the subjective consciousness (§215), so also is the possibility of knowing how in any special case the law is carried out. The course of the external proceedings should be public, and also the legal principles involved. The order of procedure is of itself a thing of general value. Though the special content of the case is of interest only to the contending parties, the universal content, involving right and a legal decision, is of interest to all. Hence is demanded the publicity of the administration of the law.

Note.—Deliberations by the members of a court amongst themselves over the judgment to be given, are only private opinions and views, and are not of public import.

Addition.—Honest common sense holds that the publicity of legal proceedings is right and just. A strong reason to the contrary was always the rank of the judiciary. They were not to be seen by everybody, and regarded themselves as the warders of a law, into which laymen ought not to intrude. But law should possess the confidence of the citizens, and this fact calls for the publicity of the sentence. Publicity is a right, because the aim of the court is justice, which as a universality belongs to all. Moreover, the citizens should be convinced that the right sentence has actually been pronounced.

225. In the application of the law by the judicial authorities to special cases are to be distinguished two separate aspects. There must be firstly an acquaintance with the direct facts of the case, whether a contract has taken place, an injurious act done, and who the doer is. In criminal law the act must be known also in its intention, which contains its substantive criminal quality (§119, *note*). In the second place the act must be brought under the law of the restoration of right. This in criminal law includes the punishment. Decisions in connection with these two aspects are two different functions.

Note.—In the constitution of the Roman law-courts these two functions occurred in this way. The *Prætor* gave his decision on the condition that the case was of such and such a kind, and then he commanded a certain *Judex* to make inquiries into its exact nature. The fixing of the exact criminal quality of an act, whether, for example, it be murder or manslaughter, is in English judicial procedure left to the insight or caprice of the accuser, and the court is restricted to his view, even if it is seen to be wrong.

226. To conduct the whole inquiry, to arrange the procedure of the parties, which is itself a right (§222), and to pass sentence, are the special functions of the judge (§225). For him, as the organ of the law, the case must be prepared and brought under some law. It must be raised out of its empirical nature, and made a recognized fact with general attributes.

227. That aspect of the case, which consists in knowing and estimating the direct facts, contains no distinctively judicial elements. The knowledge is possible to any intelligent man. When, in order that an estimate of the act may be made, the subjective factor of the insight or intention of the agent is essential (see Second Part), when the evidence concerns no abstract object of reason or the understanding, but mere particulars, circumstances, and objects of sensible perception and subjective certitude, when the case contains no absolutely objective element, and the duty of deciding must fall to subjective conviction and conscience (*animi sententia*), and when the evidence rests on depositions and statements, the oath, though a subjective confirmation, is ultimate.

Note.—In this question it is a cardinal point to keep before our eyes the nature of the available evidence, and to distinguish it from knowledge and evidence of other kinds. To prove a phase of reason, such as is the conception of right itself, that is, to recognize its necessity, requires another method than the proof of a geometrical theorem. Moreover, in a theorem the figure is determined by the understanding, and is already abstractly made according to a law. But in the case of an empirical content, such as a fact, the material for knowledge is composed of sense-perceptions, and attestations based on the subjective certitude of sense. These depositions, testimonies, and circumstances must be put together, and from them a conclusion must be drawn. With such material and such a means of making it independent and objective there is attained only partial proofs. In obedience to a true logic, which nevertheless is formally illogical, the punishments are consequently exceptional. This objective truth is quite different from the truth of a rational principle or of a proposition, whose matter has already been abstractly fixed by the understanding. In so far as an empirical truth can be recognized in the specific judicial finding of a court, and so far as in the finding can be shown to lie an unique quality, that is, an exclusive implicit right and necessity, the formal judicial court is entitled to pass judgment upon the fact as well as upon the point of law.

Addition.—There is no reason for supposing that the judge is the only one to decide upon matters of fact. For this not the legal mind alone but any man of ordinary intelligence is competent. Judgment as to matter of fact depends upon empirical circumstances, witnesses of the act, and similar data of perception. There may also be other facts, by means of which one can infer the nature and probability of the act in dispute. Here at most we reach an assurance, but not a truth in the sense of something eternal. Assurance is subjective conviction or conscience, and the question to decide is what form to give this certitude at a law court. The demand, usually made in German law, for a confession on the part of the criminal has this right, that by it satisfaction is given to the right of the subjective consciousness. The judge's decision must agree with the criminal's consciousness; and, not until the culprit has confessed, is the sentence free from an element which is foreign to him. But the criminal may deny the act, and thus imperil the course of justice. Yet it is a harsh measure to treat him according to the subjective conviction of the judge, since then he is no longer regarded as free. Hence, it is still required that the decree of guilt or innocence should come from the soul of the criminal, and this requisite is secured through trial by jury.

228. When the facts of the case have been decided on, and the judge in his sentence brings the case, so qualified, under a certain law, the accused's right of self-consciousness is not violated. In the first place, the law is known, and is itself the law of the accused. In the second place the proceedings, by which the case is brought under a certain law, are public. But when a decision is not yet reached upon the particular subjective and external content of the matter, a knowledge of which comes under the first of the two aspects given in §225, the accused's right of self-consciousness is preserved by intrusting the case to the subjectivity of jurors. This procedure is based on the equality of the jurors with the accused, both as regards class and in general.

Note.—The right of self-consciousness, or the element of subjective freedom, can be regarded as the substantive point of view in the question of the necessity of a public trial, or trial by a jury. To this point of view all that is essential and needful in these institutions may be reduced. From any other standpoint disputes may arise as to whether this or that feature is an advantage or disadvantage, but such reasonings either are of secondary consequence and decide nothing, or they are taken from other and perhaps higher spheres. It is possible that the law might be as well administered by courts of judges, or even better by them than by other institutions. But grant the possibility, or let the possibility become a probability or even a certainty, there remains always on the other hand the right of self-consciousness, which maintains its claims and must be satisfied. Because of the general nature of the law, it can happen that the knowledge of right, the course of legal proceedings, and the possibility of prosecuting the law, may become the exclusive property of a class. This class may use a language which is to those in whose interest it was made a foreign tongue. The members of a civic community, who have to rely for their subsistence upon their own activity, knowledge, and will, then become strangers not only to what is most private and personal in the law, but also to its substantive and rational essence. Hence, they fall under a kind of bodily vassalage to the legal class. They may have the right to present themselves in person before the court (*in judicio stare*), but of what use is that, if they are not present as intelligent spirits? The justice, which they receive, remains for them an external fate.

229. In the civic community the idea is lost in particularity, and dispersed by the separation of inner and outer. But in the administration of justice the community is brought back to the conception, that is, to the unity of the intrinsic universal with subjective particularity. But as subjective particularity is present only as one single case, and the universal only as abstract right, the unification is in the first instance relative. The realization of this relative unity over the whole range of particularity is the function of the police, and within a limited but concrete totality constitutes the corporation.

Addition.—In the civic community universality is only necessity. In the relation of wants, right as such is the only steadfast principle. But the sphere of this right is limited, and refers merely to the protection of what I have. To right as such, happiness is something external. Yet in the system of wants well-being is an essential element. The universal, which is at first only right, has to spread itself over the whole field of particularity. Justice, it is true, is a large factor in the civic community. The state will flourish, if it has good laws, of which free property is the fundamental condition. But since I am wholly environed by my particularity, I have a right to demand that in connecting myself with others I shall further my special happiness. Regard to my particular well-being is taken by the police and the corporation.

C. Police and Corporation

230. In the system of wants the subsistence and happiness of every individual is a possibility, whose realization is conditioned by the objective system of wants. By the administration of justice compensation is rendered for injury done to property or person. But the right, which is actualized in the particular individual, contains the two following factors. It asks firstly that person and property should be secured by the removal of all fortuitous hindrances, and secondly that the security of the indi-

vidual's subsistence and happiness, his particular well-being should be re-garded and actualized as a right.

(a) Police

231. So far as the particular will is the principle of a purpose, the force, by which the universal guarantees security, is limited to the realm of mere accident, and is an external arrangement.

232. Crimes are in their nature contingent or casual, taking the form of capricious choice of evil, and must be prevented or brought to justice by the general force. Apart from them, however, arbitrary choice must be allowed a place in connection with acts in themselves lawful, such as the private use of property. Here it comes into external relation with other individuals, and also with public institutions for realizing a common end. In this way a private act is exposed to a haphazard play of circumstances, which take it beyond my control. It thus may or actually does effect an injury or wrong to others.

233. This is, indeed, only a possibility of harm. But that no actual injury is done is now no longer a matter of accident, since the aspect of wrong in private acts is the ultimate ground for the right of police control.

234. The relations of external reality occur within the realm of the infinity created by the understanding, and have accordingly no inherent limit. Hence, as to what is dangerous and what not, what suspicious and what free from suspicion, what is to be forbidden, or kept under inspection, or pardoned with a reprimand, what is to be retained after pardon under police supervision, and what is to be dismissed on suspended sentence, no boundary can be laid down. Custom, the spirit of the constitution as a whole, the condition of the time, the danger of the moment, etc., furnish means for a decision.

Addition.—No fixed definition can here be given, or absolute boundary drawn. Here everything is personal and influenced by subjective opinion. To the spirit of the constitution or the danger of the times are due any more decisive characteristics. In time of war, *e.g.,* many things morally harmless are looked on as harmful. Because of the presence of this aspect of contingency and arbitrary personality the police are viewed with odium. They can by far-fetched conclusions draw every kind of thing within their sphere; for in anything may be found a possibility of harm. Hence, the police may go to work in a pedantic spirit, and disturb the moral life of individuals. But great as the nuisance may be, an objective limit to their action cannot be drawn.

235. Although every one relies on the untrammelled possibility of satisfying his daily wants, yet, when in the indefinite multiplication and limitation of them it is sought to procure or exchange the means and it is

desired to expedite the transaction, there comes into sight a common interest, which makes the business of one subserve the interest of all. There appear, likewise, ways and means, which may be of public utility. To oversee and foster the ways and means calculated to promote the public welfare is the function of a public power.

236. The different interests of producers and consumers may come into conflict, and, although the right relation between the two may on the whole arise of its own accord, yet the adjustment of the two calls for a regulation standing above both sides and put into operation consciously. The right to make such a regulation in any particular case (*e.g.,* taxation of the articles most necessary to sustain life), consists in this, that the public offer of goods, in wide and daily use, is not to the individual, as such, but to him as a universal, *i.e.,* to the public. The people's right to honest dealing and inspection of goods to prevent fraud may be enforced by a public functionary. But more especially does the dependence of great branches of industry upon foreign conditions and distant combinations, which the individuals engaged in these industries cannot themselves oversee, make necessary a general supervision and control.

Note.—In contrast with freedom of business and trade in the civic community stands the other extreme of the establishment and direction of the work of all by means of official regulation. Under this head comes perhaps the construction of the pyramids and other monstrous Egyptian and Asiatic works. They were built for public ends without the intervention of any work done by the individual to further his own private interests. Private interest summons the principle of freedom against interference from above, but the more blindly it is sunk in self-seeking ends, the more it stands in need of regulation, in order that it may be led back to the universal. Thus what might be a dangerous upheaval becomes largely harmless, and shorter time is left for conflicts to adjust themselves merely by unconscious necessity.

Addition.—Police control and provision are intended to intervene between the individual and the universal possibility of obtaining his wants. It takes charge of lighting the streets, building bridges, taxation of daily wants, even of health. Two main views stand out at this point. One view is that it falls to the police to look after everything, the other that the police should not interfere at all, since every one will be guided by the need of others. The individual, it is true, must have the right to earn his bread in this or the other way, but on the other hand the public has a right to ask that what is necessary shall be done. Both claims should be met, and the freedom of trade ought not to be of such a kind as to endanger the general weal.

237. The possibility of sharing in the general wealth is open to the individual and secured to him by public regulations. This security,

however, cannot be complete, and in any case the possibility of sharing in the general wealth is from the subjective side open to casualties, just in proportion as it presupposes conditions of skill, health, and capital.

238. In the first instance the family is the substantive whole. To it falls the duty of providing for the particular side of the individual's life, both in regard of the means and talents requisite for winning his maintenance out of the common stock, and in regard of subsistence and provision in case of disability. But the civic community tears the individual out of the family bonds, makes its members strangers to one another, and recognizes them as independent persons. Instead of external inorganic nature and the paternal soil, from which the individual drew subsistence, the community substitutes its own ground, and subjects the whole family to fortuitous dependence upon itself. Thus the individual has become the son of the civic community, which makes claims upon him, at the same time as he has rights to it.

Addition.—The family has, of course, to provide bread for individuals; but in the civic community the family is subordinate and merely forms a basis. After that it is no longer of such extensive efficacy. Rather is the civic community the monster, which snatches man to itself, claims from him that he should toil for it and that he should exist through it and act by means of it. If man is a member of such a community, he has just such rights in it or claims upon it as he had in and upon the family. The civic community must protect its members, and defend their rights, as they in turn are engaged to obey its mandates.

239. The civic community, in its character as universal family, has the right and duty to supersede, if necessary, the will of the parents, and superintend the education of the young, at least in so far as their education bears upon their becoming members of the community. Especially is this the case if the education is to be completed not by the parents but by others. Further, the community must undertake general arrangements for education, in so far as they can be made.

Addition.—The boundary line between the rights of parents and those of the civic community is hard to define. The parents generally suppose themselves to possess complete liberty with regard to education, and to be able to do whatever they wish. Whenever instruction is made public, the chief opposition usually comes from the parents, who cry out and make acclaim about teachers and schools merely because they are displeased with them. In spite of this, the community has the right to proceed according to tried methods, and to compel parents to send their children to school, to have them vaccinated, etc. Contests occur in France between the demands of free instruction, *i.e.,* of the pleasure of parents, on the one side, and the oversight of the state on the other.

240. Similarly, the community has the duty and right to take under its

guardianship those who wantonly squander their subsistence and that of their family. In the place of this extravagance it substitutes their real end, which it seeks to promote along with the purpose of the community.

Addition.—It was a law in Athens that every citizen should give an account of his way of life. Our view is that this is no one's business. Of course every individual is in one way independent, but he is also a member of the system of the civic community. In so far as every man has the right to ask maintenance from it, it must also protect him against himself. It is not simply that starvation must be guarded against. The wider view is that there never shall arise a rabble, or mass. Since the civic community is obliged to support individuals, it has also the right to insist that individuals should care for its subsistence.

241. Not the arbitrary will only, but accidental circumstances, which may be physical or external (§200), may bring the individual to poverty. This condition exposes him to the wants of the civic community, which has already deprived him of the natural methods of acquisition (§217), and superseded the bond of the family stock (§181). Besides, poverty causes men to lose more or less the advantage of society, the opportunity to acquire skill or education, the benefit of the administration of justice, the care for health, even the consolation of religion. Amongst the poor the public power takes the place of the family in regard to their immediate need, dislike of work, bad disposition, and other vices, which spring out of poverty and the sense of wrong.

242. The subjective element of poverty, or generally the distress, to which the individual is by nature exposed, requires subjective assistance, both in view of the special circumstances, and out of sympathy and love. Here, amidst all general arrangements, morality finds ample room to work. But since the assistance is in its own nature and in its effects casual, the effort of society shall be to discover a general remedy for penury and to do without random help.

Note.—Haphazard almsgiving and such foundations as the burning of lamps beside holy images, etc., are replaced by public poor-houses, hospitals, street lighting, etc. To charity enough still remains. It is a false view for charity to restrict its help to private methods and casual sentiment and knowledge, and to feel itself injured and weakened by regulations binding upon the whole community. On the contrary, the public system is to be regarded as all the more complete, the less remains to be done by special effort.

243. When the civic community is untrammelled in its activity, it increases within itself in industry and population. By generalizing the relations of men by the way of their wants, and by generalizing the manner in which the means of meeting these wants are prepared and procured, large fortunes are amassed. On the other side, there occur repartition and

limitation of the work of the individual labourer and, consequently, dependence and distress in the artisan class. With these drawbacks are associated callousness of feeling and inability to enjoy the larger possibilities of freedom, especially the mental advantages of the civic community.

244. When a large number of people sink below the standard of living regarded as essential for the members of society, and lose that sense of right, rectitude, and honour which is derived from self-support, a pauper class arises, and wealth accumulates disproportionately in the hands of a few.

Addition.—The way of living of the pauper class is the lowest of all, and is adopted by themselves. But with different peoples the minimum is very different. In England even the poorest man believes that he has his right, and with him this standard is different from that which satisfies the poor in other lands. Poverty does not of itself make a pauper. The pauper state implies a frame of mind, associated often with poverty, consisting in inner rebellion against the wealthy, against society, and against constituted authority. Moreover, in order to descend to the class, which is at the mercy of the changes and chances of life, men must be heedless and indifferent to work, as are the Lazzaroni in Naples. Hence, in this section of the community arises the evil thing that a man has not self-respect enough to earn his own living by his work, and still he claims support as a right. No man can maintain a right against nature. Yet, in social conditions want assumes the form of a wrong done to one or other class. The important question, how poverty is to be done away with, is one which has disturbed and agitated society, especially in modern times.

245. If upon the more wealthy classes the burden were directly laid of maintaining the poor at the level of their ordinary way of life, or if in public institutions, such as rich hospitals, foundations, or cloisters, the poor could receive direct support, they would be assured of subsistence without requiring to do any work. This would be contrary both to the principle of the civic community and to the feeling its members have of independence and honour.

Again, if subsistence were provided not directly but through work, or opportunity to work, the quantity of produce would be increased, and the consumers, becoming themselves producers, would be proportionately too few. Whether in the case of over-production, then, or in the case of direct help, the evil sought to be removed would remain, and, indeed, would by either method be enhanced. There arises the seeming paradox that the civic community when excessively wealthy is not rich enough. It has not sufficient hold of its own wealth to stem excess of poverty and the creation of paupers.

Note.—These phenomena may be studied in England, where they occur on an extensive scale. In that country may also be observed the consequences of poor rates, of vast foundations, of unlimited private benevolence, and, above all, of the discontinuance of the corporation. In England, and especially in Scotland, the most direct remedy against poverty and against laziness and extravagance, which are the cause of poverty, has been proved by practical experience to be to leave the poor to their fate, and direct them to public begging. This, too, has been found to be the best means for preserving that sense of shame and honour, which is the subjective basis of society.

246. By means of its own dialectic the civic community is driven beyond its own limits as a definite and self-complete society. It must find consumers and the necessary means of life amongst other peoples, who either lack the means, of which it has a superfluity, or have less developed industries.

247. As the firm-set earth, or the soil, is the basis of family life, so the basis of industry is the sea, the natural element which stimulates intercourse with foreign lands. By the substitution for the tenacious grasp of the soil, and for the limited round of appetites and enjoyments embraced within the civic life, of the fluid element of danger and destruction, the passion for gain is transformed. By means of the sea, the greatest medium of communication, the desire for wealth brings distant lands into an intercourse, which leads to commercial exchange. In this intercourse is found one of the chief means of culture, and in it, too, trade receives world-historical significance.

Note.—Rivers are not natural boundaries, though people have in modern times tried to make them so. Rather do they, and more especially the sea, bind men together.

That Horace (Carm. I. 3) is wrong when he says:

> ". . . deus abscidit
> Prudens Oceano dissociabili
> Terras, . . ."

is shown by the general fact that basins of rivers are inhabited by one nation or race. This is proved even more conspicuously by the relations of ancient Greece with Ionia and Magna Graecia, of Brittany with Britain, of Denmark with Norway, of Sweden with Finland and Lapland, in contrast with the slight intercourse obtaining between the inhabitants of the coast and those of the interior. We have only to compare the position of the nations, who have frequented the sea, with that of the nations who have avoided it, in order to discover what a means of culture and commerce it really is. Observe how the Egyptians and Hindoos have become dull and insensible, and are sunk in the grossest and most shameful superstitions, while all the great aspiring nations press to the sea.

248. The wider connection due to the sea becomes a means for

colonization, to which, be it sporadic or systematic, the full-grown civic community finds itself impelled. Thus for a part of its population it provides on a new soil a return to the family principle, and also procures for itself at the same time a new incentive and field for work.

Addition.—The civic society is forced to found colonies, owing to the increase of population, but more especially because production oversteps the needs of consumption, and the growing numbers cannot satisfy their needs by their work. Sporadic colonization occurs mainly in Germany, the colonists, finding a home in America or Russia, being without any connection with and of no benefit to their native land. A different kind of colonization is the systematic, which is conducted by the state consciously and with suitable appliances. Of this kind of colonization many forms occurred amongst the ancients, especially the Greeks. In Greece the citizens did not engage in severe toil, but directed their energies to public affairs. When the population grew to such an extent that it was difficult to provide for them, the youth were sent into a new neighbourhood, which was sometimes chosen for them, sometimes left to the accident of discovery. In modern times colonists have not been granted the rights possessed by the inhabitants of the parent country. The result has been war and ultimate independence, as may be read in the history of the English and Spanish colonies. The independence of the colonies has turned out to be of the greatest advantage to the mother land, just as the liberation of the slaves was of the greatest advantage to the masters.

249. The universal, which is contained in the particularity of the civic community, is realized and preserved by the external system of police supervision, whose purpose is simply to protect and secure the multitude of private ends and interests subsisting within it. It has also the higher function of caring for the interests which lead out beyond the civic community (§246). In accordance with the idea particularity itself makes the universal, which exists in its special interests, the end and object of its will and endeavour. The ethical principle thus comes back as a constituent element of the civic community. This is the corporation.

(b) The Corporation

250. In its substantive family life and life of nature the agricultural class contains directly the concrete universal in which it lives. The universal class, again, has this universal as an independent end of its activity, and as its ground and basis. The middle or commercial class is essentially engaged with the particular, and hence its peculiar province is the corporation.

251. The work of the civic community spreads in different directions in obedience to the nature of its particularity. Since the implicit equality, contained in particularity, is here realized as the common purpose of an

association, the particular and self-seeking end becomes something actively universal. Each member of the civic community is with his special talent a member of the corporation. The universal aim of the corporation is accordingly quite concrete, and has no wider application than what lies in trade and its distinctive interests.

252. In keeping with this view, the corporation, under the oversight of the public authority, has the right to look after its own clearly-defined interests, according to the objective qualifications of skill and rectitude to adopt members, whose number is determined by the general system, to make provision for its adherents against fortuitous occurrences, and to foster the capacity necessary in any one desiring to become a member. In general it must stand to its members as a second family, a position which remains more indefinite than the family relation, because the general civic community is at a farther remove from individuals and their special needs.

Note.—The tradesman is different from the day-labourer, as well as from him who is ready for any casual employment. The trader, be he employer or employee, is a member of an association, not for mere accidental gain but for the whole circuit of gain, or the universal involved in his particular maintenance. The privileges, which are rights of a corporate branch of the civic community, are not the same as special privileges in the etymological sense of the term. Special privileges are haphazard exceptions to a general law, but the other privileges are legal phases of the particularity of an essential branch of the community.

253. The corporation provides for the family a basis and steady means (§170), by securing for it a subsistence varying according to capacity. Moreover, both security and capacity are in the corporation publicly recognized. Hence, the member of a corporation does not need to certify his capacity or the reality of his regular income to any larger outside organization. It is also recognized that he belongs to and has active interest in a whole, whose aim is to promote the welfare of society in general. Thus, in his class he has honour.

Note.—The corporation, in making secure the means of the family, corresponds to agriculture and private property in another sphere (§203, *note*).—When it is complained that the luxury and extravagance of the commercial class give rise to paupers (§244), it must not be overlooked that these conditions have an ethical or social basis in such causes as the increasingly mechanical nature of work. If the individual is not a member of an authorized corporation, and no combination can be a corporation unless it is authorized, he has no class-honour. By limiting himself to the self-seeking side of trade and his own subsistence and enjoyments, he loses standing. He perhaps seeks, in that case, to obtain recognition by displaying his success in his trade; but his display has no limit, because he has no desire to live in a way becoming his class. Indeed, he has no class at all, since only what is of general purport really exists in a civic community, and can be established and recognized. As he has no class, he has not the more universal life characteristic of the class.—In the corporation the assistance received by poverty loses its lawless character, and the humiliation wrongly associated with it. The opulent, by performing their duty to their associates, lose their pride, and cease to stir up envy in others. Integrity receives its due honour and recognition.

254. The corporation sets a limit to the so-called natural right to make acquisitions by the exercise of any skill, only so far as the limit is a rational one. This right is thus freed from mere opinion and random influences, and from danger to itself and others. In this way it wins recognition and an assured place, and is exalted to the level of a conscious effort to attain a common purpose.

255. As the family was the first, so the corporation, grounded upon the civic community, constitutes the second ethical root or basis of the state. The family contains the elements of subjective particularity and objective universality in substantive unity. Then, in the civic community, these elements are in the first instance dissociated and become on the one side a particularity of want and satisfaction, which is turned back into itself, and on the other side abstract legal universality. The corporation joins these two in an internal way, so that particular well-being exists and is realized as a right.

Note.—Sanctity in the marriage tie and honour in the corporation are the points which the disorganizing forces of the civic community assail.

Addition.—In modern times the corporation has been superseded, with the intention that the individual should care for himself. Grant that the intention is wise, yet the obligation of the individual to procure his own livelihood is not by the corporation altered. In our modern states the citizens participate only slightly in the general business. It is, however, needful to provide the ethical man with a universal activity, one above his private ends. This universal, with which the modern state does not always supply him, is given by the corporation. We have already seen that the individual, while maintaining himself in the civic community, acts also for others. But this unconscious necessity is not enough. It is in the corporation that a conscious and reflective ethical reality is first reached. The superintendence of the state is higher, it is true, and must be given an upper place; otherwise the corporation would become fossilized; it would waste itself upon itself, and be reduced to the level of a wretched club. But the corporation is not in its absolute nature a secret society, but rather the socializing of a trade, which without it would stand in isolation. It takes the trade up into a circle, in which it secures strength and honour.

256. The limited and finite end of the corporation has its truth in the absolutely universal end and the absolute actuality of this end. This actualized end is also the truth of the division involved in the external system of police, which is merely a relative identity of the divided elements. Thus, the sphere of the civic community passes into the state.

Note.—City and country are the two as yet ideal constituents, out of which the state proceeds. The city is the seat of the civic society, and of the reflection which goes into itself and causes separation. The country is the seat of the ethical, which rests upon nature. The one comprises the individuals, who gain their livelihood by virtue of their relation to other persons possessed of rights. The other comprises the family. The state is the true meaning and ground of both.

The development of simple ethical observance into the dismemberment marking the civic community, and then forward into the state, which is shown to be the true foundation of these more abstract phases, is the only scientific proof of the conception of the state.—Although in the course of the scientific exposition the state has the appearance of a result, it is in reality the true foundation and cause. This appearance and its process are provisional, and must now be replaced by the state in its direct existence. In actual fact the state is in general primary. Within it the family grows into the civic community, the idea of the state being that which sunders itself into these two elements. In the development of the civic community the ethical substance reaches its infinite form, which contains the following elements:—(1) infinite differentiation even to the point at which consciousness as it is in itself exists for itself, and (2) the form of universality, which in civilization is the form of thought, that form by which spirit is itself in its laws and institutions. They are its thought will, and it and they together become objective and real in an organic whole.

THIRD SECTION
The State

257. The state is the realized ethical idea or ethical spirit. It is the will which manifests itself, makes itself clear and visible, substantiates itself. It is the will which thinks and knows itself, and carries out what it knows, and in so far as it knows. The state finds in ethical custom its direct and unreflected existence, and its indirect and reflected existence in the self-consciousness of the individual and in his knowledge and activity. Self-consciousness in the form of social disposition has its substantive freedom in the state, as the essence, purpose, and product of its activity.

Note.—The Penates are the inner and lower order of gods; the spirit of a nation, Athene, is the divinity which knows and wills itself. Piety is feeling, or ethical behaviour in the form of feeling; political virtue is the willing of the thought-out end, which exists absolutely.

258.—The state, which is the realized substantive will, having its reality in the particular self-consciousness raised to the plane of the universal, is absolutely rational. This substantive unity is its own motive and absolute end. In this end freedom attains its highest right. This end has the highest right over the individual, whose highest duty in turn is to be a member of the state.

Note.—Were the state to be considered as exchangeable with the civic society, and were its decisive features to be regarded as the security and protection of property and personal freedom, the interest of the individual as such would be the ultimate purpose of the social union. It would then be at one's option to be a member of the state.—But the state has a totally different relation to the individual. It is the objective spirit, and he has his truth, real existence, and ethical status only in being a member of it. Union, as such, is itself the true content and end, since the individual is intended to pass a universal life. His particular satisfactions, activities, and way of life have in this authenticated substantive principle their origin and result.

Rationality, viewed abstractly, consists in the thorough unity of universality and individuality. Taken concretely, and from the standpoint of the content, it is the unity of objective freedom with subjective freedom, of the general substantive will with the individual consciousness and the individual will seeking particular ends. From the standpoint of the form it consists in action determined by thought-out or universal laws and principles.—This idea is the absolutely eternal and necessary being of spirit.—The idea of the state is not concerned with the historical origin of either the state in general or of any particular state with its special rights and characters. Hence, it is indifferent whether the state arose out of the patriarchal condition, out of fear or confidence, or out of the corporation. It does not care whether the basis of state rights is declared to be in the divine, or in positive right, or contract, or custom. When we are dealing simply with the science of the state, these things are mere appearances, and belong to history. The causes or grounds of the authority of an actual state, in so far as they are required at all, must be derived from the forms of right, which have validity in the state.

Philosophic investigation deals with only the inner side of all this, the thought conception. To Rousseau is to be ascribed the merit of discovering and presenting a principle, which comes up to the standard of the thought, and is indeed thinking itself, not only in its form, such as would be a social impulse or divine authority, but in its very essence. This principle of Rousseau is will. But he conceives of the will only in the limited form of the individual will, as did also Fichte afterwards, and regards the universal will not as the absolutely reasonable will, but only as the common will, proceeding out of the individual will as conscious. Thus the union of individuals in a state becomes a contract, which is based upon caprice, opinion, and optional, explicit consent. Out of this view the understanding deduces consequences, which destroy the absolutely divine, and its absolute authority and majesty. Hence, when these abstractions attained to power, there was enacted the most tremendous spectacle which the human race has ever witnessed. All the usages and institutions of a great state were swept away. It was then proposed to begin over again, starting from the thought, and as the basis of the state to will only what was judged to be rational. But as the undertaking was begun with abstractions void of all ideas, it ended in scenes of tragic cruelty and horror.

As against the principle of the individual will we must bear in mind the fundamental conception that the objective will is in itself rational in its very conception, whether or not it be known by the individual or willed as an object of his good pleasure. We must also keep in mind that the opposite principle, the subjectivity of freedom, *i.e.,* such knowing and willing as are retained in that principle, contains only one, and that a one-sided factor of the idea of the reasonable will. The will is reasonable only if it is so both in itself and when it is actualized.

The other contrary of the thought, which apprehends the state as an embodiment of reason, is the theory which takes such external appearances as the accidents of distress, need, protection, strength, and wealth, for the substance of the state, when they are mere elements of its historical development. Moreover, it is in unique and isolated individuals that the principle of knowledge is here said to be found, not however in their thought, but in the attributes of their merely empirical personalities, such as strength or weakness, wealth or poverty. The freak of disregarding what is absolutely infinite and reasonable in the state and of banishing thought from the constitution of the state's inner nature has never appeared so undisguisedly as in Mr. v. Haller's "Restauration der Staatswissenschaft." In all genuine attempts to reach the real nature of the state, though the principles adduced be ever so one-sided and superficial, there is yet implied that rightly to conceive of the state is to attain to thoughts and universal characters. But in the book alluded to, the author not only consciously renounces both the rational content, which is the state, and the form of thought, but passionately inveighs against them. One of what he himself calls the far-reaching effects of his work is due to the circumstance that in his inquiry he knew how to fasten the whole into one piece without the help of thought. Hence, he says, are absent the confusion and disturbance, which arise when into a discussion of the contingent is foisted a suggestion about the substantive, and into a discussion of the empirical and external is injected a reminder of the uni-

versal and rational. Hence, when engaged with the inadequate and imperfect he is not continually reminding his readers of what is higher and
infinite.—Yet even this method of inquiry has consequences. Since the
fortuitous is taken as the essence of the state, and not the substantive,
there results from the absence of thought an incoherence, which jogs on
without looking back, and finds itself quite at home in the very opposite
of what it had commended a moment before.[6]

---

[6]This book is of an original kind. The ill-humour of the author might in itself be not ig-
noble, since he was stirred to indignation by the false theories, to which is attached especially the name of Rousseau, and by the attempt to put them in operation. But Mr. v.
Haller, in order to save himself, has thrown himself into a counter-position, which is
wholly void of thought, and cannot, therefore, be said to have any standing-ground. He
expresses the bitterest hatred of all law, legislation, and all formally and legally constituted
right. Hatred of the law, and of legally constituted right is the shibboleth, by means of
which are revealed and may be infallibly recognized fanaticism, mental imbecility, and the
hypocrisy of good intentions, let them disguise themselves as they will.

Such an originality as that of Mr. v. Haller's is always a noteworthy phenomenon, and
for those of my readers who do not yet know the work, I shall quote a few passages in
proof of my contention. Mr. v. H. (p. 342 ff., vol. i.) thus exhibits his fundamental proposition: "In the inorganic realm the greater oppresses the smaller, and the mighty the feeble; so is it also with animals, and the same law in more honourable forms, and often indeed in dishonourable forms, appears again in man." "It is the eternal, unchangeable decree of God that the more powerful rules, must rule, and will ever rule." From these sentences, and from those given further on, it may be seen in what sense the word "power"
is here used. It not the power of right and the ethical, but the contingent force of nature.
This he proceeds to make good upon this amongst other grounds (p. 365 and fol.), that
by an admirable and wise provision of nature the feeling of one's own superiority irre-
sistibly enriches the character, and favours the development of the very virtues which are
most necessary in dealing with subordinates. He asks, with much rhetoric, "whether in
the kingdom of science it is the strong or the weak, who are the more inclined to use
authority and trust, in order to aid their low selfish purposes, and for the ruin of confiding men, whether the majority of the lawyers are not pettifoggers and pedants, who be-
tray the hopes of confiding clients, make white black and black white, use the law as a
vehicle of wrong, bring those who seek their protection to beggary, and, like the hungry
vulture, tear in pieces the innocent lamb, etc." Mr. v. H. has here forgotten that he is em-
ploying this rhetoric in support of his sentence that the rule of the stronger is the eternal ordinance of God, the very same ordinance by virtue of which the vulture tears to
pieces the innocent lamb. He seems to say that the stronger are quite right in using their
knowledge of the law to plunder the feeble trusting clients. But it would be asking too
much of him to bring two thoughts into relation when he has not one.

It is self-evident that Mr. v. H. is an enemy of statute-books. Civil laws in general are
in his view "unnecessary, since they issue as self-evident from natural law." States, since
states there are, would be saved the trouble devoted to laws, law-books, and the study of
legal right, if they would simply repose on the principle that everything is self-evident.
"But on the other side the laws are not properly speaking given to private persons. They
are instructions for the judges, who are by them made acquainted with the will of the
rulers. The administration of the law (vol. i. p. 297; pt. i. p. 254, and elsewhere) is not a
duty of the state, but a donation or assistance by the strong, and is merely supplementary.
Of the means for the protection of rights the employment of law is not the most

Addition.—The state as a completed reality is the ethical whole and the actualization of freedom. It is the absolute purpose of reason that freedom should be actualized. The state is the spirit, which abides in the world and there realizes itself consciously; while in nature it is realized only as the other of itself or the sleeping spirit. Only when it is present in consciousness, knowing itself as an existing object, is it the state. In thinking of freedom we must not take our departure from individuality or the individual's self-consciousness, but from the essence of self-consciousness. Let man be aware of it or not, this essence realizes itself as an independent power, in which particular persons are only phases. The state is the march of God in the world; its ground or cause is the power of reason realizing itself as will. When thinking of the idea of the state, we must not have in our mind any particular state, or particular institution, but must rather contemplate the idea, this actual God, by itself. Although a state may be declared to violate right principles and to be defective in various ways, it always contains the essential moments of its existence, if, that is to say, it belongs to the full formed states of our own time. But as it is more easy to detect short-comings than to grasp the positive meaning, one easily falls into the mistake of dwelling so much upon special aspects of the state as to overlook its inner organic being. The state is not a work of art. It is in the world, in the sphere of caprice, ac-

complete, but is rather uncertain and insecure. It leaves us with only our modern law-scholars, and robs us of the three other means, which lead most quickly and certainly to the end, the means which friendly nature has given man for the security of his rightful freedom." These three are (what do you think?) "(1) Private obedience and enforcement of the natural law, (2) Resistance to wrong, and (3) Flight, when there is no other remedy." How unfriendly are the jurists in comparison with friendly nature! "But the natural divine law (vol. i. p. 292), which all-bountiful nature has given to every one, is: Honour every one as thy equal." (According to the author's principle this should read: Honour him who is not thy equal, but the stronger.) "Wrong no man who does not wrong thee. Demand nothing but what he owes thee." (But what does he owe?) "Yes, and more, love thy neighbour and use him when thou canst." It is to be the planting of this law which is to make legislation and constitutions useless. It would be worth seeing how Mr. v. H. makes it intelligible that, irrespective of this planting, legislation and constitutions have come into the world.

In vol. iii. p. 362 fol., the author reaches the "so-called national liberties," that is, the laws and constitutions of nations. Every legally constituted right is in this larger use of the word a liberty. Of these laws he says this, amongst other things, "that their content is usually very insignificant, although in books great stress is laid upon these documentary liberties." When we realize that the author means the national liberties of the German Empire and of the English nation (the *Charta Magna*, "which, however, is little read, and, because of its antiquated expressions, less understood," and the *Bill of Rights*), and the national liberties of the people of Hungary and other lands, we are surprised to learn that he regards these so highly-valued possessions as insignificant. As great a surprise is it to hear that the laws, which are of daily and hourly concern, dealing with every piece of cloth that is worn and every piece of bread that is eaten, should have a value merely in books.

cident, and error. Evil behaviour can doubtless disfigure it in many ways, but the ugliest man, the criminal, the invalid, the cripple, are living men. The positive thing, the life, is present in spite of defects, and it is with this affirmative that we have here to deal.

259. (a) The idea of the state has direct actuality in the individual state. It, as a self-referring organism, is the constitution or internal state-organization or polity.

(b) It passes over into a relation of the individual state to other states. This is its external organization or polity.

(c) As universal idea, or kind, or species, it has absolute authority over individual states. This is the spirit which gives itself reality in the process of world-history.

Addition.—The state as an actual thing is pre-eminently individual, and, what is more, particular. Individuality as distinguished from particularity is an element of the idea of the state itself, while particularity belongs to history. Any two states, as such, are independent of each other. Any relation between the two must be external. A third must therefore stand above and unite them. Now this third is the spirit, which gives itself reality in world-history, and constitutes itself absolute judge over states. Several states indeed might form an alliance and pass judgment upon others, or interstate relations may arise of the nature of the Holy Alliance. But these things are always relative and limited, as was the ever-

As for the general statute-book of Prussia, to quote only one thing more, Mr. v. H. has not one good word to say for it (vol. i. p. 185 fol.), because upon it the unphilosophical errors (not as yet the Kantian philosophy, at any rate, I must add, against which Mr. v. H. inveighs most bitterly of all) have had a bad effect, especially in the matters of the state, national wealth, the end of the state, the head of the state, his duties, the servants of the state, and such things. What most annoys Mr. v. H. is "the right to levy contributions upon private possessions, occupations, productions, and consumptions, in order to defray the expenses of the state. As state-wealth is not the private possession of the prince, but is qualified as the wealth of the state, neither the king himself nor any Prussian citizen has anything his own, neither body nor goods, and all the subjects become legal bond-men. They dare not withdraw themselves from the service of the state."

In all this incredible crudity there is a touch of the ludicrous in the unspeakable pleasure which Mr. v. H. feels in his own revelations (vol. i., *preface*). It was "a joy, such as only a friend of truth can feel, when he after an honest investigation is assured that he has hit upon as it were" (yes, indeed, *As it were!*) "the voice of nature or the word of God." (The word of God is in its revelation quite distinct from the voice of nature and of the natural man.) "And when he might have sunk down in sheer amazement, a stream of joyous tears sprang from his eyes, and from that moment living religiosity arose within him." Mr. v. H. ought rather, in his religiosity, to have wept over his fate as the hardest chastisement of God. It is the most severe punishment which can be experienced to wander so far from thought and reason, from reverence for the law and from the knowledge of how infinitely important and divine it is that the duties of the state and the rights of the citizens, as also the rights of the state and the duties of the citizens, should be legally determined, to wander so far from this as to substitute an absurdity for the word of God.

lasting peace. The sole, absolute judge, which always avails against the particular, is the self-caused self-existing spirit, which presents itself as the universal and efficient leaven of world-history.

A. Internal Polity

260. The state is the embodiment of concrete freedom. In this concrete freedom, personal individuality and its particular interests, as found in the family and civic community, have their complete development. In this concrete freedom, too, the rights of personal individuality receive adequate recognition. These interests and rights pass partly of their own accord into the interest of the universal. Partly, also, do the individuals recognize by their own knowledge and will the universal as their own substantive spirit, and work for it as their own end. Hence, neither is the universal completed without the assistance of the particular interest, knowledge, and will, nor, on the other hand, do individuals, as private persons, live merely for their own special concern. They regard the general end, and are in all their activities conscious of this end. The modern state has enormous strength and depth, in that it allows the principle of subjectivity to complete itself to an independent extreme of personal particularity, and yet at the same time brings it back into the substantive unity, and thus preserves particularity in the principle of the state.

Addition.—The peculiarity of the idea of the modern state is that it is the embodiment of freedom, not according to subjective liking, but to the conception of the will, the will, that is, in its universal and divine character. Incomplete states are they, in which this idea is still only a germ, whose particular phases are not permitted to mature into self-dependence. In the republics of classical antiquity universality, it is true, is to be found. But in those ages particularity had not as yet been released from its fetters, and led back to universality or the universal purpose of the whole. The essence of the modern state binds together the universal and the full freedom of particularity, including the welfare of individuals. It insists that the interests of the family and civic community shall link themselves to the state, and yet is aware that the universal purpose can make no advance without the private knowledge and will of a particularity, which must adhere to its right. The universal must be actively furthered, but, on the other side, subjectivity must be wholly and vitally developed. Only when both elements are present in force is the state to be regarded as articulate and truly organized.

261. In contrast with the spheres of private right and private good, of the family and of the civic community, the state is on one of its sides an external necessity. It is thus a higher authority, in regard to which the laws and interests of the family and community are subject and dependent. On the other side, however, the state is the indwelling end of these

things, and is strong in its union of the universal end with the particular interests of individuals. Thus, just so far as people have duties to fulfil towards it, they have also rights (§155).

Note.—We have already noticed (§3, *note*) that Montesquieu in his famous work, "The Spirit of the Laws," has kept before his mind, and sought to prove in detail, the thought that the laws, especially those of private right, are dependent upon the character of the state. He has maintained the philosophic view that the part is to be regarded only in relation to the whole.

Duty is, in the first instance, a relation to something, which is for me a substantial and self-subsisting universal. Right, on the other hand, is in general some embodiment of this substantive reality, and hence brings to the front its particular side and my particular freedom. These two things, treated formally, appear as deputed to different phases or persons. But the state as ethical, implying thorough interpenetration of the substantive and the particular, brings into light the fact that my obligation to the substantive reality is at the same time the realization of my particular freedom. In the state, duty and right are bound together in one and the same reference. But because in the state the elements of right and duty attain their peculiar shape and reality, the difference between them once more becomes manifest. While they are identical in themselves or formally, they differ in content. In private right and morals the necessity inherent in the relation fails to be realized. The abstract equality of content is alone brought forward. In this abstract region what is right for one is right for another, and what is one man's duty is also another man's duty. This absolute identity of right and duty occurs, when transferred to the content, simply as equality. This content, which is now to rank as the complete universal and sole principle of duty and right, is the personal freedom of men. Hence, slaves have no duties, because they have no rights, and *vice versâ*, religious duties, of course, falling outside of this discussion.

But when we turn from abstract identity to the concrete idea, the idea which develops itself within itself, right and duty are distinguished, and at once become different in content. In the family, for example, the rights of the son are not the same in content as his duties towards his father, nor are the rights of the citizen the same in content as his duties to his prince or government.—The conception of the union of duty and right is one of the most important features of states, and to it is due their internal strength.—The abstract treatment of duty insists upon casting aside and banishing the particular interest as something unessential and even unworthy. But the concrete method, or the idea, exhibits particularity as essential, and the satisfaction of the particular as a sheer necessity. In carrying out his duty the individual must in some way or other discover his own interest, his own satisfaction and recompense. A right must accrue to him out of his relation to the state, and by this right the universal concern becomes his own private concern. The particular interest shall in truth be neither set aside nor suppressed, but be placed in open concord with the universal. In this concord both particular and universal are inclosed. The individual, who from the point of view of his duties is a subject, finds, in fulfilling his civic duties, protection of person and property, satisfaction of his real self, and the consciousness and self-respect implied in his being a member of this whole. Since the citizen discharges his duty as a performance and business for the state, the state is permanently preserved. Viewed from the plane of abstraction, on the other hand, the interest of the universal would be satisfied, if the contracts and business, which it demands of him, are by him fulfilled simply as duties.

Addition.—Everything depends on the union of universality and particularity in the state. In the ancient states the subjective end was out-and-out one with the volition of the state. In modern times, on the contrary, we demand an individual view, and individual will and conscience. Of these things the ancients had none in the same sense. For them the final thing was the will of the state. While in Asiatic despotisms the individual had no inner nature, and no self-justification, in the modern world man's inner self is honoured. The conjunction of duty and right has the twofold aspect that what the state demands as duty should forthwith be the right of individuality, since the state's demand is nothing other than the organization of the conception of freedom. The prevailing characters of the individual will are by the state brought into objective reality, and in this way first attain to their truth and realization. The state is the sole and essential condition of the attainment of the particular end and good.

262. The actual idea, the spirit, divides itself, as we have said, into the two ideal spheres of its conception, the family and the civic community. It descends into its two ideal and finite spheres, that it may out of them become actually infinite and real. Hence, spirit distributes to individuals as a mass the material of its finite realization in these spheres, in such a way that the portion of the individual has the appearance of being occasioned by his circumstances, caprice, and private choice (§185, and *note*).

Addition.—In the Platonic state subjective freedom has not as yet any place, since in it the rulers assigned to individuals their occupations. In many oriental states occupation depends upon birth. But subjective freedom, which must be respected, demands free choice for individuals.

263. In these two spheres, in which the elements of spirit, individuality, and particularity, have in one their direct and in the other their reflected reality, spirit is their objective universality in the form of appear-

ance. It is the power of the rational in the region of necessity (§184), and becomes the institutions, which have already been passed in review.

Addition.—The state, as spirit, divides itself according to the particular determining attributes of its conception, in order to exist in its own way. We may adduce an illustration out of the region of nature. The nerve-system is especially the sensitive system; it is the abstract element which aims, so to speak, to exist by itself, and in this existence to have its own identity. Now feeling, when analyzed, furnishes two separate sides, dividing itself so that the differences appear as complete systems. On one side is the abstract sense of feeling, which withdraws by itself; it is the smothered movement going on internally in reproduction, internal self-nourishment, assimilation, and digestion. On the other hand this withdrawal into oneself has over against itself the element of difference, or the movement outwards; and this outward movement of feeling is irritability. These two form a system of their own, and there are lower orders of animals, in which this system alone is developed, being without that unity of feeling which marks the complete soul. If we compare these facts of nature with the facts of spirit, we may place together family and sensibility on the one side, civic community and irritability on the other. The third is the state, corresponding to the actual nervous system as an internally organized whole. But it is a living unity only in so far as both elements, the family and the civic community, are developed within it. The laws which govern these two are the institutions of the rational; it makes its appearance in them. The foundation and final truth of these institutions is the spirit, which is their universal purpose and conscious object. The family is, indeed, also ethical, but its purpose is not a conscious one. In the civic community, on the other hand, separation is the definitive feature.

264. The individuals of a multitude are spiritual beings, and have a twofold character. In them is the extreme of the independently conscious and willing individuality, and also the extreme of the universality, which knows and wills what is substantive. They obtain the rights of both these aspects, only in so far as they themselves are actual, both as private persons and as persons substantive. One right they have directly in the family, the other in the civic community. In these two institutions, which implicitly universalize all particular interests, individuals have their real self-conscious existence. And in the corporation they provide for these particular interests a wider scope, and an activity directed to a universal end.

265. These institutions comprise in detail the constitution, that is, the developed and actualized rationality. They are the steadfast basis of the state, determining the temper of individuals towards the state, and their confidence in it. They are, moreover, the foundation-stones of public freedom, because in them particular freedom becomes realized in a

rational form. They thus involve an intrinsic union of freedom and necessity.

Addition.—It has been already remarked that both the sanctity of marriage, and also the institutions, in which the ethical character of the civic community makes its appearance, constitute the stability of the whole. The universal is the concern of every particular person. Everything depends on the law of reason being thoroughly incorporated with the law of particular freedom. My particular end thus becomes identical with the universal. In any other case the state is a mere castle in the air. In the general self-consciousness of individuals the state is actual, and in the identity of particularity and universality it has its stability. It has often been said that the end of the state is the happiness of the citizens. That is indeed true. If it is not well with them, if their subjective aim is not satisfied, if they find that the state as such is not the medium through which comes their satisfaction, the state stands upon an insecure footing.

266. But spirit is realized and becomes its own object, not only as this necessity and as a kingdom of appearances, but as their ideality or inner being. Substantive universality is thus an object and end for itself, and necessity assumes the form of freedom.

267. By the necessity, which lies within this ideality, is meant the development of the idea within itself. As subjective substantiality the idea is a political temper of mind, and in distinction from this it, as objective, is the organism of the state, *i.e.,* the strictly political state, and its constitution.

Addition.—The unity of the freedom, which knows and wills itself, exists in the first instance as necessity. Here the substantive is found as the subjective existence of individuals. But there is a second necessity, and that is the organism. In this case spirit is a process within itself, makes within itself distinctions, divides itself into organic members, through which it passes in living circulation.

268. Political disposition, or, in general terms, patriotism, may be defined as the assurance which stands on truth, and the will which has become a custom. Mere subjective assurance does not proceed out of truth, and is only opinion. Genuine patriotism is simply a result of the institutions which subsist in the state as in the actuality of reason. Hence, patriotic feeling is operative in the act, which is in accord with these institutions. Political sentiment is, in general, a confidence, which may pass over into a more or less intelligent insight; it is a consciousness that my substantive and particular interest is contained and preserved in the interest and end of another, here the state, in its relation to me, the individual. Wherefore the state is for me forthwith not another, and I in this consciousness am free.

Note.—By patriotic feeling is frequently understood merely a readiness to submit to exceptional sacrifices or do exceptional acts. But in reality it is the sentiment which arises in ordinary circumstances and ways of life, and is wont to regard the commonweal as its substantive basis and end. This consciousness is kept intact in the routine of life, and upon it the readiness to submit to exceptional effort is based. But as men would rather be magnanimous than merely right, they easily persuade themselves that they possess this extraordinary patriotism, in order to spare themselves the burden of the true sentiment, and to excuse the lack of it. If this feeling be regarded as something, which provides its own beginning, and can proceed out of subjective imaginations and thoughts, it is confounded with mere opinion, and in that case is devoid of its true basis in objective reality.

Addition.—Uneducated men delight in surface-reasonings and fault-findings. Fault-finding is an easy matter, but hard is it to know the good and its inner necessity. Education always begins with fault-finding, but when full and complete sees in everything the positive. In the case of religion one may say off-hand that this or that is superstition, but it is infinitely harder to conceive of the truth involved in it. Political sentiment, as a mere appearance, is also to be distinguished from what men truly will. They will in fact the real matter, but they hold fast to bits, and delight in the vanity of making improvements. Men trust in the stability of the state, and suppose that in it only the particular interest can come into being. But custom makes invisible that upon which our whole existence turns. If any one goes safe through the streets at night, it does not occur to him that it could be otherwise. The habit of feeling secure has become a second nature, and we do not reflect that it is first brought about by the agency of special institutions. Often it is imagined that force holds the state together, but the binding cord is nothing else than the deep-seated feeling of order, which is possessed by all.

269. Political disposition is given definite content by the different phases of the organism of the state. This organism is the development of the idea into its differences, which are objectively actualized. These differences are the different functions, affairs, and activities of state. By means of them the universal uninterruptedly produces itself, by a process which is a necessary one, since these various offices proceed from the nature of the conception. The universal is, however, none the less self-contained, since it is already presupposed in its own productive process. This organism is the political constitution.

Addition.—The state is an organism or the development of the idea into its differences. These different sides are the different functions, affairs and activities of state by means of which the universal unceasingly produces itself by a necessary process. At the same time it is self-contained, since it is presupposed in its own productive activity. This organism is the political constitution. It proceeds eternally out of the state, just as the state in turn is self-contained by means of the constitution. If these two things fall apart, and make the different aspects independent, the unity produced by the constitution is no longer established. The true relation is illustrated by the fable of the belly and the limbs. Although the parts of an organism do not constitute an identity, yet it is of such a nature that, if one of its parts makes itself independent, all must be harmed. We cannot by means of predicates, propositions, etc., reach any right estimate of the state, which should be apprehended as an organism. It is much the same with the state as with the nature of God, who cannot be through predicates conceived, whose life rather is within itself and must be perceived.

270. (1) The abstract actuality or substantiality of the state consists in this, that the end pursued by the state is the general interest, which, being the substance of all particular interests, includes the preservation of them also. (2) But the actuality of the state is also the necessity of the state, since it breaks up into the various distinctions of state-activity, which are implied in the conception. By means of the state's substantiality these distinctions become real and tangible as the different public offices. (3) This substantiality, when thoroughly permeated by education, is the spirit which knows and wills itself. Hence, what the state wills it knows, and knows it in its universality as that which is thought out. The state works and acts in obedience to conscious ends, known principles and laws, which are not merely implied, but expressly before its consciousness. So, too, it works with a definite knowledge of all the actual circumstances and relations, to which the acts refer.

Note.—We must here touch upon the relation of the state to religion. In modern times it is often repeated that religion is the foundation of the state, and accompanying this assertion is the dogmatic claim that outside of religion nothing remains to political science. Now, no assertion can be more confusing. Indeed, it exalts confusion to the place of an essential element in the constitution of the state, and of a necessary form of knowledge.—In the first place it may seem suspicious that religion is principally commended and resorted to in times of public distress, disturbance, and oppression; it is thought to furnish consolation against wrong, and the hope of compensation in the case of loss. A proof of religious feeling is considered to be indifference to worldly affairs and to the course and tenor of actual life. But the state is the spirit, as it abides in the world. To refer people to religion is far from calculated to exalt the interest and business of the state into a really earnest purpose. On the contrary, state concerns are held to be a matter of pure caprice, and are therefore rejected. The ground for this step is that in the state only the purposes of passion and unlawful power prevail, or that religion, when taken by itself,

is sufficient to control and decide what is right. It would surely be regarded as a bitter jest if those who were oppressed by any despotism were
referred to the consolations of religion; nor is it to be forgotten that religion may assume the form of a galling superstition, involving the most
abject servitude, and the degradation of man below the level of the
brute. Amongst the Egyptians and Hindoos animals are revered as higher
creatures than man. Such a fact leads us to observe that we cannot speak
of religion in general, and that when it assumes certain forms security
must be found against it in some power which will guarantee the rights
of reason and self-consciousness.

But the ultimate judgment upon the connection of religion with the
state is obtained only when we go back to their conception. Religion has
as its content absolute truth, and, therefore, also the highest kind of feeling. Religion, as intuition, feeling, or imaginative thought, the object of
whose activity is God, the unlimited basis and cause of all things, ad-
vances the claim that everything should be apprehended in reference to
it, and in it should receive its confirmation, justification, and certitude. By
this relation state and laws, as well as duties, attain for consciousness to
their highest verification and most binding power, since they, as a determinate reality, pass up into and rest upon a higher sphere. (See
"Encyclopædia of the Philosophical Sciences.") For this reason in all the
changes and chances of life religion preserves the consciousness of the
unchanging and of the highest freedom and contentment.[7]

Religion, so interpreted, is the foundation of the ethical system, and
contains the nature of the state as the divine will; yet it is only the foundation. This is the point at which state and religion separate. The state is
the divine will as a present spirit, which unfolds itself in the actual shape
of an organized world.

They who adhere to the form of religion, as opposed to the state, conduct themselves like persons who in knowledge think that they are right
when they cling to a mere abstract essence and never proceed to reality,
or like those who will only the abstract good, and arbitrarily postpone
deciding what in fact is good (§140, note). Religion is the relation to the
absolute in the form of feeling, imagination, faith; and within its all-
embracing circumference everything is merely accidental and transient.

---

[7]Religion, knowledge, and science have as principles forms peculiar to themselves and different from that of the state. Hence, they enter the state partly as aids to education and
sentiment, partly as ends for themselves, having an external reality. In both cases the principles of the state are merely applied to these spheres. In a fully concrete treatise on the
state these spheres, as well as art and the mere natural relations, would have to be considered, and given their proper place. But in this treatise, where the principle of the state is
traversed in its own peculiar sphere in accordance with its idea, these other principles, and
the application to them of the right of the state, can receive only a passing notice.

If this form is obstinately maintained to be the only real and valid determination for the state, the state, as an organization developed into stable differences, laws, and regulations, is handed over as booty to feebleness, uncertainty, and disorder. By enveloping everything definite this vague form becomes a subjective principle. In contrast with it, the laws, instead of having validity and self-subsistence as the objective and universal, are counted as something merely negative. There result the following practical maxims: "The righteous man is not subject to law; only be pious and you may do what you please; you may yield to your own arbitrary will and passion, and direct those, who suffer harm by your acts, to the comfort and hope of religion, or you may brand them as irreligious." But this negative relation sometimes refuses to remain merely an inner sentiment, and makes itself felt in external reality. There then arises the form of religious fanaticism, which, like political fanaticism, regards all state-management and lawful order as restrictive barriers, and discards them as unsuited to the inner life and infinitude of feeling. It banishes private property, marriage, and the relations and tasks of the civic community, as unworthy of love and of the freedom of feeling. But since in daily walk and action some decision must be made, then here, as is always the case with the subjective will, whose subjectivity is aware of itself as absolute (§140), the decision proceeds from subjective picture-thinking, that is, from opinion and arbitrary inclination.

In opposition to that kind of truth which wraps itself up in the subjectivity of feeling and imagination, the real truth consists in the tremendous transition of the inner into the outer, of the visions of reason into reality. By this process the whole of world-history has been wrought out, and civilized man has at length won the actuality and the consciousness of a reasonable political life. There are those who, as they say, seek the Lord, and in their untutored opinion assure themselves of possessing all things directly. They make no effort to raise their subjective experience into a knowledge of the truth and a consciousness of objective right and duty. From such persons can proceed nothing except abomination and folly, and the demolition of all ethical relations. These consequences are inevitable, if religious sentiment holds exclusively to its form, and turns against reality and the truth, which is present in the form of the universal, that is, of the laws.

Still, this sentiment may not invade reality. On the contrary, it may retain its merely negative character, thus remaining something internal, suiting itself to the laws and affairs of state, and acquiescing either with sighs or with scorn and wishing. It is not strength, but weakness, which has in our times made religiosity a polemic kind of piety, be it conjoined with a true need, or with nothing but discontented vanity. Instead of moulding one's opinion through study, and subjecting one's will to discipline, and thus exalting it to free obedience, it is much the cheaper plan to take a less arduous course. We renounce all knowledge of objective truth, treasure up a feeling of oppression and pride, and claim to possess beforehand all the holiness requisite for discerning the laws and institutions of state, for prejudging them, and specifying what their nature ought to be. The ground for this behaviour is that everything issues from the pious heart unquestionably and infallibly. Thus, as intentions and assertions go to religion for their support, neither by exposing their shallowness nor their erroneousness is it possible to prevail against them.

In so far as religion is of a true sort, not displaying a negative and hostile spirit towards the state, but rather recognizing and supporting it, it has its own special place and station. Public worship consists in acts and doctrine; it needs possessions and property, and likewise individuals devoted to the service of the congregation. Out of this arises between church and state a relation, which it is not difficult to define. It is in the nature of the case that the state fulfils a duty by giving assistance and protection to the religious ends of a congregation. More than that, since to the deepest religious feeling there is present the state as a whole, it may fairly be demanded by the state that every individual should connect himself with some congregation. Of course, with its special character, depending on inner imaginative thinking, the state cannot interfere. When well organized and strong, the state can afford to be liberal in this matter, and may overlook small details affecting itself. It may even give room within itself to congregations, whose creed prevents them from recognizing any direct duties to it. But this concession must depend upon the numerical strength of the sects in question. The members of these religious bodies the state is content to leave to the laws of the civic community, and to accept a passive fulfilment of their direct duties to it by means of substitutes.[8]

---

[8] Of Quakers, Anabaptists, etc., it may be said that they are merely active members of the civic community, having as private persons only private relations with others. Even here, however, they have been permitted to forego the use of the oath. Direct state duties they fulfil passively. To one of the most important of these, that of defence against an enemy, they openly refuse to submit, and are granted release from it on condition of their substituting some other service. Towards these sects the state is expected to exercise toleration. Since they do not recognize their duties to it, they cannot claim the right to be members of it. Once in a North American Congress, when the abolition of the slavery of the negroes was being strongly advocated, a deputy from the Southern States made the apposite remark, "Let us have negroes; we let you have Quakers."—Only because the state is otherwise strong can it overlook and tolerate these anomalies. It relies upon the strength of its moral observances, and upon the inner reason of its institutions to diminish and overcome divisions, which it would nevertheless be within its strict right to abolish. So, too, states have had a formal right against the Jews in regard to the concession to them of even civil rights, because they are not merely a religious body, but claim to look upon themselves as a foreign nation. But the outcry raised against them on this and other

So far as the ecclesiastical body owns property, performs overt acts of worship, and maintains individuals for this service, it leaves the inner realm and enters that of the world. Hence it places itself directly under the jurisdiction of the state. The oath, ethical observances generally, as well as marriage, all carry with them the inner reconstruction and elevation of that disposition of mind which finds in religion its deepest confirmation. Since ethical relations are essentially relations of actual rationality, the rights of these relations are the first to be maintained in reality, and to them is added ecclesiastical confirmation, simply as their inner and more abstract side.—As to other forms of ecclesiastical communion, such as doctrine, the internal is more important than the external. The same is true of overt acts of worship and kindred matters, whose legal side appears as independent, and belongs to the state. The ministers and property of churches, it is true, are exempt from the power and jurisdiction of the state. Churches have also assumed jurisdiction over worldly persons in all matters involving the co-operation of religion, such as divorce and the administration of the oath.—In all affairs bearing the aspects of both church and state, the political side, owing to its nature, is ill-defined. This is observable even in relation to acts which are wholly civic (§234). In so far as individuals, assembling for religious worship, have formed themselves into a congregation or corporation, they come under the supervision of the superior officers of state.

Doctrine has its province in conscience, and is founded upon the right of the subjective freedom of self-consciousness. This is the inner region, which as such does not come within the sphere of the state. However, the state also has a doctrine, in which its regulations, and whatever in right, in the constitution, etc., is valid generally, exist essentially in the form of thought, as law. And as the state is not a mechanism, but the reasonable life of self-conscious freedom and the system of the ethical world, so sentiment or feeling for it, and the conscious expression of this feeling in the form of principles, are an essential element in the actual state. Then, again, the doctrine of the church is not merely the edict of conscience, but in the form of doctrine is rather an outward expression,

---

grounds has overlooked the fact that they are first of all men, and that to be a man is more than a superficial abstract qualification (§209, *note*). The civil rights implied in it give rise to a feeling of self-respect, the sense of counting as a lawful person in the civic community. This feeling of being infinite and free from all others is the root out of which springs the needed balance of the various kinds of thought and sentiment. The isolation with which the Jews have been blamed it is better to preserve. It would have been a reproach and wrong for any state to have excluded them for this reason. To do so would be to misunderstand its own principle, the nature and power of its objective institutions (§268, *end of note*). To expel the Jews on the pretence that this course is in accordance with the highest justice, has proved an unwise measure, while the actual method employed by the government has been shown to be wise and honourable.

and that, too, regarding a content, which has the most intimate connection with ethical principles and the laws, and may directly concern them. Here also church and state meet either harmoniously or in opposition. The difference between the two realms may be driven by the church to extreme antagonism. It, containing as it does the absolute content of religion, may contemplate the spiritual element and therefore the ethical element also, as its own, and may regard the state as a mere mechanical scaffolding for unspiritual, external ends. It may esteem itself as the kingdom of God or at least as the way to it and its forecourt, and the state as the kingdom of this world, the sphere of the transient and finite. It may count itself as end for itself, and the state as merely a means. United with such a presumptuous attitude is the demand of the church that the state should let it have its own way, and should show to its doctrines unreserved respect, simply because they are doctrines, no matter what the substance of them may be. The reason advanced by the church is that the formation of doctrine is exclusively its function. Just as the church makes this claim on the wide ground that the spiritual has been entrusted solely to its keeping, science and knowledge generally may occupy a similar position. Like the church, they may fashion themselves into an independent, exclusive organization, and may with even greater justice look upon themselves as filling the place of the church. Hence would be asked for science also independence of the state; the state would be only a means for it, while it would be its own end.

In this connection it is unimportant whether the individuals and representatives, who minister to the congregation, have gone the length of secluding themselves, leaving only the congregations at large in subjection to the state, or whether they abide in the state, and withdraw only their church character. This general position, it may first of all be observed, coincides with the view that the state in its fundamentals takes into its protection and care the life, property, and free-will of every person, simply in so far as he does not injure the life, property, and free-will of any other The state is thus considered as answering simply to our needs. The higher spiritual element, absolute truth, is counted as subjective religiosity or theoretical science, and placed outside of the state. The state is merely the laity, and must be absolutely respectful. That which is peculiarly ethical falls beyond its reach. Now it is a matter of history that there have been barbaric times and circumstances, in which all high spiritual matters had their seat in the church, and the state was only a worldly rule of force, lawlessness, and passion. Abstract opposition was then the main principle of actuality (§358). But it is too blind and shallow a proceeding to consider this view as true and in accordance with the idea. The development of the idea has rather demonstrated that the spirit as free and rational is in itself ethical, that the true idea is actualized rationality, and that this rationality exists as the state. From this idea it is quite easy to infer that its ethical truth assumes for the thinking consciousness a content, which is worked up into the form of universality, and is realized as law. The state in general knows its own ends, recognizes them with a clear consciousness, and busies itself with them in accordance with fundamental principles.

As before remarked, religion has truth for its universal object, but this content is merely given, and its fundamental principles are not recognized through thinking and conceptions. Thus the individual is under an obligation, which is grounded upon authority, and the testimony of his own spirit and heart, in which is contained the element of freedom, takes the form of faith and feeling. But it is philosophic insight, which clearly recognizes that church and state are not opposed to each other on the question of truth and rationality, but differ only in form. There were, it is true, and still are, churches, which have nothing more than a form of public worship; but there are others, which, though in them the form of worship is the main thing, have also doctrine and instruction. Whenever the church takes up the point of doctrine, and deals in its teaching with objective thought and the principles of the ethical and rational, it passes over into the province of the state. It pronounces authoritatively upon the ethical and right, upon the law and institutions, and its utterance is believed. In contrast with faith and the authority of the church, in contrast also with the subjective convictions which it requires, the state is that which knows. In its principles the content does not remain in the form of feeling and faith, but belongs to the formed thought.

In so far as the self-caused and self-existing content makes its appearance in religion as a particular content, namely, in the form of doctrines peculiar to the church as a religious community, it does not fall within the scope of the state. In Protestantism, it may be said, there are no clergy who are considered to be the sole depositary of church doctrine, because in this form of religion there is no laity. Since ethical and political principles pass over into the realm of religion, and not only are established, but must be established, in reference to religion, the state is thus on the one hand furnished with religious confirmation. On the other hand there remains to the state the right and the form of self-conscious objective rationality, the right, that is, to maintain objective reason against the assertions, which have their source in the subjective form of truth, no matter what depth of certitude and authority surrounds them. Because the principle of the state's form is universal, and hence essentially the thought, freedom of thought and scientific investigation issue from the state. It was a church that burnt Giordano Bruno, and forced Galileo, who advocated the Copernican system, to recant upon his knees.[9] Hence science, also, has its place on the side of the state, as it has the same element of form as the state; its end is knowledge, and indeed thought out objective truth and rationality. Thought knowledge may, it is true, fall from science to mere opinion, and from principles to mere reasonings. Applying itself to ethical objects and the organization of the state, it may oppose their fundamental principles. This it may do with something of the same pretentious claims, as the church makes with regard to its peculiar belongings. It may rely upon mere opining, as if it were reason, and upon the right, advanced by subjective self-consciousness, to be in its opinion and conviction free.

Already (§140, *note*) the principle of the subjectivity of knowledge has been examined, and only a single remark need now be added. On the one hand the state may treat with infinite indifference opinion, in so far as it is mere opinion, and has hence a mere subjective content. This opinion, let it plume itself to any extent it pleases, contains no true strength or force. The state is in the position of the painter, who in his work confines himself to the three ground colours, and may treat with indifference the school-wisdom which maintains that there are seven. But there is another side to the question. This opining of bad principles constitutes it-

[9]Laplace, in his "Darstellung des Weltsystems," Book V, ch. 4, writes, "When Galileo published his discoveries, to which he was assisted by the telescope and the phases of Venus, he proved incontestably that the earth moved. But the view that the earth is in motion was declared by an assembly of cardinals to be heretical. Whereupon Galileo, the famous advocate of this view, was summoned before the Inquisition, and compelled to retract on pain of a severe imprisonment. In a man of mind the passion for truth is one of the strongest passions.—Galileo, convinced by his own observations of the motion of the earth, thought for a long time upon a new work in which he would undertake to develop all the proofs of his theory. But in order at the same time to escape the persecution, of which he would have been the victim, he resolved to issue his work in the form of a dialogue between three persons. Naturally, the advantage lay with the advocate of the Copernican system. But since Galileo did not decide between them, and gave every possible weight to the objections of the follower of Ptolemaus, he had a right to expect that he would not be disturbed in the enjoyment of that rest which his great age and services deserved. But in his sixtieth year he was a second time summoned before the tribunal of the Inquisition, was imprisoned, and again asked to retract his views under the threat of the punishment which is meted out to a heretic twice fallen. They induced him to subscribe to the following form of abjuration: 'I, Galileo, who in my sixtieth year find myself in person before the court, kneeling and looking upon the holy Gospels, which I touch with my hands, forswear, abjure, and execrate with honest heart and true faith, the preposterous, false, and heretical doctrine of the motion of the earth, etc.' What a spectacle! An honourable old man, celebrated through a long life devoted to the investigation of nature, against the witness of his own conscience, recants upon his knees the truth, which he had so convincingly proved. By the sentence of the Inquisition he was condemned to perpetual imprisonment. A year afterwards, through the mediation of the Grand-duke of Florence, he was set at liberty.—He died in 1642. His loss was deplored by Europe, which had been enlightened by his labours and stirred to indignation by the sentence passed by so detested a tribunal upon so great a man."

self a universal fact and corrodes actuality. It is manifested as the formalism of unconditioned subjectivity, which would adopt as a basis the scientific starting-point, would exalt the state-academies to the presumptuous level of a church, and would then turn them against the state. In opposition to this proceeding the state must take under its protection objective truth and the principle of the ethical life; and on the other side, in opposition to the church, which claims unlimited and unconditional authority, the state has to uphold as a general thing the formal right of self-consciousness to its own insight, conviction, and thought of what shall be reckoned as objective truth.

There may also be mentioned here the unity of state and church, a union which is much canvassed in modern times, and praised as the highest ideal. If the essential unity of these two is the unity of true principles with sentiment, it is also essential that along with this unity should come into specific existence the difference, which is in the form of their consciousness. In an oriental despotism there already exists the so frequently wished for unity of church and state. Yet in it the state is not present, at least not that self-conscious form of it, which is alone worthy of spirit and includes right, free ethical life and organic development. If the state is to have reality as the ethical self-conscious realization of spirit, it must be distinguished from the form of authority and faith. But this distinction arises only in so far as the ecclesiastical side is in itself divided into separate churches. Then only is the state seen to be superior to them, and wins and brings into existence the universality of thought as the principle of its form. To understand this we must know what universality is, not only in itself, but also in its existence. It is far from being a weakness or misfortune for the state that the church has been divided. Only through this division has the state been able to develop its true character, and become a self-conscious, rational, and ethical reality. This division was an event of the happiest augury, telling in behalf of the freedom and rationality of the church, and also in behalf of the freedom and rationality of thought.

Addition.—The state is real. Its reality consists in its realizing the interest of the whole in particular ends. Actuality is always the unity of universality and particularity. Universality exists piecemeal in particularity. Each side appears as if self-sufficient, although it is upheld and sustained only in the whole. In so far as this unity is absent, the thing is unrealized, even though existence may be predicated of it. A bad state is one which merely exists. A sick body also exists, but it has no true reality. A hand, which is cut off, still looks like a hand and exists, though it is not real. True reality is necessity. What is real is in itself necessary. Necessity consists in this, that the whole is broken up into the differences contained in the conception. Then, as so broken up, it furnishes a fast and enduring character, not that of the fossil, but of that which in giving itself up always begets itself anew.

To the complete state essentially belong consciousness and thought. Hence the state knows what it wills, and knows it as something thought. Since consciousness has its seat only in the state, science has its place also there, and not in the church. In despite of that, much has in modern times been said to the effect that the state has sprung into existence out of religion. The state is the developed spirit, and exhibits its elements in the daylight of consciousness. Owing to the fact that what lies in the idea walks forth into visible being, the state appears to be something finite, whose province is of this world, while religion represents itself as the realm of the infinite. Thus, the state seems to be subordinate, needing, since the finite cannot subsist by itself, the basis of the church. As finite, it is thought to have no verification, and only in and through religion to become holy and appertain to the infinite. But this version of the matter is highly one-sided. The state is certainly in its essence of the world and finite, having particular ends and functions. But its being worldly is only one side of it. Only to a perception, which is void of spirit, is the state merely finite. The state has a vital soul, and this vitalizing power is subjectivity, which both creates distinctions and yet preserves their unity. In the kingdom of religion there are also distinctions and finitudes. God is triune. Thus there are three determinations, whose unity alone is the spirit. If we would apprehend in a concrete way the divine nature, we do so only through distinctions. In the divine kingdom as in the worldly occur limits, and it is a one-sided view to say that the worldly spirit or the state is merely finite, for reality is nothing irrational. A bad state is indeed purely finite and worldly, but the rational state is in itself infinite.

Secondly, it is said that the state must accept its justification from religion. The idea, as present in religion, is spirit in the inner condition of feeling, but this same idea it is which gives itself worldliness in the state, and procures for itself in consciousness and will an outward place and reality. If we say that the state must be grounded on religion, we mean only that the state must rest upon and proceed from rationality. But this sentence can be understood wrongly to mean that when the spirit of man is bound by a religion which is not free, he is most adroitly brought to political obedience. The Christian religion, however, is the religion of freedom. Yet even Christianity may be infected by superstition, and converted into an instrument of bondage. Thus, the doctrine that the state should be founded on religion is perverted, when it is interpreted to mean that individuals must have religion in order that their spirit, enchained by it, may be the more readily oppressed in the state. But if we mean that reverence should be felt for the state as the whole, of which individuals are the branches, this feeling flows most easily from philosophic insight into the nature of the state, although if that insight should be lacking, religious sentiment may lead to the same result. So the state may need religion and faith. It yet remains essentially distinguished from religion in that its commands are a legal duty, it being a matter of indifference in what spirit the duty is performed, while the empire of religion, on the contrary, is the internal. Just as the state, if it were to make such a claim as religion makes, would endanger the right of the inner mind, so the church degenerates into a tyrannical religion, if it acts as a state and imposes punishments.

A third distinction, related to the foregoing, is that the content of religion is and remains veiled; feeling, sensibility, and fancy are the ground on which it is built, and on this ground everything has the form of subjectivity. The state, on the other hand, actualizes itself, and gives its phases a solid reality. If religiosity were to insist upon making itself good within the state, as it is wont to do in its own territory, it would overturn the political organization. Each several distinction has a broad and fair field in the state, while in religion everything is always referred to the totality. If this totality were to seize upon all the political relations, it would be fanaticism. It would be bent upon having the whole in every particular part, and could not accomplish its desire except by the destruction of the particular. Fanaticism will not allow particular differences to have their way. The expression, "The pious are subject to no law," is nothing more than the decree of fanaticism. Piety, when it replaces the state, cannot tolerate that which is definitely constituted and destroys it. A kindred type of mind is shown by him who permits conscience or internality to judge, and does not decide on general grounds. This internality does not in its development proceed to principles, and gives itself no justification. If piety is counted as the reality of the state, all laws are cast to the winds, and subjective feeling legislates. This feeling may be nothing but caprice, and yet this cannot be ascertained except by its acts. But in so far as it becomes acts or commands, it assumes the shape of laws, and is directly opposed to subjective feeling. God, who is the object of this feeling, may also be regarded as a being who determines. But God is the universal idea, and is in feeling the undetermined, which is not mature enough to determine what actually exists in a developed form in the state. The fact that everything in the state is firm and secure is a bulwark against caprice and positive opinion. So religion, as such, ought not to rule.

271. The political constitution is (1) the organization of the state and the process of its organic life in reference to its own self. In this process the state distinguishes within itself its elements, and unfolds them into self-subsistence.

(2) It is a single, exclusive individuality, and as such is related to another. It turns its distinctive features towards foreign states, and in so doing es-

tablishes its self-subsisting distinctions within itself in their ideality.

Addition.—Just as irritability in the living organism is in one of its phases something internal, belonging to the organism as such, so here also the reference to foreign states has a bearing upon what is within. The internal state as such is the civil power; the direction outwards is the military power, which, however, has a definite side within the state itself. To balance both phases is one of the chief matters of statesmanship. Sometimes the civil power has been wholly extinguished, and rests only upon the military power, as happened during the time of the Roman emperors and Pretorian Guards. Sometimes, as in modern days, the military power proceeds only out of the civil power, as when all citizens are bound to bear arms.

I. INTERNAL CONSTITUTION

272. The constitution is rational in so far as the active working divisions of the state are in accord with the nature of the conception. This occurs when every one of its functions is in itself the totality, in the sense that it effectually contains the other elements. These elements, too, though expressing the distinctions of the conception, remain strictly within its ideality, and constitute one individual whole.

Note.—Concerning the constitution, as concerning reason itself, there has in modern times been an endless babble, which has in Germany been more insipid than anywhere else. With us there are those who have persuaded themselves that it is best even at the very threshold of government to understand before all other things what a constitution is. And they think that they have furnished invincible proof that religion and piety should be the basis of all their shallowness. It is small wonder if this prating has made for reasonable mortals the words reason, illumination, right, constitution, liberty, mere empty sounds, and men should have become ashamed to talk about a political constitution. At least as one effect of this superfluity, we may hope to see the conviction becoming general, that a philosophic acquaintance with such topics cannot proceed from mere reasonings, ends, grounds, and utilities, much less from feeling, love, and inspiration, but only out of the conception. It will be a fortunate thing, too, if those who maintain the divine to be inconceivable and an acquaintance with the truth to be wasted effort, were henceforth to refrain from breaking in upon the argument. What of undigested rhetoric and edification they manufacture out of these feelings can at least lay no claim to philosophic notice.

Amongst current ideas must be mentioned, in connection with §269, that regarding the necessary division of the functions of the state. This is a most important feature, which, when taken in its true sense, is rightly regarded as the guarantee of public freedom. But of this those, who think to speak out of inspiration and love, neither know nor will know anything, for in it lies the element of determination through the way of reason. The principle of the separation of functions contains the essential element of difference, that is to say, of real rationality. But as apprehended by the abstract understanding it is false when it leads to the view that these several functions are absolutely independent, and it is one-sided when it considers the relation of these functions to one another as negative and mutually limiting. In such a view each function in hostility to or fear of the others acts towards them as towards an evil. Each resolves to oppose the others, effecting by this opposition of forces a general balance, it may be, but not a living unity. But the internal self-direction of the conception, and not any other purpose or utility, contains the absolute source of the different functions. On their account alone the political organization exists as intrinsically rational and as the image of eternal reason.

From logic, though indeed not of the accepted kind, we know how the conception, and in a concrete way the idea, determine themselves of themselves, and thereby abstractly set up their phases of universality, particularity, and individuality. To take the negative as the point of departure, and set up as primary the willing of evil and consequent mistrust, and then on this supposition cunningly to devise breakwaters, which in turn require other breakwaters to check their activity, any such contrivance is the mark of a thought, which is at the level of the negative understanding, and of a feeling, which is characteristic of the rabble (§244).—The functions of the state, the executive and the legislative, as they are called, may be made independent of each other. The state is, then, forthwith overthrown, an occurrence which we have witnessed on a vast scale. Or, in so far as the state is essentially self-contained, the struggle of one function to bring the other into subjection effects somehow or other a closer unity, and thus preserves only what is in the state essential and fundamental.

Addition.—In the state we must have nothing which is not an expression of rationality. The state is the world, which the spirit has made for itself. Hence it has a definite self-begun and self-related course. Often we speak of the wisdom of God in nature, but we must not therefore believe that the physical world of nature is higher than the world of spirit. Just so high as the spirit stands above nature, the state stands above the physical life. We must hence honour the state as the divine on earth, and learn that if it is difficult to conceive of nature, it is infinitely harder to apprehend the state. That we in modern times have attained definite views concerning the state in general, and are perpetually engaged in speaking about and manufacturing constitutions, is a fact of much importance. But that does not settle the whole matter. It is necessary further that we approach a reasonable question in the mind of rational beings, that we know what is essential, and distinguish it from what is merely striking. Thus, the functions of the state must indeed be distinguished; and yet each must of itself form a whole, and also contain the other elements. When we speak of the distinctive activity of any function, we must not fall into the egregious error of supposing that it should exist in abstract independence, since it should rather be distinguished merely as an element of the conception. If the distinctions were to subsist in abstract independence, it is as clear as light that two independent things are not able to constitute a unity, but must rather introduce strife. As a result, either the whole world would be cast into disorder, or the unity would be restored by force. Thus, in the French Revolution at one time the legislative function had swallowed up the executive, at another time the executive had usurped the legislative function. It would be stupid in such a case to present the moral claim of harmony. If we cast the responsibility of the matter upon feeling, we have indeed got rid of the whole trouble. But, necessary as ethical feeling is, it cannot evolve from itself the functions of state. Whence it comes to pass that since the definite functions are the whole implicitly, they comprise in their actual existence the total conception. We usually speak of the three functions of state, the legislative, executive, and judicial. The legislative corresponds to universality, and the executive to particularity; but the judicial is not the third element of the conception. The individuality uniting the other two lies beyond these spheres.

273. The political state is divided into three substantive branches:

(a) The power to fix and establish the universal. This is legislation.

(b) The power, which brings particular spheres and individual cases under the universal. This is the function of government.

(c) The function of the prince, as the subjectivity with which rests the final decision. In this function the other two are brought into an individual unity. It is at once the culmination and beginning of the whole. This is constitutional monarchy.

Note.—The perfecting of the state into a constitutional monarchy is the work of the modern world, in which the substantive idea has attained the infinite form. This is the descent of the spirit of the world into itself, the free perfection by virtue of which the idea sets loose from itself its own elements, and nothing but its own elements, and makes them totalities; at the same time it holds them within the unity of the conception, in which is found their real rationality. The story of this true erection of the ethical life is the subject matter of universal world-history.

The old classification of constitutions into monarchy, aristocracy, and democracy is based upon the substantive unity which has not yet been divided. This unity has no internal distinctions, is not an intrinsically developed organization, and has not attained depth and concrete rationality. From the standpoint of the ancient world the classification is correct, because the unity of the ancient state was a substantive whole, not as yet fully mature and unfolded. The distinctions predicated of it must hence be external, and refer merely to the number of persons in whom this substantive unity should find an abode. But these various forms of the state, which belong in this way to different wholes, are in constitutional monarchy lowered to their proper place as elements. In monarchy we have a single person, in its executive several, in legislation the multitude. But, as we have said, such merely quantitative distinctions are superficial, and do not account for the conception. Similarly, it is not to the point to speak so much as we do of the democratic or aristocratic element in the monarchy for the phases, described by these terms, just in so far as they occur in a monarchy, are no longer democratic and aristocratic.

It is thought by some that the state is a mere abstraction which orders and commands, and that it may be left undecided, or be regarded as a trifle, whether one or several or all stand in the chief place in the state.— "All these forms," says Fichte ("Naturrecht," Pt. I., p. 196), "are right, and can produce and preserve universal right, if only there be present an ephorat." The ephorat was invented by Fichte, and defined as a needful counterpoise to the highest power. Such a view springs from a shallow conception of the state. It is true, indeed, that in a primitive condition of society these distinctions have little or no meaning. So Moses, when giving rules to the people in the case of their choosing a king, made no other alteration in the institutions than to command that the king's horses and wives should not be too numerous, or his treasure of gold and silver too large (Deut. xvii. 16, and fol.).—Further, it is true that in one sense these three forms are even for the idea a matter of no concern. I mean monarchy in its limited and exclusive signification, in accordance with which it stands by the side of democracy and aristocracy. But such a remark has a meaning the opposite of Fichte's. It would mean that these forms are a matter of indifference, because they collectively are not in accordance with the idea in its rational development (§272); nor can the idea in any one of them attain its right and actuality. Hence, it is idle to ask which of these forms is to be preferred. We speak of them now as having only an historical interest.

Here, as in so many other places, must be recognized the penetrating vision of Montesquieu, who discusses this question in his celebrated description of the principles of these forms of government. But this description we must not misunderstand, if we are to do it justice. He, as is well known, stated that virtue was the principle of democracy. Democracy does in fact rest upon sentiment as upon a form which is merely substantive. And it is still under this form that the rationality of the absolute will exists in democracy. But he goes on to say that England in the seventeenth century proved by a beautiful spectacle that its efforts to found a democracy were unavailing owing to a lack of virtue in the leaders. And he adds that, when in a republic virtue disappears, ambition seizes upon those whose minds are capable of it, and greed seizes upon all, and the state, becoming a general prey, maintains its strength only through the power of some individuals and the extravagance of all. Upon this view it must be remarked that when society becomes civilized, and the powers of particularity are developed and freed, the virtue of the rulers is not enough. Not mere sentiment, but the form of rational law is required, if the whole is to be able to keep itself together, and give to the developed powers of particularity the right to expand positively as well as negatively.

Similarly should be set aside the misconception that, since in a democratic republic the sentiment of virtue is the substantive form, it is wanting, or at least unnecessary, in a monarchy; and also the misconception that the legally constituted agencies of a systematized organization are opposed to and incompatible with virtue.

Moderation, or the principle of aristocracy, implies the incipient separation of public power and private interest. And yet these two are here in such close contact that aristocracy is always by its very nature on the verge of passing into the severest form of tyranny or anarchy, and so bringing on itself destruction. Witness Roman history.

Montesquieu, by crediting monarchy with the principle of honour, refers, it is clear, not to the patriarchal or any of the ancient monarchies, nor, on the other side, to the monarchy which has developed into an objective constitution, but to a feudal monarchy, in which the relations of political right to lawful private property and the privileges of individuals and corporations are confirmed. Since in this form of constitution state-life depends upon privileged persons, in whose liking is laid a large part of what must be done for the maintenance of the state, the objective element of these transactions is grounded not on duty but on imaginative thought and opinion. Thus, instead of duty it is only honour which keeps the state together.

Here it is natural to put a second question:—Who shall frame the constitution? This question seems intelligible at first glance, but on closer examination turns out to be meaningless. It presupposes that no constitution exists, but merely a collection of atomic individuals. How a heap of individuals is to obtain a constitution, whether by its own efforts or by means of others, whether by goodness, thought, or force, must be left to itself to decide, for with a mere mass the conception has nothing to do. If the question, however, takes for granted the existence of an actual constitution, then to make a constitution means only to modify it, the previous existence of the constitution implying that any change must be made constitutionally. But it is strictly essential that the constitution, though it is begotten in time, should not be contemplated as made. It is rather to be thought of as above and beyond what is made, as self-begotten and self-centred, as divine and perpetual.

Addition.—The principle of the modern world as a whole is freedom of subjectivity, the principle that all essential aspects of the spiritual whole should attain their right by self-development. From this stand-point one can hardly raise the idle question, as to which form is the better, monarchy or democracy. We venture to reply simply that the forms of all constitutions of the state are one-sided, if they are not able to contain the principle of free subjectivity, and do not know how to correspond to completed reason.

274. Spirit is real only in what it knows itself to be. The state, which is the nation's spirit, is the law which permeates all its relations, ethical observances, and the consciousness of its individuals. Hence the constitution of a people depends mainly on the kind and character of its self-consciousness. In it are found both its subjective freedom and the actuality of the constitution.

Note.—To think of giving to a people a consitution *à priori* is a whim, overlooking precisely that element which renders a constitution something more than a product of thought. Every nation, therefore, has the constitution which suits it and belongs to it.

Addition.—The state must in its constitution penetrate all its aspects. Napoleon insisted upon giving to the Spanish a constitution *à priori,* but the project failed. A constitution is not a mere manufacture, but the work of centuries. It is the idea and the consciousness of what is reasonable, in so far as it is developed in a people. Hence no constitution is merely created. That which Napoleon gave to the Spanish was more rational than what they had before, yet they viewed it as something foreign to them, and rejected it because they were not sufficiently developed. In a constitution a people must embody their sense of right and reproduce their conditions. Otherwise the constitution may exist externally, but it has no significance or truth. Often, indeed, the need of and longing for a better constitution may arise in individuals, but that is different from the whole multitude's being saturated by such a notion. This general conviction comes later. The principle of morality and inner conviction advocated by Socrates came of necessity into being in his day; but time had to elapse before it could reach general self-consciousness.

(a) The Function of the Prince

275. The function of the prince contains of itself the three elements of the totality (§272), (1) the universality of the constitution and the

laws; (2) counsel, or reference of the particular to the universal; and (3) the final decision, or the self-determination, into which all else returns and from which it receives the beginning of its actuality. This absolute self-determination, constituting the distinguishing principle of the princely function, as such, must be the first to be considered.

Addition.—We begin with the princely function or the factor of individuality, because in it the three phases of the state are inter-related as a totality. The I is at once the most individual and the most universal. The individual occurs also in nature, but there reality is equal to non-ideality, and its parts exist externally to one another. Hence it is not self-complete existence; in it the different individualities subsist side by side. In spirit, on the other hand, all differences exist only as ideal or as a unity. The state as spiritual is the interpretation of all its elements, but individuality is at the same time the soul, the vital and sovereign principle, which embraces all differences.

276. (1) The basal principle of the political state is the substantive unity, which is the ideality of its elements. (α) In this ideality the particular functions and offices of the state are just as much dissolved as retained. Indeed, they are retained only as having no independent authority, but such and so extensive an authority as is yielded them in the idea of the whole. They proceed, therefore, from the power of the state, and are the flexible limbs of the state as of their own simplified self.

Addition.—This ideality of elements is like the life of an organized body. Life exists in every part. There is but one life in all points, and there is no opposition to it. Any part separated from it is dead. Such is also the ideality of all individual occupations, functions, and corporations, great as may be their impulse to subsist and do for themselves. It is as in the organism, where the stomach assumes independence, and yet is at the same time superseded and sacrificed by becoming a member of one whole.

277. (β) The particular offices and agencies of the state, being its essential elements, are intimately connected with it. To the individuals, who manage and control them, they are attached in virtue not of their direct personality but of their objective and universal qualities. With particular personality, as such, they are joined only externally and accidentally. The business and functions of the state cannot therefore be private property.

Addition.—The agencies of the state are attached to individuals, who nevertheless are not authorized to discharge their offices through natural fitness, but by reason of their objective qualification. Capacity, skill, character, belong to the particularity of the individual, who must, however, be adapted to his special business by education and training. An office can, therefore, be neither sold nor bequeathed. Formerly in France seats in parliament were saleable, and this is still the case with any position of officer in the English army below a certain grade. These facts depended, or depend, upon the mediæval constitution of certain states, and are now gradually vanishing.

278. These two characteristics, namely (β) that the particular offices and functions of the state have independent and firm footing neither in themselves, nor in the particular will of individuals, but (α) ultimately in the unity of the state as in their simple self, constitute the sovereignty of the state.

Note.—This is sovereignty on its inner side. It has an outer side also, as we shall see.—In the older feudal monarchy the state had an outer aspect, but on its inner side not only was the monarch at no time sovereign, but neither was the state. Partly were the several offices and functions of the state and civic life dispersed in independent corporations and communities (§273, *note*), while the whole was rather an aggregate than an organism. Partly, too, were these functions the private property of individuals who, when it was proposed that they should act, consulted their own opinion and wish.

The idealism, which constitutes sovereignty, is that point of view in accordance with which the so-called parts of an animal organism are not parts but members or organic elements. Their isolation or independent subsistence would be disease. The same principle occurs in the abstract conception of the will (see *note* to next §) as the negativity, which by referring itself to itself reaches a universality, which definitely moulds itself into individuality (§7). Into this concrete universality all particularity and definiteness are taken up, and receive a new significance. It is the absolute self-determining ground. To apprehend it we must be at home with the conception in its true substance and subjectivity.

Because sovereignty is the ideality of all particular powers, it easily gives rise to the common misconception, which takes it to be mere force, empty wilfulness, and a synonym for despotism. But despotism is a condition of lawlessness, in which the particular will, whether of monarch or people (ochlocracy) counts as law, or rather instead of law. Sovereignty, on the contrary, constitutes the element of the ideality of particular spheres and offices, in a condition which is lawful and constitutional. No particular sphere is independent and self-sufficient in its aims and methods of working. It does not immerse itself in its own separate vocation. On the contrary, its aims are led by and dependent upon the aim of the whole, an aim which has been named in general terms and indefinitely the well-being of the state.

This ideality is manifested in a twofold way. (1) In times of peace the particular spheres and businesses go their way of satisfying their particular offices and ends. According to mere unconscious necessity self-seeking here veers round to a contribution in behalf of mutual preservation and the preservation of the whole (§183). But, also, through a direct influence from above is it that these employments are continually brought back and limited by the aim of the whole (see "Function of Government," §289), and led to make direct efforts for its preservation. (2) In circumstances of distress, internal or external, the organism consisting of its particulars, comes together into the simple conception of sovereignty, to which is intrusted the safety of the state, even at the sacrifice of what is at other times justifiable. It is here that idealism attains its peculiar realization (§321).

279. (2) Sovereignty, at first only the universal thought of this ideality, exists merely as a subjectivity assured of itself, and as the abstract and so far groundless self-direction and ultimate decision of the will; by virtue of this quality the state is individual and one. But in the next place subjectivity exists in its truth only as a subject, and personality as a person. In the constitution, which has matured into rational reality, each of the three elements of the conception has its own independent, real, and separate embodiment. Hence, the element which implies absolute decision is not individuality in general but one individual, the monarch.

Note.—The internal development of a science, whose whole content is deduced out of the simple conception—the only method which is deserving of the name philosophic,—reveals the peculiarity that one and the same conception, here the will, which at the beginning is abstract because it is the beginning, yet contains itself, condenses of itself its own characteristics, and in this way acquires a concrete content. Thus it is fundamental in the personality, which is at first in simple right abstract. It then develops itself through the different forms of subjectivity, and at last in absolute right, the state or the complete, concrete objectivity of the will, attains to the personality of the state and its conscious assurance of itself. This final term gives to all particularities a new form by taking them up into its pure self. It ceases to hesitate between reasons *pro* and *con.,* and deciding by an "I will," initiates all action and reality.

Personality, further, or subjectivity generally, as infinite and self-referring, has truth only as a person or independent subject. This independent existence must be one, and the truth which it has is of the most direct or immediate kind. The personality of the state is actualized only as a person, the monarch.—Personality expresses the conception as such, while person contains also the actuality of the conception. Hence the conception becomes the idea or truth, only when it receives this additional character.—A so-called moral person, a society, congregation, or family, be it as concrete as it may, possesses personality only as an element and abstractly. It has not reached the truth of its existence. But the state is this very totality, in which the moments of the conception gain reality in accordance with their peculiar truth.—All these phases of the idea have been already explained, both in their abstract and in their concrete forms, in the course of this treatise. Here, however, they need to be repeated, because we, while easily admitting them piecemeal in their particular forms, do not so readily recognise and apprehend them in their true place as elements of the idea.

The conception of monarch offers great difficulty to abstract reasonings and to the reflective methods of the understanding. The understanding never gets beyond isolated determinations, and ascribes merit to mere reasons, or finite points of view and what can be derived from them. Thus the dignity of the monarch is represented as something derivative not only in its form but also in its essential character. But the conception of the monarch is not derivative, but purely self-originated. Akin to this mistaken notion is the idea that the right of the monarch is based upon and receives its unconditional nature from divine authority. The misconceptions that are allied to this idea are well-known; besides, philosophy sets itself the task of conceiving the divine.

The phrase "sovereignty of the people," can be used in the sense that a people is in general self-dependent in its foreign relations, and constitutes its own state. Such are the people of Great Britain, for example. But the people of England, Scotland, Ireland, Venice, Genoa, or Ceylon, have ceased to be a sovereign people, since they no longer have independent princes, and the chief government is not exclusively their own. Further, it may be said that internal sovereignty resides in the people if, as was already pointed out (§§277–278), we speak in general terms, and mean that sovereignty accrues to the whole state. But the sovereignty of the people is usually in modern times opposed to the sovereignty of the monarch. This view of the sovereignty of the people may be traced to a confused idea of what is meant by "the people." The people apart from their monarch, and the common membership necessarily and directly associated with him, is a formless mass. It is no longer a state. In it occur none of the characteristic features of an equipped whole, such as sovereignty, government, law-courts, magistrates, professions, etc., etc. When these elements of an organized national life make their appearance in a people, it ceases to be that undefined abstraction, which is indicated by the mere general notion "people."

If by the phrase "sovereignty of the people" is to be understood a republic, or more precisely a democracy, for by a republic we understand various empirical mixtures which do not belong to a philosophic treatise, all that is necessary has already been said (§273, *note*). There can no longer be any defence of such a notion in contrast with the developed idea.—When a people is not a patriarchal tribe, having passed from the primitive condition, which made the forms of aristocracy and democracy possible, and is represented not as in a wilful and unorganized condition, but as a self-developed truly organic totality, in such a people sovereignty is the personality of the whole, and exists, too, in a reality, which is proportionate to the conception, the person of the monarch.

The element of the ultimate self-determining decision of will does not appear as an immanent vital element of the actual state in its peculiar reality, so long as the classification of constitutions into democracy, aristocracy, and monarchy can be made. When this classification prevails we are, as we have said, at the stage of the undeveloped substantive unity, which has not yet reached infinite difference and self-immersion. But even in these incomplete forms of the state the summit must be occupied by an individual. Either he appears in actual fact, as in those monarchies, which are of this type. Or, under aristocratic, or more especially under democratic governments, he appears in the person of statesmen or generals, according to accident and the particular need of the time. Here all overt action and realization have their origin and completion in the unity of the leader's decision. But this subjectivity of decision, confined within a primitive and unalloyed unity of functions, must be accidental in its origin and manifestation, and also on the whole subordinate. Accordingly, a pure and unmixed decision was looked for outside of and beyond this conditional summit, and was found in a fate which pronounced judgment from without. As an element of the idea it had to enter actual existence, but yet it had its root outside of human freedom, and the compass of the state.—To this source is to be traced the need of oracles, the *daimon* of Socrates, the consultation of the entrails of animals, the flight of birds, and their way of eating, etc., methods resorted to on great occasions, when it was necessary to have final judgment upon weighty affairs of state. As mankind had not yet realized the profundity of self-consciousness, or come forth from the pure virginity of the substantive unity into self-conscious existence, they had not yet strength to discover such a judgment within the pale of human existence.—In the *daimon* of Socrates (§138) we can discern the beginning of a change; we can see that the will, formerly set upon an object wholly outside of itself, has begun to transfer itself into itself, and recognize itself within itself. This is the beginning of self-conscious and therefore true freedom. This real freedom of the idea, since it gives its own present self-conscious reality to every one of the elements of rationality, imparts to the function of consciousness the final self-determining certitude, which in the conception of the will is the cope-stone. But this final self-determination can fall within the sphere of human liberty only in so far as it is assigned to an independent and separate pinnacle, exalted above all that is particular and conditional. Only when so placed, has it a reality in accordance with the conception.

Addition.—In the organization of the state, that is to say, in constitu-

tional monarchy, we must have before us nothing except the inner necessity of the idea. Every other point of view must disappear. The state
must be regarded as a great architectonic building, or the hieroglyph of
reason, presenting itself in actuality. Everything referring merely to utility, externality, etc., must be excluded from a philosophic treatment. It is
easy for one to grasp the notion that the state is the self-determining and
completely sovereign will, whose judgment is final. It is more difficult to
apprehend this "I will" as a person. By this is not meant that the monarch
can be wilful in his acts. Rather is he bound to the concrete content of
the advice of his councillors, and, when the constitution is established, he
has often nothing to do but sign his name. But this name is weighty. It is
the summit, over which nothing can climb. It may be said that an articulated organization has already existed in the beautiful democracy of
Athens. Yet we see that the Greeks extracted the ultimate judgment from
quite external phenomena, such as oracles, entrails of sacrificial animals,
and the flight of birds, and that to nature they held as to a power, which
in these ways made known and gave expression to what was good for
mankind. Self-consciousness had at that time not yet risen to the abstraction of subjectivity, or to the fact that concerning the matter to be
judged upon must be spoken a human "I will." This "I will" constitutes
the greatest distinction between the ancient and the modern world, and
so must have its peculiar niche in the great building of state. It is to be
deplored that this characteristic should be viewed as something merely
external, to be set aside or used at pleasure.

280. (3) This ultimate self of the state's will is in this its abstraction an
individuality, which is simple and direct. Hence its very conception implies that it is natural. Thus the monarch as a specific individual is abstracted from all other content, and is appointed to the dignity of
monarch in a directly natural way, by natural birth.

Note.—This transition from the conception of pure self-determination
to direct existence, and so to simple naturalness, is truly speculative in its
nature. A systematic account of it belongs to logic. It is on the whole the
same transition which is well-known in the nature of the will. It is the
process of translation of a content out of subjectivity, as represented end,
into tangible reality (§8). But the peculiar form of the idea and of the
transition, here passed in review, is the direct conversion of the pure self-
determination of the will, the simple conception itself, into a specific object, a "this," or natural visible reality, without the intervention of any
particular content, such as an end of action.

In the so-called ontological proof of the existence of God there is the
same conversion of the absolute conception into being. This conversion
has constituted the depth of the idea in modern times, although it has
been recently pronounced to be inconceivable. On such a theory, since

the unity of conception and embodiment is the truth (§23), all knowledge of the truth must be renounced. Although the understanding does not find this unity in its consciousness, and harps upon the separation of the two elements of the truth, it still permits a belief in a unity. But since the current idea of the monarch is regarded as issuing out of the ordinary consciousness, the understanding, with its astute reasonings, holds all the more tenaciously to the principle of separation and its results. It thereupon denies that the element of ultimate decision in the state is absolutely, that is, in the conception of reason, conjoined with direct nature. It maintains, on the contrary, the merely accidental character of the conjunction of these two, and hence regards as rational their absolute divergence. Finally, from the irrationality of the co-relation of these two phases proceed other consequences, which destroy the idea of the state.

Addition.—It is often maintained that the position of monarch gives to the affairs of state a haphazard character. It is said that the monarch may be ill-educated, and unworthy to stand at the helm of state, and that it is absurd for such a condition of things to exist under the name of reason. It must be replied that the assumption on which these objections proceed is of no value, since there is here no reference to particularity of character. In a completed organization we have to do with nothing but the extreme of formal decision, and that for this office is needed only a man who says "Yes," and so puts the dot upon the "i." The pinnacle of state must be such that the private character of its occupant shall be of no significance. What beyond this final judgment belongs to the monarch devolves upon particularity, with which we have no concern. There may indeed arise circumstances, in which this particularity alone has prominence, but in that case the state is not yet fully, or else badly constructed. In a well-ordered monarchy only the objective side of law comes to hand, and to this the monarch subjoins merely the subjective "I will."

281. Both elements, the final motiveless self of the will, and the like motiveless existence on the side of nature, indissolubly unite in the idea of that which is beyond the reach of caprice, and constitute the majesty of the monarch. In this unity lies the actualized unity of the state. Only by means of its unmotived directness on both its external and its internal side is the unity taken beyond the possibility of degradation to the wilfulness, ends, and views of particularity. It is thus removed also from the enfeeblement and overthrow of the functions of state and from the struggle of faction against faction around the throne.

Note.—Right of birth and right of inheritance constitute the basis of legitimacy, not as regards positive right merely, but likewise in the idea.— Through the self-determined or natural succession to the vacant throne all factious disputes are avoided. This has rightly been reckoned as one of the advantages of inheritance. However, it is only a consequence, and to assign it as a motive is to drag majesty down into the sphere of mere reasonings. The character of majesty is unmotived directness, and final self-involved existence. To speak of grounds is to propound as its basis not the idea of the state, which is internal to it, but something external in its nature and alien, such as the thought of the well-being of the state or of the people. By such a method inheritance can indeed be deduced through *medii termini*; but there might be other *medii termini* with quite other consequences. And it is only too well known what consequences may be drawn from the well-being of the people (*salut du peuple*).— Hence, philosophy ventures to contemplate majesty only in the medium of thought. Every other method of inquiry, except the speculative method of the infinite self-grounded idea, absolutely annuls the nature of majesty.

Freely to elect the monarch is readily taken as the most natural way. It is closely allied to the following shallow thought:—"Because it is the concern and interest of the people which the monarch has to provide for, it must be left to the people to choose whom it will depute to provide for them, and only out of such a commission arises the right of governing." This view, as well as the idea that the monarch is chief-officer of state, and also the idea of a contract between him and the people, proceed from the will of the multitude, in the form of inclination, opinion, and caprice. These views, as we long ago remarked, first make themselves good, or rather seek to do so, in the civic community. They can make no headway against the principle of the family, still less that of the state, or, in general, the idea of the ethical system.—That the election of a monarch is the worst of proceedings may be even by ratiocination detected in the consequences, which to it appear only as something possible or probable, but are in fact inevitable. Through the relation involved in free choice the particular will gives the ultimate decision, and the constitution becomes a free-capitulation, that is, the abandonment of the functions of state to the discretion of the particular will. The specific functions of state are thus transformed into private property, and there ensue the enfeeblement and injury of the sovereignty of the state, its internal dissolution and external overthrow.

Addition.—If we are to apprehend the idea of the monarch, it is not sufficient for us to say that God has established kings, since God has made everything, even the worst of things. Nor can we proceed very far under the guidance of the principle of utility, since it is always open to point out disadvantages. Just as little are we helped by regarding monarchy as positive right. That I should have property is necessary, but this specific possession is accidental. Accidental also appears to be the right that one man should stand at the helm of state, if this right, too, be regarded as abstract and positive. But this right is present absolutely, both as a felt want and as a need of the thing itself. A monarch is not remarkable for bodily strength or intellect, and yet millions permit themselves to be ruled by him. To say that men permit themselves to be governed contrary to their interests, ends, and intentions is preposterous, since men are not so stupid. It is their need and the inner power of the idea which urge them to this in opposition to their seeming consciousness, and retain them in this relation.

Although the monarch comes forward as summit and essential factor of the constitution, it must be admitted that in the constitution a conquered people is not identical with the prince. An uprising occurring in a province conquered in war is different from a rebellion in a well-organized state. The conquered are not rising against their prince, and commit no crime against the state, because they are not joined with their master in the intimate relation of the idea. They do not come within the inner necessity of the constitution. In that case only a contract is to the fore, and not a state-bond. "*Je ne suis pas votre prince, je suis votre maître,*" replied Napoleon to the delegation from Erfurt.

282. Out of the sovereignty of the monarch flows the right of pardoning criminals. Only to sovereignty belongs that realization of the power of the spirit, which consists in regarding what has happened as not having happened, and cancels crime by forgiving and forgetting.

Note.—The right of pardon is one of the highest recognitions of the majesty of spirit. This right belongs to the retrospective application of the character of a higher sphere to a lower and antecedent one.—Similar applications are found in the special sciences, which treat of objects in their empirical environment (§270, *footnote*).—It belongs to applications of this kind that injury done to the state generally or to the sovereignty, majesty, and personality of the prince, should fall under the conception of crime, as it has already been discussed (§§95–102), and should indeed be declared to be a specific crime of the gravest character.

Addition.—Pardon is the remission of punishment, but does not supersede right. Rather right remains, and the pardoned is a criminal as much after the pardon as he was before. Pardon does not imply that no wrong has been committed. Remission of the penalty may occur in religion, for by and in spirit what has occurred can be made not to have occurred. But in so far as remission of penalty is completed in the world, it has place only in majesty, and can be effected only by its unmotived edict.

283. The second element contained in the princely function is that of particularity, involving a definite content and the subsumption of it under the universal. In so far as it receives a particular existence, it is the supreme council, and is composed of individuals. They present to the

monarch for his decision the content of the affairs, as they arise, and of the legal cases which necessarily spring out of actual wants. Along with these they furnish also their objective sides, namely, the grounds for decision, the laws which bear on the case, the circumstances, etc. As the individuals who discharge this office have to do with the monarch's immediate person, their appointment and dismissal lie in his unlimited, free, arbitrary will.

284. The objective side of decision, including knowledge of the special content and circumstances, and the legal and other evidence, is alone responsible. It, that is to say, is alone able to furnish proof of objectivity. It must, therefore, come before a council other than the personal will of the monarch, as such. These councils, advising boards or individual advisers, are alone answerable. The peculiar majesty of the monarch, as the final deciding subjectivity, is exalted above all responsibility for the acts of government.

285. The third element of the princely function concerns the absolutely universal, which consists subjectively in the conscience of the monarch, objectively in the whole constitution and the laws. The princely function presupposes these other elements, just as much as they presuppose it.

286. The objective guarantee of the princely office, or the securing of the lawful succession to the throne by inheritance, lies in the fact that, just as this office has a reality distinct from the other elements determined by reason, so the others have also their independent and peculiar rights and duties. Every member of a rational organism, while preserving itself in independence, preserves also the peculiarities of the others.

Note.—One of the later results of history is such a modification of the monarchical constitution that the succession to the throne is determined by the law of primogeniture. This is, as it were, a return to the patriarchal principle, out of which this mode of succession has historically arisen, although it now bears the higher form of an absolute pinnacle of an organically developed state. This result has a most significant bearing upon public liberty, and is one of the most important elements in a rational constitution, although, as has already been observed, it is not so generally understood as it is respected. The earlier and merely feudal monarchies, and despotism also, reveal in their history the alternation of revolutions, high-handed dealings of princes, rebellion, overthrow of princely individuals and houses, and a general desolation and destruction, internal and external. The reason is that their division of state offices, entrusted as they were to vassals, pashas, etc., was only mechanical. It was not a distinction inherent in the essential character and form, but one of merely greater or less power. Accordingly, each part, preserving and producing only itself, did not preserve and produce the rest. All the elements were thus completely isolated and independent.

In the organic relation, in which members, and not parts, are related to one another, each one preserves the rest while fulfilling its own sphere. The preservation of the other members is the substantial end and product of each one in preserving itself. The guarantees asked for, be they for the stability of succession, for the stability of the princely office generally, or for justice and public liberty, are secured in institutions. Love of the people, character, oaths, force, etc., may be regarded as subjective guarantees; but when we speak of a constitution, we are engaged with only objective guarantees, institutions, or organically intertwined and self-conditioned elements. Thus, public freedom and hereditary succession are mutual guarantees, and are absolutely connected. Public liberty is the rational constitution, and hereditary succession of the princely function lies, as has been shown, in the conception of the constitution.

(b) The Executive

287. Decision is to be distinguished from its execution and application, and in general from the prosecution and preservation of what has been already resolved, namely, the existing laws, regulations, establishments for common ends, and the like. This business of subsumption or application is undertaken by the executive, including the judiciary and police. It is their duty directly to care for each particular thing in the civic community, and in these private ends make to prevail the universal interest.

288. Common interests of private concern occur within the civic community, and fall outside of the self-constituted and self-contained universal of the state (§256). They are administered in the corporations (§251) of the societies, trades, and professions, by their superintendents and representatives. The affairs, overseen by them, are the private property and interest of these particular spheres, whose authority depends upon the mutual trust of the associates, and confidence in the securities. Yet these circles must be subordinate to the higher interest of the state. Hence, in filling these posts generally, there will occur a mingling of the choice of the interested parties with the ratification of a higher authority.

289. To secure the universal interest of the state and to preserve the law in the province of particular rights, and also to lead these rights back to the universal interest, require the attention of subordinates of the executive. These subordinates are on one side executive officers and on the other a college of advisers. These two meet together in the highest offices of all, which are in contact with the monarch.

Note.—The civic community is, as we saw, the arena for the contest of the private interests of all against all. It is also the seat of battle between private interest and the collective special interest, and likewise of both private and collective special interests with the higher standpoint and order of the state. The spirit of the corporation, begotten in the course of regulating the particular spheres, becomes by a process internal to itself converted into the spirit of the state. It finds the state to be the means of preserving particular ends. This is the secret of the patriotism of the citizens in one of its phases. They are aware that the state is their substantive being, because it preserves their particular spheres, sustains their authority, and considers their welfare. Since the spirit of the corporation contains directly the riveting of the particular to the universal, it exhibits the depth and strength of the state as it exists in sentiment.

The administration of the business of the corporation through its own representatives is often clumsy, because, while they see and know their own peculiar interests and affairs, they do not discern the connection with remote conditions or the universal standpoint. Other elements contribute to this result, as, e.g., an intimate private relation between the representatives and their subordinates. Circumstances often tend to equalize these two classes which are in many ways mutually dependent. This peculiar territory can be looked on as handed over to the element of formal freedom, in which the knowledge, judgment, and practice of individuals, as also their small passions and fancies, may have room to wrestle with one another. This may all the more easily happen, the more trivial from the universal side of the state is the mismanaged affair, especially when the mismanagement stands of itself in direct relation to the satisfaction and opinion, which are derived from it.

290. In the business of the executive also there is a division of labour (§198). The organized executive officers have therefore a formal though difficult task before them. The lower concrete civil life must be governed from below in a concrete way. And yet the work must be divided into its abstract branches, specially officered by middlemen, whose activity in connection with those below them must from the lowest to the highest executive offices take the form of a continuous concrete oversight.

Addition.—The main point which crops up in connection with the executive is the division of offices. This division is concerned with the transition from the universal to the particular and singular; and the business is to be divided according to the different branches. The difficulty is that the different functions, the inferior and superior, must work in harmony. The police and the judiciary proceed each on its own course, it is true, but they yet in some office or other meet again. The means used to effect this conjunction often consists in appointing the chancellor of state and the prime minister, ministers in council. The matter is thus simplified on its upper side. In this way also everything issues from above out of the ministerial power, and business is, as they say, centralized. With this are associated the greatest possible despatch and efficiency in regard to what may affect the universal interests of state. This *régime* was introduced by the French Revolution, developed by Napoleon, and in France is found to this day. But France, on the other hand, has neither corporations nor communes, that is to say, the sphere in which particular and general interests coincide. In the Middle Ages this sphere had acquired too great an independence. Then there were states within the state, who persisted in behaving as if they were self-subsistent bodies. Though this ought not to occur, yet the peculiar strength of states lies in the communities. Here the government meets vested interests, which must be respected by it. These interests are inspected, and may be assisted by the government. Thus the individual finds protection in the exercise of his rights, and so attaches his particular interest to the preservation of the whole. For some time past the chief task has been that of organization carried on from above: while the lower and bulky part of the whole was readily left more or less unorganized. Yet it is of high importance that it also should be organized, because only as an organism is it a power or force. Otherwise it is a mere heap or mass of broken bits. An authoritative power is found only in the organic condition of the particular spheres.

291. The offices of the executive are of an objective nature, which is already independently marked out in accordance with their substance (§287). They are at the same time conducted by individuals. Between the objective element and individuals there is no direct, natural connecting tie. Hence individuals are not set aside for these offices by natural personality or by birth. There is required in them the objective element, namely, knowledge and proof of fitness. This proof guarantees to the state what it needs, and, as it is the sole condition, makes it possible for any citizen to devote himself to the universal class.

292. The subjective side is found in this, that out of many one individual must be chosen, and empowered to discharge the office. Since in this case the objective element does not lie in genius, as it does in art, the number of persons from whom the selection may be made is necessarily indefinite, and whom finally to prefer is beyond the possibility of absolute determination. The junction of individual and office, two phases whose relation is always accidental, devolves upon the princely power as decisive and sovereign.

293. The particular state-business, which monarchy transfers to executive officers, constitutes the objective side of the sovereignty inherent in the monarch. The distinguishing feature of this state-business is found in the nature of its matter. Just as the activity of the officers is the discharge of a duty, so their office is not subject to chance but a right.

294. The individual, who by the act of the sovereign (§292) is given an official vocation, holds it on the condition that he discharges his duty,

which is the substantive factor in his relation. By virtue of this factor the individual finds in his official employment his livelihood and the assured satisfaction of his particularity (§264), and in his external surroundings and official activity is free from subjective dependence and influences.

Note.—The state cannot rely upon service which is capricious and voluntary, such, for example, as the administration of justice by knights-errant. This service reserves to itself the right to act in accordance with subjective views, and also the right to withhold itself at will, or to realize subjective ends. The opposite extreme to the knight-errant in reference to public service would be the act of the public servant, who was attached to his employment merely by want, without true duty or right.

The public service requires the sacrifice of independent self-satisfaction at one's pleasure, and grants the right of finding satisfaction in the performance of duty, but nowhere else. Here is found the conjunction of universal and particular interests, a union which constitutes the conception and the internal stability of the state (§260).

Official position is not based upon contract (§75), although it involves the consent of the two sides and also a double performance. The public servant is not called to a single chance act of service, as is the attorney, but finds in his work the main interest of both his spiritual and his particular existence. So also it is not a matter merely external and particular, the performance of which is intrusted to him. The value of such a matter on its inner side is different from the externality of it, and thus is not as yet injured, as a stipulation is (§77), merely by non-performance. That which the public servant has to perform is as it stands of absolute value. Hence positive injury or non-performance, either being opposed to the essence of service, is a wrong to the universal content (§95, a negative-infinite judgment), and therefore a fault or crime.

The assured satisfaction of particular want does away with external need. There is no occasion to seek the means for alleviating want at the cost of official activity and duty. In the universal function of state those who are commissioned with the affairs of state are protected also against the other subjective side, the private passion of subjects, whose private interests, etc., may be injured by the furtherance of the universal.

295. Security for the state and its subjects against misuse of power by the authorities and their officers is found directly in their responsibility arising out of their nature as a hierarchy. But it is also found in the legitimate societies and corporations. They hold in check the inflow of subjective wilfulness into the power of the officers. They also supplement from below the control from above, which cannot reach down to the conduct of individuals.

Note.—In the conduct and character of the officers the laws and decisions of government touch individuality, and are given reality. On this depend the satisfaction and confidence of the citizens in the government. On this also depends the execution of the government's intentions, or else the weakening and frustration of them, since the manner in which the intention is realized is by sensibility and sentiment easily estimated more highly than the act itself, even though it be a tax. It is due to this direct and personal contact that the control from above may incompletely attain its end. This end may find an obstacle in the common interest of the official class, which is distinct from both subjects and superiors. Especially when institutions are perhaps not yet perfected, the higher interference of sovereignty for the removal of these hindrances (as for example that of Friedrich II. in the famous Müller-Arnold affair) is demanded and justified.

296. Whether or no integrity of conduct, gentleness, and freedom from passion pass into social custom depends upon the nature of the direct ethical life and thought. These phases of character maintain the spiritual balance over against the merely mental acquisition of the so-called sciences, dealing with the objects of these spheres of government, against also the necessary practice of business, and the actual labour of mechanical and other trades. The greatness of the state is also a controlling element, by virtue of which the importance of family relations and other private ties is diminished, and revenge, hate, and the like passions become inoperative and powerless. In concern for the great interests of a large state, these subjective elements sink out of sight, and there is produced an habitual regard for universal interests and affairs.

297. The members of the executive and the state officials constitute the main part of the middle class, in which are found the educated intelligence and the consciousness of right of the mass of a people. The institutions of sovereignty operating from above and the rights of corporations from below prevent this class from occupying the position of an exclusive aristocracy and using their education and skill wilfully and despotically.

Note.—At one time the administration of justice, whose object is the peculiar interest of all individuals, had been converted into an instrument of gain and despotism. The knowledge of law was concealed under a pedantic or foreign speech, and the knowledge of legal procedure under an involved formalism.

Addition.—The state's consciousness and the most conspicuous education are found in the middle class, to which the state officials belong. The members of this class, therefore, form the pillars of the state in regard to rectitude and intelligence. The state, if it has no middle class, is still at a low stage of development. In Russia, for example, there is a multitude of serfs and a host of rulers. It is of great concern to the state that a middle class should be formed, but this can be effected only in an organization such as we have described, namely, by the legalization of particular circles, which are relatively independent, and by a force of officials, whose wilfulness has no power over these legalized circles. Action in accordance with universal right, and the habit of such action, are consequences of the opposition produced by these self-reliant independent circles.

(c) *The Legislature*

298. The legislature interprets the laws and also those internal affairs of the state whose content is universal. This function is itself a part of the constitution. In it the constitution is presupposed, and so far lies absolutely beyond direct delimitation. Yet it receives development in the improvement of the laws, and the progressive character of the universal affairs of government.

Addition.—The constitution must unquestionably be the solid ground, on which the legislature stands. Hence, the prime essential is not to set to work to make a constitution. It exists, but yet it radically becomes, that is, it is formed progressively. This progress is an alteration which is not noticed, and has not the form of an alteration. For example, the wealth of princes and their families was at first a private possession in Germany; then, without any struggle or opposition it was converted into domains, that is, state wealth. This came about through the princes feeling the need of an undivided possession and demanding from the country, and the landed classes generally, security for the same. There was in this way developed a kind of possession, over which the princes had no longer the sole disposition. In a similar way, the emperor was formerly judge, and travelled about in his kingdom giving the law. Through the merely seeming or external progress of civilization, it has become necessary that the emperor should more and more delegate this office of judge to others. Thus the judicial function passed from the person of the prince to colleagues. So the progress of any condition of things is a seemingly calm and unnoticed one. In the lapse of time a constitution attains a position quite other than it had before.

299. These objects are defined in reference to individuals more precisely in two ways, (α) what of good comes to individuals to enjoy at the hands of the state, and (β) what they must perform for the state. The first division embraces the laws of private right in general, also the rights of societies and corporations. To these must be added universal institutions, and indirectly (§298) the whole of the constitution. But that which, on the other hand, is to be performed, is reduced to money as the existing universal value of things and services. Hence, it can be determined only in so equitable a way that the particular tasks and services, which the individual can perform, may be effected by his private will.

Note.—The object-matter of universal legislation may be in general distinguished from that of the administrative and executive functions in this way. Only what is wholly universal in its content falls under legislation, while administration deals with the particular and also the special way of carrying it out. But this distinction is not absolute, since the law, as it is a law, and not a mere general command such as "Thou shalt not kill" (§140, *note,* p. 142), must be in itself definite, and the more definite it is, the more nearly its content approaches the possibility of being carried out as it is. But at the same time such a complete settlement of the laws would give them an empirical side, which in actual execution would make them subject to alteration. This would be detrimental to their character as laws. The organic unity of the functions of state implies that one single spirit both fixes the nature of the universal and also carries it out to its definite reality.

It may occur that the state lays no direct claim upon the many kinds of skill, possessions, talents, faculties, with the manifold personal wealth which is contained in them and is tinged with subjective sentiment, but only upon that form of wealth which appears as money.—The services referring to the defence of the state against enemies belong to the duty discussed in the next section of this treatise. Money is, in fact, not a special kind of wealth, but the universal element in all kinds, in so far as they in production are given such an external reality as can be apprehended as an object. Only at this external point of view is it possible and just to estimate performances quantitatively.

Plato in his "Republic" allows the rulers to appoint individuals to their particular class, and assign to them their particular tasks (§185, *note*). In feudal-monarchy vassals had to perform a similarly unlimited service, and simply in their particularity to discharge such a duty as that of a judge. Services in the East, such as the vast undertakings in architecture in Egypt, are also in quality particular. In all these relations there is lacking the principle of subjective freedom. In accordance with this principle, the substantive act of the individual, which even in the abovementioned services is in its content particular, should proceed from his particular will. This right is possible only when the demand for work rests upon the basis of universal value. Through the influence of this right the substitution of money for services has been introduced.

Addition.—The two aspects of the constitution refer to the rights and the services of individuals. The services are now almost all reduced to money. Military duty is perhaps the only remaining personal service. In former times claim was made to the concrete individual, who was summoned to work in accordance with his skill. Now the state buys what it needs. This may seem abstract, dead, and unfeeling. It may also seem as if to be satisfied with abstract services were for the state a retrograde step. But the principle of the modern state involves that everything which the individual does should be occasioned by his will. By means of money the justice implied in equality can be much better substantiated. The talented would be more heavily taxed than the man without talents if respect were had to concrete capacity. But now, out of reverence for subjective liberty, the principle is brought to light that only that shall be laid hold upon which is of a nature to be laid hold upon.

300. In the legislative function in its totality are active both the monarchical element and the executive. The monarchical gives the final decision, and the executive element advises. The executive element has concrete knowledge and oversight of the whole in its many sides and in the actual principles firmly rooted in them. It has also acquaintance with the wants of the offices of state. In the legislature are at last represented the different classes or estates.

Addition.—It proceeds from a wrong view of the state to exclude the members of the executive from the legislature, as was at one time done by the constituent assembly. In England the ministers are rightly members of parliament, since those who share in the executive should stand in connection with and not in opposition to the legislature. The idea that the functions of government should be independent contains the fundamental error that they should check one another. But this independence is apt to usurp the unity of the state, and unity is above all things to be desired.

301. By admitting the classes the legislature gives not simply implicit but actual existence to matters of general concern. The element of subjective formal freedom, the public consciousness, or the empirical universality of the views and thoughts of the many, here becomes a reality.

Note.—The expression "The Many" (οἱ πολλοὶ) characterizes the empirical universality better than the word "All," which is in current use. Under this "all," children, women, etc., are manifestly not meant to be included. Manifestly, therefore, the definite term "all" should not be employed, when, it may be, some quite indefinite thing is being discussed.

There are found in current opinion so unspeakably many perverted and false notions and sayings concerning the people, the constitution, and the classes, that it would be a vain task to specify, explain, and correct them. When it is argued that an assembly of estates is necessary and advantageous, it is meant that the people's deputies, or, indeed, the people itself, must best understand their own interest, and that it has undoubtedly the truest desire to secure this interest. But it is rather true that the people, in so far as this term signifies a special part of the citizens, does not know what it wills. To know what we will, and further what the absolute will, namely reason, wills, is the fruit of deep knowledge and insight, and is therefore not the property of the people.

It requires but little reflection to see that the services performed by the classes in behalf of the general well-being and public liberty cannot be traced to an insight special to these classes. The highest state officials have necessarily deeper and more comprehensive insight into the workings and needs of the state, and also greater skill and wider practical experience. They are able without the classes to secure the best results, just as it is they who must continually do this when the classes are in actual assembly. General well-being does not therefore depend upon the particular insight of the classes, but is rather the achievement of the official deputies. They can inspect the work of the officers who are farthest removed from the observation of the chief functionaries of state. They, too, have a concrete perception of the more urgent special needs and defects. But to this intelligent oversight must be added the possibility of public censure. This possibility has the effect of calling out the best insight upon public affairs and projects, and also the purest motives; its influence is felt by the members of the classes themselves. As for the conspicuously good will, which is said to be shown by the classes towards the general interest, it has already been remarked (§272, *note*) that the masses, who in general adopt a negative standpoint, take for granted that the will of the government is evil or but little good. If this assumption were replied to in kind, it would lead to the recrimination that the classes, since they originate in individuality, the private standpoint and particular interests, are apt to pursue these things at the expense of the universal interest; while the other elements of the state, being already at the point of view of the state, are devoted to universal ends. As for the pledge to respect the public welfare and rational freedom, it should be given especially by the classes, but is shared in by all the other institutions of state. This guarantee is present in such institutions as the sovereignty of the monarch, hereditary succession, and the constitution of the law-courts, much more pronouncedly than in the classes. The classes, therefore, are specially marked out by their containing the subjective element of universal liberty. In them the peculiar insight and peculiar will of the sphere, which in this treatise has been called the civic community, is actualized in relation to the state. It is here as elsewhere by means of the philosophic point of view that this element is discerned to be a mark of the idea when developed to a totality. This inner necessity is not to be confounded with the external necessities and utilities of this phase of state activity.

Addition.—The attitude of the government to the classes must not be in its essence hostile. The belief in the necessity of this hostile relation is a sad mistake. The government is not one party which stands over against another, in such a way that each is seeking to wrest something from the other. If the state should find itself in such a situation, it must be regarded as a misfortune and not as a sign of health. Further, the taxes, to which the classes give their consent, are not to be looked upon as a gift to the state, but are contributed for the interest of the contributors. The peculiar significance of the classes or estates is this, that through them the state enters into and begins to share in the subjective consciousness of the people.

302. The classes, considered as a mediating organ, stand between the government and the people at large in their several spheres and individual capacities. This specific designation of the classes requires of them a sense and sentiment both for the state and government and for the interests of special circles and individuals. This position of the classes has, in common with the organized executive, a mediatorial function. It neither isolates the princely function as an extreme, causing it to appear as a mere ruling power acting capriciously, nor does it isolate the particular interests of communities, corporations, and individuals. Furthermore, individuals are not in it contrasted with the organized state, and thus are not presented as a mass or heap, as unorganized opinion and will, or as a mere collective force.

Note.—It is one of the fundamental principles of logic, that a definite element, which, when standing in opposition, has the bearing of an extreme, ceases to be in opposition and becomes an organic element, when it is observed to be at the same time a mean. In this present question it is all the more important to make prominent this principle, since the prejudice is as common as it is dangerous, which presents the classes as essentially in opposition to the government. Taken organically, that is, in its totality, the element of the classes proves its right only through its office of mediation. Thus the opposition is reduced to mere appearance. If it, in so far as it is manifested, were not concerned merely with the superficial aspect of things but became a substantive opposition, the state would be conceived of as in decay.—That the antagonism is not of this radical kind is shown by the fact that the objects, against which it is directed, are not the essential phases of the political organism, but things that are more special and indifferent. The passion, which attaches itself to this opposition, becomes mere party seeking for some subjective interest, perhaps for one of the higher offices of state.

Addition.—The constitution is essentially a system of mediation. In despotic lands where there are only princes and people, the people act, if they act at all, in such a way as to disturb or destroy the political organization. But when the multitude has an organic relation to the whole, it obtains its interests in a right and orderly way. If this middle term is not present, the utterance of the masses is always violent. Therefore, the despot treats the people with indulgence, while his rage affects only those in his immediate neighbourhood. So also the people in a despotism pay light taxes, which in a constitutional state become larger through the people's own consciousness. In no other land are taxes so heavy as they are in England.

303. The universal class, the class devoted to the service of the government, has directly in its structure the universal as the end of its essential activity. In that branch of the legislative function, which contains the classes, the private individual attains political significance and efficiency. Hence, private persons cannot appear in the legislature either as a mere undistinguished mass, or as an aggregate of atoms. In fact, they already exist under two distinct aspects. They are found in the class, which is based on the substantive relation, and also in the class based upon particular interests and the labour by which they are secured (§201 and fol.). Only in this way is the actual particular in the state securely attached to the universal.

Note.—This view makes against another widespread idea, that since the private class is in the legislature exalted to participation in the universal business, it must appear in the form of individuals, be it that representatives are chosen for this purpose, or that every person shall exercise a voice. But even in the family this abstract atomic view is no longer to be found, nor in the civic community, in both of which the individual makes his appearance only as a member of a universal. As to the state, it is essentially an organization, whose members are independent spheres, and in it no phase shall show itself as an unorganized multitude. The many, as individuals, whom we are prone to call the people, are indeed a collective whole, but merely as a multitude or formless mass, whose movement and action would be elemental, void of reason, violent, and terrible. When in reference to the constitution we still hear the people, that is, this unorganized mass, spoken of, we may take it for granted that we shall be given only generalities and warped declamations.

The view leading to the disintegration of the common existence found in the various circles, which are elements in the political world or highest concrete universality, would seek to divide the civic from the political life. The basis of the state would then be only the abstract individuality of wilfulness and opinion, a foundation which is merely accidental, and not absolutely steadfast and authoritative. That would be like building political life in the air. Although in these so-called theories the classes of the civic community generally and the classes in their political significance lie far apart, yet speech has retained their unity, a union which indeed existed long ago.

304. The distinction of classes, which is already present in the earlier spheres, is contained also within the strict circumference of the political classes generally. Their abstract position is the extreme of empirical universality in opposition to the princely or monarchical principle. In this abstract position there is only the possibility of agreement, and hence quite as much the possibility of antagonism. It becomes a reasonable relation, and leads to the conclusion of the syllogism (§302, *note*), only if its

middle term, or element of mediation, becomes a reality. Just as from the side of the princely function the executive (§300) has already this character of reconciliation, so also from the side of the classes should one of their elements be converted into a mediating term.

305. Of the classes of the civic community one contains the principle, which is really capable of filling this political position. This is the class, whose ethical character is natural. As its basis it has family life, and as regards subsistence it has the possession of the soil. As regards its particularity it has a will, which rests upon itself, and, in common with the princely function, it bears the mark of nature.

306. In its political position and significance this class becomes more clearly defined, when its means are made as independent of the wealth of the state as they are of the uncertainty of trade, the desire for gain, and the fluctuations of property. It is secure from the favour at once of the executive and of the multitude. It is further secured even from its own caprice, since the members of this class, who are called to this office, do without the rights exercised by the other citizens. They do not freely dispose of their property, nor do they divide it equally among their children, whom they love equally. This wealth becomes an inalienable inheritance burdened by primogeniture.

Addition.—This class has a more independent volition. The class of property owners is divided into two broad parts, the educated and the peasants. In contradistinction to these two kinds stand both the industrial class, which is dependent on and directed by the general wants, and the universal class, which is essentially dependent upon the state. The security and stability of this propertied class may be increased still more by the institution of primogeniture. This, however, is desirable only in reference to the state, since it entails a sacrifice for the political purpose of giving to the eldest son an independent life. Primogeniture is instituted that the state may reckon upon, not the mere possibility belonging to sentiment, but upon something necessary. Now sentiment, it is true, is not bound up with a competence. But it is relatively necessary that some having a sufficient property and being thereby freed from external pressure, should step forth without hindrance and use their activity for the state. But to establish and foster primogeniture where there are no political institutions would be nothing but a fetter clogging the freedom of private right. Unless this freedom is supplemented by the political sense, it goes to meet its dissolution.

307. The right of this part of the substantive class is based upon the nature-principle of the family. But through heavy sacrifices for the state this principle is transformed, and by the transformation this class is set apart for political activity. Hence it is called and entitled to this sphere by birth, without the accident of choice. It thus receives a stable substantive

situation intermediate between the subjective caprice and the accidents of the two extremes. While it resembles the princely function (§306), it participates in the wants and rights of the other extreme. It thus becomes a support at once to the throne and to the community.

308. Under the other part of the general class element is found the fluctuating side of the civic community, which externally because of its numerous membership, and necessarily because of its nature and occupation, takes part in legislation only through deputies. If the civic community appoints these deputies, it does so in accordance with its real nature. It is not a number of atoms gathering together merely for a particular and momentary act without any further bond of union, but a body systematically composed of constituted societies, communities, and corporations. These various circles receive in this way political unity. Through the just claim of this part to be represented by a deputation to be summoned by the princely power, and also through the claim of the first part to make an appearance (§307), the existence of the classes and of their assembly finds its peculiar constitutional guarantee.

Note.—It is held that all should share individually in the counsels and decisions regarding the general affairs of state. The reason assigned is that all are members of the state, its affairs are the affairs of all, and for the transaction of these affairs all with their knowledge and will have a right to be present. This is a notion which, although it has no reasonable form, the democratic element would insert into the organism of state, notwithstanding the fact that the state is an organism only because of its reasonable form. This superficial view fastens upon and adheres to the abstraction "member of the state." But the rational method, the consciousness of the idea, is concrete and is combined with the true practical sense, which is itself nothing else than the rational sense or the sense for the idea. Yet this sense is not to be confounded with mere business routine, or bounded by the horizon of a limited sphere. The concrete state is the whole, articulated into its particular circles, and the member of the state is the member of a circle or class. Only his objective character can be recognized in the state. His general character contains the twofold element, private person and thinking person, and thinking is the consciousness and willing of the universal. But consciousness and will cease to be empty only when they are filled with particularity, and by particularity is meant the characteristic of a particular class. The individual is species, let us say, but has his intrinsic general actuality in the species next above it. He attains actual and vital contact with the universal in the sphere of the corporations and societies (§251). It remains open to him by means of his skill to make his way into any class, for which he has the capacity, including the universal class. Another assumption, found in the current idea that all should have a share in the business of state, is that all understand this business. This is as absurd as it, despite its absurdity, is widespread. However, through the channel of public opinion (§316) every one is free to express and make good his subjective opinion concerning the universal.

309. Counsels and decisions upon universal concerns require delegates, who are chosen under the belief that they have a better understanding of state business than the electors themselves. They are trusted to prosecute not the particular interest of a community or a corporation in opposition to the universal, but the universal only. Hence, to the deputies are not committed specific mandates or explicit instructions. But just as little has the assembly the character merely of a lively gathering of persons, each of whom is bent upon instructing, convincing, and advising the rest.

Addition.—In the case of representation consent is not given directly by all, but by those who are qualified, since here the individual voter is no longer a mere infinite person. Representation is based upon confidence; but confidence is different from simply casting a vote. To be guided by the majority of votes is antagonistic to the principle that I must meet my duty as a particular person. We have confidence in a person when we believe in his insight and his willingness to treat my affair as his own according to the best light of his knowledge and conscience. The principle of the individual subjective will also disappears, for confidence is concerned with a thing, the guiding ideals of a man, his behaviour, his acts, his concrete understanding. A representative must have a character, insight, and will capable of participating in universal business. He speaks not in his character as an abstract individual, but as one who seeks to make good his interests in an assembly occupied with the universal. And the electors merely ask for some guarantee that the delegate shall carry out and further this universal.

310. Independent means has its right in the first part of the classes. The guarantee implied in a qualification and sentiment adequate to public ends is found in the second part, which arises out of the fluctuating, variable element of the civic community. It is chiefly found in sentiment, skill, and practical knowledge of the interests of the state and civic community, all of which qualities are acquired through actual conduct of business in the magistracies and public offices, and are preserved by practical use. It is found present, too, in the official or political sense, which is fashioned and tested by actual experience.

Note.—Subjective opinion readily finds the demand for guarantees superfluous or injurious, when it is made upon the so-called people. But the state contains the objective as its distinguishing trait, and not subjective opinion with its self-confidence. Individuals can be for the state only what in them is objectively recognizable and approved. Since this second part of the class-element has its root in particular interests and concerns, where accident, change, and caprice have the right to disport themselves, the state must here look the more closely after the objective.

The external qualification of a certain property appears, when taken abstractly, a one-sided external extreme, in contrast with the other just as one-sided extreme, namely, the mere subjective confidence and opinion of the electors. Each in its abstraction is distinguished from the concrete qualifications, indicated in §302, which are required of those who advise concerning the business of state.—Nevertheless, in the choice of a magistrate or other officer of a society or an association, a property qualification is rightly made a condition, especially as much of the business is administered without remuneration. This qualification has also direct value in regard to the political business of the classes, if the members receive no salary.

311. Deputies from the civic community should be acquainted with the particular needs and interests of the body which they represent, and also with the special obstacles which ought to be removed. They should therefore be chosen from amongst themselves. Such a delegation is naturally appointed by the different corporations of the civic community (§308) by a simple process, which is not disturbed by abstractions and atomistic notions. Thus they fulfil the point of view of the community directly, and either an election is altogether superfluous, or the play of opinion and caprice is reduced to a minimum.

Note.—It is a manifest advantage to have amongst the delegates individuals who represent every considerable special branch of the community, such as trade, manufacture, etc. These individuals must be thoroughly acquainted with their branch and belong to it. In the idea of a loose, indefinite election this important circumstance is given over to accident. Every branch, however, has an equal right to be represented. To regard the deputies as representatives has a significance that is organic and rational, only if they are not representatives of mere separate individuals or of a mere multitude, but of one of the essential spheres of the community and of its larger interests. Representation no longer means that one person should take the place of another. Rather is the interest itself actually present in the person of the representative, since he is there in behalf of his own objective nature.

Of elections by means of many separate persons it may be observed that there is necessarily little desire to vote, because one vote has so slight an influence. Even when those who are entitled to vote are told how extremely valuable their privilege is, they do not vote. Hence occurs just the opposite of what is sought. The selection passes into the hands of a few, a single party, or a special accidental interest, which should rather be neutralized.

312. Of the two elements comprised under the classes, each brings into council a particular modification. As one of these elements has within the sphere of the classes the peculiar function of mediation, and that, too, between two things which both exist, it has a separate existence. The assembly of the classes is thus divided into two chambers.

313. By this separation the number of courts is increased, and there is a greater certainty of mature judgment. Moreover, an accidental decision, secured on the spur of the moment by a simple majority of the votes, is rendered much less probable. But these are not the main advantages. There is, besides, smaller opportunity or occasion for direct opposition to arise between the class element and the government. Or in the case when the mediating element is also found on the side of the lower chamber, the insight of this lower house becomes all the stronger, since it in this case appears to be more unpartisan and its opposition to be neutralized.

314. The classes are not the sole investigators of the affairs of state and sole judges of the general interest. Rather do they form merely an addition (§301). Their distinctive trait is that, as they represent the members of the civic community who have no share in the government, it is through their co-operating knowledge, counsel, and judgment that the element of formal freedom attains its right. Besides, a general acquaintance with state affairs is more widely extended through the publicity given to the transactions of the classes.

315. By means of this avenue to knowledge public opinion first attains to true thoughts, and to an insight into the condition and conception of the state and its concerns. It thus first reaches the capacity of judging rationally concerning them. It learns, besides, to know and esteem the management, talents, virtues, and skill of the different officers of state. While these talents by receiving publicity are given a strong impulse towards development and an honourable field for exhibiting their worth, they are also an antidote for the pride of individuals and of the multitude, and are one of the best means for their education.

Addition.—To open the proceedings of the assembly of classes to the public is of great educational value, especially for the citizens. By it the people learn most certainly the true nature of their interests. There prevails extensively the idea that everybody knows already what is good for the state, and that this general knowledge is merely given utterance to in a state assembly. But, indeed, the very opposite is the fact. Here, first of all are developed virtues, talents, skill, which have to serve as examples. Indeed, these assemblies may be awkward for the ministers, who must here buckle on their wit and eloquence to resist the attacks of their opponents. Publicity is the greatest opportunity for instruction in the state interests generally. Amongst a people, where publicity is the rule, there is seen quite a different attitude towards the state than in those places where state assemblies are not found or are secret. By the publication of every proceeding, the chambers are first brought into union with the larger general opinion. It is shown that what a man fancies when he is at home with his wife and friends is one thing, and quite another thing what occurs in a great gathering where one clever stroke annihilates the preceding.

316. Formal subjective freedom, implying that individuals as such should have and express their own judgment, opinion, and advice concerning affairs of state, makes its appearance in that aggregate, which is called public opinion. In it what is absolutely universal, substantive, and true is joined with its opposite, the independent, peculiar, and particular opinions of the many. This phase of existence is therefore the actual contradiction of itself; knowledge is appearance, the essential exists directly as the unessential.

Addition.—Public opinion is the unorganized means through which what a people wills and thinks is made known. That which is effective in the state must indeed be in organic relation to it; and in the constitution this is the case. But at all times public opinion has been a great power, and it is especially so in our time, when the principle of subjective freedom has such importance and significance. What now shall be confirmed is confirmed no longer through force, and but little through use and wont, but mainly by insight and reasons.

317. Public opinion contains therefore the eternal substantive principles of justice, the true content and result of the whole constitution, of legislation, and of the universal condition in general. It exists in the form of sound human understanding, that is, of an ethical principle which in the shape of prepossessions runs through everything. It contains the true wants and right tendencies of actuality.

But when this inner phase comes forth into consciousness, it appears to imaginative thinking in the form of general propositions. It claims to be of interest partly on its own separate account; but it also comes to the assistance of concrete reasoning upon felt wants and upon the events, arrangements, and relations of the state. When this happens, there is brought forward also the whole range of accidental opinion, with its ignorance and perversion, its false knowledge and incorrect judgment. Now, as to the consciousness of what is peculiar in thought and knowledge, with which the present phenomenon has to do, it may be said that the worse an opinion is, the more peculiar and unique it is. The bad is in its content wholly particular and unique; the rational, on the contrary, is the absolutely universal. Yet it is the unique upon which opinion founds its exalted self-esteem.

Note.—Hence it is not to be regarded merely as a difference in the subjective point of view when it is declared on one side

"Vox populi, vox dei;"

and on the other side (in Ariosto, for example),[10]

"Che 'l Volgare ignorante ogn' un riprenda
E parli più di quel che meno intenda;"

both phases are found side by side in public opinion. Since truth and endless error are so directly united in it, either the one or the other is not truly in earnest. It may seem hard to decide which is in earnest; and it would still be hard, even if we were to confine ourselves to the direct expression of public opinion. But since in its inner being public opinion is the substantive, it is truly in earnest only about that. Yet the substantive cannot be extracted from public opinion; it, by its very nature as substantive, can be known only out of itself and on its own account. No matter what passion is expended in support of an opinion, no matter how seriously it is defended or attacked, this is no criterion of its practical validity. Yet least of all would opinion tolerate the idea that its earnestness is not earnest at all.

A great mind has publicly raised the question, whether it be permitted to deceive a people. We must answer that a people does not allow itself to be deceived in regard to its substantive basis, or the essence and definite character of its spirit; but in regard to the way in which it knows this, and judges of its acts and phases, it deceives itself.

Addition.—The principle of the modern world demands that what every man is bound to recognize must seem to him justified. He, moreover, has had a voice in the discussion and decision. If he has given his word and indicated that he is responsible, his subjectivity is satisfied, and he allows many things to go unchallenged. In France freedom of speech has always proved less dangerous than silence. One fears that if a man is silent he will retain his aversion to an object; but reasoning upon it furnishes a safety-valve and brings satisfaction, while the object, in the meantime, pursues its way unmolested.

318. Public opinion deserves, therefore, to be esteemed and despised; to be despised in its concrete consciousness and expression, to be esteemed in its essential basis. At best, its inner nature makes merely an appearance in its concrete expression, and that, too, in a more or less trou-

---

[10]Or in Goethe:

"Zuschlagen kann die Masse,
Da ist sie respektabel;
Urtheilen gelingt ihr miserabel."

bled shape. Since it has not within itself the means of drawing distinctions, nor the capacity to raise its substantive side into definite knowledge, independence of it is the first formal condition of anything great and reasonable, whether in actuality or in science. Of any reasonable end we may be sure that public opinion will ultimately be pleased with it, recognize it, and constitute it one of its prepossessions.

Addition.—In public opinion all is false and true, but to find out the truth in it is the affair of the great man. He who tells the time what it wills and means, and then brings it to completion, is the great man of the time. In his act the inner significance and essence of the time is actualized. Who does not learn to despise public opinion, which is one thing in one place and another in another, will never produce anything great.

319. The liberty of taking part in state affairs, the pricking impulse to say and to have said one's opinion, is directly secured by police laws and regulations, which, however, hinder and punish the excess of this liberty. Indirect security is based upon the government's strength, which lies mainly in the rationality of its constitution and the stability of its measures, but partly also in the publicity given to the assemblies of the classes. Security is guaranteed by publicity in so far as the assemblies voice the mature and educated insight into the interests of the state, and pass over to others what is less significant, especially if they are disabused of the idea that the utterances of these others are peculiarly important and efficacious. Besides, a broad guarantee is found in the general indifference and contempt, with which shallow and malicious utterances are quickly and effectually visited.

Note.—One means of freely and widely participating in public affairs is the press, which, in its more extended range, is superior to speech, although inferior in vivacity.—To define the liberty of the press as the liberty to speak and write what one pleases is parallel to the definition of liberty in general, as liberty to do what one pleases. These views belong to the undeveloped crudity and superficiality of fanciful theorizing. Nowhere so much as in this matter does formalism hold its ground so obstinately, and so little permits itself to be influenced by reasons. And this was to be expected, because the object is here the most transient, accidental, and particular in the whole range of opinion, with its infinite variety of content and aspect. Of course, there is no obscurity about a direct summons to steal, murder, or revolt. But, aside from that, much depends on the manner and form of expression. The words may seem to be quite general and undefined, and yet may conceal a perfectly definite significance. Besides, they may have consequences, which are not actually expressed. Indeed, it may even be debated whether these consequences are really in the expression and properly follow from it. This indefiniteness in the form and in the substance does not admit of the laws attaining in this case the precision usually demanded of laws. Since in this field crime, wrong, and injustice have their most particular and subjective shape, the indefiniteness of the wrong causes the sentence also to be completely subjective. Besides, the injury is in this matter sought to be done to and make itself real in the thought, opinion, and will of others. But it thus comes into contact with the freedom of others, upon whom it depends whether the act is actually an injury or not.

Hence, the laws are open to criticism because of their indefiniteness. By the skilful use of terms they may be evaded; or, on the other hand, it may be contended that the sentence is merely subjective. It may be maintained further that an expression is not a deed but only an opinion, or thought, or a simple saying. Thus, from the mere subjectivity of content and from the insignificance of a mere opinion or saying the inference is drawn that these words should pass unpunished. Yet in the same breath there is demanded as great a respect and esteem for that very opinion of mine as for my real mental possession, and for the utterance of that opinion as for the deliberate utterance of a mental possession.

The fact remains that injury to the honour of individuals generally, as libel, abuse, disdainful treatment of the government, its officials and officers, especially the person of the prince, contempt for the laws, incitement to civil broil, etc., are all crimes or faults of different magnitudes. The greater indefiniteness of these acts, due to the element in which they find utterance, does not annul their real character. It simply causes the subjective ground, on which the offence is committed, to decide the nature and shape of the reaction. It is this subjective nature of the offence, which in the reaction converts subjectivity and uncertainty into necessity, whether this reaction be mere prevention of crime by the police or specific punishment. Here, as always, formalism relies on isolated aspects, belonging to the external appearance, and seeks by these abstractions of its own creation to reason away the real and concrete nature of the thing.

As to the sciences, they, if they are sciences in reality, are not found in the region of opinion and subjective thought, nor does their method of presentation consist in the adroit use of terms, or allusions, or half-uttered, half-concealed opinions, but in the simple, definite, and open expression of the sense and meaning. Hence, the sciences do not come under the category of public opinion (§316).

For the rest, the element in which public opinion finds utterance and becomes an overt and tangible act is, as we have already observed, the intelligence, principles, and opinions of others. It is this element which determines the peculiar effect of these acts or the danger of them to individuals, the community or the state (§218), just as a spark, if thrown upon a heap of gunpowder, is much more dangerous than if thrown on the ground, where it goes out and leaves no trace.—Hence, as the right of science finds security in the content of its matter, so also may an uttered wrong find security, or, at least, toleration, in the contempt with which it is received. Offences, which are in strictness punishable at law, may thus partly come under a kind of nemesis. Internal impotence, by opposing itself to the talents and virtues, by which it feels oppressed, comes in this way to itself, and gives self-consciousness to its own nothingness. A more harmless form of nemesis was found amongst the Roman soldiers in the satirical songs directed against their emperors on the triumphal march. Having gone through hard service, and yet failing to secure mention in the list of honours, they sought to get even with the emperor in this jesting way. But even the nemesis which is bad and malevolent is, when treated with scorn, deprived of its effect. Like the public, which to some extent forms a circle for this kind of activity, it is limited to a meaningless delight in others' misfortunes and to a condemnation, which is inherent in itself.

320. There is the subjectivity, which is the dissolution of the established state life. It has its external manifestation in the opinion or reasoning, which, in seeking to make good its own random aims, destroys itself. This subjectivity has its true reality in its opposite, namely, in that subjectivity, which, being identical with the substantive will, and constituting the conception of the princely power, is the ideality of the whole. This higher subjectivity has not as yet received in this treatise its right and visible embodiment.

Addition.—We have already regarded subjectivity as existing in the monarch, and in that capacity occupying the pinnacle of the state. The other side of subjectivity manifests itself arbitrarily and quite externally in public opinion. The subjectivity of the monarch is in itself abstract, but it should be concrete, and should as concrete be the ideality which diffuses itself over the whole. In the state which is at peace, all branches of the civic life have their subsistence, but this subsistence beside and outside of one another the branches have only as it issues out of the idea of the whole. This process or idealization of the whole must also have its own manifestation.

II. External Sovereignty

321. Internal sovereignty (§278) is this ideality in so far as the elements of spirit, and of the state as the embodiment of spirit, are unfolded in their necessity, and subsist as organs of the state. But spirit, involving a reference to itself, which is negative and infinitely free, becomes an independent existence, which has incorporated the subsistent differences, and hence is exclusive. So constituted, the state has an individuality, which exists essentially as an individual, and in the sovereign is a real, direct individual (§279).

322. Individuality, as exclusive and independent existence, appears as a relation to other self-dependent states. The independent existence of the actual spirit finds an embodiment in this general self-dependence, which is, therefore, the first freedom and highest dignity of a people.

Note.—Those who, out of a desire for a collective whole, which will constitute a more or less self-dependent state, and have its own centre, are willing to abandon their own centre and self-dependence, and form with others a new whole, are ignorant of the nature of a collective whole, and underrate the pride of a people in its independence.—The force, which states have on their first appearance in history, is this self-dependence, even though it is quite abstract and has no further internal development. Hence, in its most primitive manifestation, the state has at its head an individual, whether he be patriarch, chief, or what not.

323. In actual reality, this negative reference of the state to itself appears as reference to each other of two independent things, as though the negative were some external thing. This negative reference has, therefore, in its existence the form of an event, involving accidental occurrences coming from without. But it is in fact its own highest element, its real infinitude, the idealization of all its finite materials. The substance, as the absolute power, is here brought into contrast with all that is individual and particular, such as life, property, the rights of property, or even wider circles, and makes their relative worthlessness a fact for consciousness.

324. The phase, according to which the interest and right of individuals is made a vanishing factor, is at the same time a positive element, forming the basis of their, not accidental and fleeting, but absolute individuality. This relation and the recognition of it constitute their substantial duty. Property and life, not to speak of opinions and the ordinary routine of existence, they must sacrifice, if necessary, in order to preserve the substantive individuality, independence, and sovereignty of the state.

Note.—It is a very distorted account of the matter when the state, in demanding sacrifices from the citizens, is taken to be simply the civic community, whose object is merely the security of life and property. Security cannot possibly be obtained by the sacrifice of what is to be secured.

Herein is to be found the ethical element in war. War is not to be regarded as an absolute evil. It is not a merely external accident, having its accidental ground in the passions of powerful individuals or nations, in acts of injustice, or in anything which ought not to be. Accident befalls that which is by nature accidental, and this fate is a necessity. So from the standpoint of the conception and in philosophy the merely accidental vanishes, because in it, as it is a mere appearance, is recognized its essence, namely, necessity. It is necessary that what is finite, such as life and property, should have its contingent nature exposed, since contingency is inherent in the conception of the finite. This necessity has in one phase of it the form of a force of nature, since all that is finite is mortal and transient. But in the ethical life, that is to say, the state, this force and nature are separated. Necessity becomes in this way exalted to the work of freedom, and becomes a force which is ethical. What from the standpoint of nature is transient, is now transient because it is willed to be so; and that, which is fundamentally negative, becomes substantive and distinctive individuality in the ethical order.

It is often said, for the sake of edification, that war makes short work of the vanity of temporal things. It is the element by which the idealization of what is particular receives its right and becomes an actuality. Moreover, by it, as I have elsewhere expressed it, "finite pursuits are rendered unstable, and the ethical health of peoples is preserved. Just as the movement of the ocean prevents the corruption which would be the result of perpetual calm, so by war people escape the corruption which would be occasioned by a continuous or eternal peace."—The view that this quotation contains merely a philosophical idea, or, as it is sometimes called, a justification of providence, and that actual war needs another kind of justification, will be taken up later. The idealization, which comes to the surface in war, viewed as an accidental foreign relation, is the same as the ideality by virtue of which the internal state functions are organic elements of the whole. This principle is found in history in such a fact as that successful wars have prevented civil broils and strengthened the internal power of the state. So, too, peoples, who have been unwilling or afraid to endure internal sovereignty, have been subjugated by others, and in their struggles for independence have had honour and success small in proportion to their failure to establish within themselves a central political power; their freedom died through their fear of its dying. Moreover, states, which have no guarantee of independence in the strength of their army, states, e.g., that are very small in comparison with their neighbours, have continued to subsist because of their internal constitution, which merely of itself would seem to promise them neither internal repose nor external security. These phenomena are illustrations of our principle drawn from history.

Addition.—In peace the civic life becomes more and more extended. Each separate sphere walls itself in and becomes exclusive, and at last there is a stagnation of mankind. Their particularity becomes more and more fixed and ossified. Unity of the body is essential to health, and where the organs become hard death ensues. Everlasting peace is frequently demanded as the ideal towards which mankind must move. Hence, Kant proposed an alliance of princes, which should settle the controversies of states, and the Holy Alliance was probably intended to be an institution of this kind. But the state is individual, and in individuality negation is essentially implied. Although a number of states may make themselves into a family, the union, because it is an individuality, must create an opposition, and so beget an enemy. As a result of war peoples are strengthened, nations, which are involved in civil quarrels, winning repose at home by means of war abroad. It is true that war occasions insecurity of possessions, but this real insecurity is simply a necessary commotion. From the pulpit we hear much regarding the uncertainty, vanity, and instability of temporal things. At the very same time every one, no matter how much he is impressed by these utterances, thinks that he will manage to retain his own stock and store. But if the uncertainty comes in the form of hussars with glistening sabres, and begins to work in downright earnest, this touching edification turns right about face, and hurls curses at the invader. In spite of this, wars arise, when they lie in the nature of the matter. The seeds spring up afresh, and words are silenced before the earnest repetitions of history.

325. Sacrifice for the sake of the individuality of the state is the substantive relation of all the citizens, and is, thus, a universal duty. It is ideality on one of its sides, and stands in contrast to the reality of particular subsistence. Hence it itself becomes a specific relation, and to it is dedicated a class of its own, the class whose virtue is bravery.

326. Dissensions between states may arise out of any one specific side of their relations to each other. Through these dissensions the specific part of the state devoted to defence receives its distinguishing character. But if the whole state, as such, is in danger of losing its independence, duty summons all the citizens to its defence. If the whole becomes a single force, and is torn from its internal position and goes abroad, defence becomes converted into a war of conquest.

Note.—The weaponed force of the state constitutes its standing army. The specific function of defending the state must be intrusted to a separate class. This proceeding is due to the same necessity by which each of the other particular elements, interests, or affairs, has a separate place, as in marriage, the industrial class, the business class, and the political class. Theorizing, which wanders up and down with its reasons, goes about to contemplate the greater advantages or the greater disadvantages of a standing army. Mere opinion decides against an army, because the conception of the matter is harder to understand than are separate and external sides. Another reason is that the interests and aims of particularity, expenses, consequent higher taxation, etc., are counted of greater concern by the civic community than is the absolutely necessary. On this view the necessary is valuable only as a means to the preservation of the various special civic interests.

327. Bravery taken by itself is a formal virtue, since in it freedom is farthest removed from all special aims, possessions, and enjoyments, and

even from life. But it involves a negation or renunciation of only external realities, and does not carry with it a completion of the spiritual nature. Thus, the sentiment of courage may be based upon any one of a variety of grounds, and its actual result may be not for the brave themselves, but only for others.

Addition.—The military class is the class of universality. To it are assigned the defence of the state and the duty of bringing into existence the ideality implicit in itself. In other words it must sacrifice itself. Bravery is, it is true, of different sorts. The courage of the animal, or the robber, the bravery due to a sense of honour, the bravery of chivalry, are not yet the true forms of it. True bravery in civilized peoples consists in a readiness to offer up oneself in the service of the state, so that the individual counts only as one amongst many. Not personal fearlessness, but the taking of one's place in a universal cause, is the valuable feature of it. In India five hundred men conquered twenty thousand, who were by no means cowardly but lacked the sense of co-operation.

328. The content of bravery as a sentiment is found in the true absolute final end, the sovereignty of the state. Bravery realizes this end, and in so doing gives up personal reality. Hence, in this feeling are found the most rigorous and direct antagonisms. There is present in it a self-sacrifice, which is yet the existence of freedom. In it is found the highest self-control or independence, which yet in its existence submits to the mechanism of an external order and a life of service. An utter obedience or complete abnegation of one's own opinion and reasonings, even an absence of one's own spirit, is coupled with the most intense and comprehensive direct presence of the spirit and of resolution. The most hostile and hence most personal attitude towards individuals is allied with perfect indifference, or even, it may be, a kindly feeling towards them as individuals.

Note.—To risk one's life is indeed something more than fear of death, but it is yet a mere negative, having no independent character and value. Only the positive element, the aim and content of the act, gives significance to the feeling of fearlessness. Robbers or murderers, having in view a crime, adventurers bent upon gratifying merely their own fancy, risk their lives without fear.—The principle of the modern world, that is, the thought and the universal, have given bravery a higher form. It now seems to be mechanical in its expression, being the act not of a particular person, but of a member of the whole. As antagonism is now directed, not against separate persons, but against a hostile whole, personal courage appears as impersonal. To this change is due the invention of the gun; and this by no means chance invention has transmuted the merely personal form of bravery into the more abstract.

329. The state has a foreign aspect, because it is an individual subject.

Hence, its relation to other states falls within the princely function. Upon this function it devolves solely and directly to command the armed force, to entertain relations with other states through ambassadors, to decide upon peace and war, and to conduct other negotiations.

Addition.—In almost all European countries the individual summit is the princely function, which has charge of foreign affairs. Wherever the constitution requires the existence of classes or estates, it may be asked whether the classes, which in any case control the supplies, should not also resolve upon war and peace. In England, for example, no unpopular war can be waged. But if it is meant that princes and cabinets are more subject to passion than the houses, and hence that the houses should decide whether there should be war or peace, it must be replied, that often whole nations have been roused to a pitch of enthusiasm surpassing that of their princes. Frequently in England the whole people have insisted upon war, and in a certain measure compelled the ministers to wage it. The popularity of Pitt was due to his knowing how to meet what the nation willed. Not till afterwards did calm give rise to the consciousness that the war was utterly useless, and undertaken without adequate means. Moreover, a state is connected not only with another but with several others, and the complications are so delicate that they can be managed only by the highest power.

B. International Law

330. International law arises out of the relation to one another of independent states. Whatever is absolute in this relation receives the form of a command, because its reality depends upon a distinct sovereign will.

Addition.—A state is not a private person, but in itself a completely independent totality. Hence, the relation of states to one another is not merely that of morality and private right. It is often desired that states should be regarded from the standpoint of private right and morality. But the position of private persons is such that they have over them a law court, which realizes what is intrinsically right. A relation between states ought also to be intrinsically right, and in mundane affairs that which is intrinsically right ought to have power. But as against the state there is no power to decide what is intrinsically right and to realize this decision. Hence, we must here remain by the absolute command. States in their relation to one another are independent and look upon the stipulations which they make one with another as provisional.

331. The nation as a state is the spirit substantively realized and directly real. Hence, it is the absolute power on earth. As regards other states it exists in sovereign independence. Hence, to exist for and be recognized by another as such a state is its primary absolute right. But this right is yet only formal, and the state's demand to be recognized, when

based on these external relations, is abstract. Whether the state exists absolutely and in concrete fact, depends upon its content, constitution, and condition. Even then the recognition, containing the identity of both inner and outer relations, depends upon the view and will of another.

Note.—Just as the individual person is not real unless related to others (§71 and elsewhere), so the state is not really individual unless related to other states (§322). The legitimate province of a state in its foreign relations, and more especially of the princely function, is on one side wholly internal; a state shall not meddle with the internal affairs of another state. Yet, on the other side, it is essential for its completeness that it be recognized by others. But this recognition demands as a guarantee that it shall recognize those who recognize it, and will have respect for their independence. Therefore they cannot be indifferent to its internal affairs.— In the case of a nomadic people, or any people occupying a lower grade of civilization, the question arises how far it can be considered as a state. The religious opinions formerly held by Jews and Mahomedans may contain a still higher opposition, which does not permit of the universal identity implied in recognition.

Addition.—When Napoleon, before the peace of Campoformio, said, "The French Republic needs recognition as little as the sun requires to be recognized," he really indicated the strength of the existence, which already carried with it a guarantee of recognition, without its having been expressed.

332. The direct reality, in which states stand to one another, sunders itself into various relations, whose nature proceeds from independent caprice on both sides, and hence has as a general thing the formal character of a contract. The subject matter of these contracts is, however, of infinitely narrower range than of those in the civic community. There individuals are dependent upon one another in a great variety of ways, while independent states are wholes, which find satisfaction in the main within themselves.

333. International law, or the law which is universal, and is meant to hold absolutely good between states, is to be distinguished from the special content of positive treaties, and has at its basis the proposition that treaties, as they involve the mutual obligations of states, must be kept inviolate. But because the relation of states to one another has sovereignty as its principle, they are so far in a condition of nature one to the other. Their rights have reality not in a general will, which is constituted as a superior power, but in their particular wills. Accordingly the fundamental proposition of international law remains a good intention, while in the actual situation the relation established by the treaty is being continually shifted or abrogated.

Note.—There is no judge over states, at most only a referee or mediator, and even the mediatorial function is only an accidental thing, being due to particular wills. Kant's idea was that eternal peace should be secured by an alliance of states. This alliance should settle every dispute, make impossible the resort to arms for a decision, and be recognized by every state. This idea assumes that states are in accord, an agreement which, strengthened though it might be by moral, religious, and other considerations, nevertheless always rested on the private sovereign will, and was therefore liable to be disturbed by the element of contingency.

334. Therefore, when the particular wills of states can come to no agreement, the controversy can be settled only by war. Owing to the wide field and the varied relations of the citizens of different states to one another, injuries occur easily and frequently. What of these injuries is to be viewed as a specific breach of a treaty or as a violation of formal recognition and honour remains from the nature of the case indefinite. A state may introduce its infinitude and honour into every one of its separate compartments. It is all the more tempted to make or seek some occasion for a display of irritability, if the individuality within it has been strengthened by long internal rest, and desires an outlet for its pent-up activity.

335. Moreover, the state as a spiritual whole cannot be satisfied merely with taking notice of the fact of an injury, because injury involves a threatened danger arising from the possible action of the other state. Then, too, there is the weighing of probabilities, guesses at intentions, and so forth, all of which have a part in the creation of strife.

336. Each self-dependent state has the standing of a particular will; and it is on this alone that the validity of treaties depends. This particular will of the whole is in its content its well-being, and well-being constitutes the highest law in its relation to another. All the more is this so since the idea of the state involves that the opposition between right or abstract freedom on one side and the complete specific content or well-being on the other is superseded. It is to states as concrete wholes that recognition (§331) is first granted.

337. The substantive weal of the state is its weal as a particular state in its definite interests and condition, its peculiar external circumstances, and its particular treaty obligations. Thus the government is a particular wisdom and not universal providence (§324, *note*). So, too, its end in relation to other states, the principle justifying its wars and treaties, is not a general thought, such as philanthropy, but the actually wronged or threatened weal in its definite particularity.

Note.—At one time a lengthy discussion was held with regard to the opposition between morals and politics, and the demand was made that politics should be in accordance with morality. Here it may be remarked merely that the commonweal has quite another authority than the weal of the individual, and that the ethical substance or the state has directly its reality or right not in an abstract but in a concrete existence. This existence, and not one of the many general thoughts held to be moral commands, must be the principle of its conduct. The view that politics in this assumed opposition is presumptively in the wrong depends on a shallow notion both of morality and of the nature of the state in relation to morality.

338. Although in war there prevails force, contingency, and absence of right, states continue to recognize one another as states. In this fact is implied a covenant, by virtue of which each state retains absolute value. Hence, war, even when actively prosecuted, is understood to be temporary, and in international law is recognized as containing the possibility of peace. Ambassadors, also, are to be respected. War is not to be waged against internal institutions, or the peaceable family and private life, or private persons.

Addition.—Modern wars are carried on humanely. One person is not set in hate over against another. Personal hostilities occur at most in the case of the pickets. But in the army as an army, enmity is something undetermined, and gives place to the duty which each person owes to another.

339. For the rest, the capture of prisoners in time of war, and in time of peace the concession of rights of private intercourse to the subjects of another state, depend principally upon the ethical observances of nations. In them is embodied that inner universality of behaviour, which is preserved under all relations.

Addition.—The nations of Europe form a family by virtue of the universal principle of their legislation, their ethical observances, and their civilization. Amongst them international behaviour is ameliorated, while there prevails elsewhere a mutual infliction of evils. The relation of one state to another fluctuates; no judge is present to compose differences; the higher judge is simply the universal and absolute spirit, the spirit of the world.

340. As states are particular, there is manifested in their relation to one another a shifting play of internal particularity of passions, interests, aims, talents, virtues, force, wrong, vice, and external contingency on the very largest scale. In this play even the ethical whole, national independence, is exposed to chance. The spirit of a nation is an existing individual having in particularity its objective actuality and self-consciousness. Because of this particularity it is limited. The destinies and deeds of states in their connection with one another are the visible dialectic of the finite nature of these spirits. Out of this dialectic the universal spirit, the spirit of the world, the unlimited spirit, produces itself. It has the highest right of all, and exercises its right upon the lower spirits in world-history. The history of the world is the world's court of judgment.

C. World-History

341. The universal spirit exists concretely in art in the form of perception and image, in religion in the form of feeling and pictorial imaginative thinking, and in philosophy in the form of pure free thought. In world-history this concrete existence of spirit is the spiritual actuality in the total range of its internality and externality. It is a court of judgment because in its absolute universality the particular, namely, the Penates, the civic community, and the national spirit in their many-coloured reality are all merely ideal. The movement of spirit in this case consists in visibly presenting these spheres as merely ideal.

342. Moreover, world-history is not a court of judgment, whose principle is force, nor is it the abstract and irrational necessity of a blind fate. It is self-caused and self-realized reason, and its actualized existence in spirit is knowledge. Hence, its development issuing solely out of the conception of its freedom is a necessary development of the elements of reason. It is, therefore, an unfolding of the spirit's self-consciousness and freedom. It is the exhibition and actualization of the universal spirit.

343. The history of spirit is its overt deeds, for only what it does it is, and its deed is to make itself as a spirit the object of its consciousness, to explain and lay hold upon itself by reference to itself. To lay hold upon itself is its being and principle, and the completion of this act is at the same time self-renunciation and transition. To express the matter formally, the spirit which again apprehends what has already been grasped and actualized, or, what is the same thing, passes through self-renunciation into itself, is the spirit of a higher stage.

Note.—Here occurs the question of the perfection and education of humanity. They who have argued in favour of this idea, have surmised something of the nature of spirit. They have understood that spirit has Γνῶθι σεαυτὸν as a law of its being, and that when it lays hold upon what it itself is, it assumes a higher form. To those who have rejected this idea, spirit has remained an empty word and history a superficial play of accidental and so-called mere human strife and passion. Though in their use of the words "providence" and "design of providence," they express their belief in a higher control, they do not fill up the notion, but announce that the design of providence is for them unknowable and inconceivable.

344. States, peoples, and individuals are established upon their own particular definite principle, which has systematized reality in their constitutions and in the entire compass of their surroundings. Of this systematized reality they are aware, and in its interests are absorbed. Yet are they the unconscious tools and organs of the world-spirit, through whose inner activity the lower forms pass away. Thus the spirit by its

own motion and for its own end makes ready and works out the transition into its next higher stage.

345. Justice and virtue, wrong, force, and crime, talents and their results, small and great passions, innocence and guilt, the splendour of individuals, national life, independence, the fortune and misfortune of states and individuals, have in the sphere of conscious reality their definite meaning and value, and find in that sphere judgment and their due. This due is, however, as yet incomplete. In world-history, which lies beyond this range of vision, the idea of the world-spirit, in that necessary phase of it which constitutes at any time its actual stage, is given its absolute right. The nation, then really flourishing, attains to happiness and renown, and its deeds receive completion.

346. Since history is the embodiment of spirit in the form of events, that is, of direct natural reality, the stages of development are present as direct natural principles. Because they are natural, they conform to the nature of a multiplicity, and exist one outside the other. Hence, to each nation is to be ascribed a single principle, comprised under its geographical and anthropological existence.

347. To the nation, whose natural principle is one of these stages, is assigned the accomplishment of it through the process characteristic of the self-developing self-consciousness of the world-spirit. In the history of the world this nation is for a given epoch dominant, although it can make an epoch but once (§346). In contrast with the absolute right of this nation to be the bearer of the current phase in the development of the world-spirit, the spirits of other existing nations are void of right, and they, like those whose epochs are gone, count no longer in the history of the world.

Note.—The special history of a world-historic nation contains the unfolding of its principle from its undeveloped infancy up to the time when, in the full manhood of free ethical self-consciousness, it presses in upon universal history. It contains, moreover, the period of decline and destruction, the rise of a higher principle being marked in it simply as the negative of its own. Hence, the spirit passes over into that higher principle, and thus indicates to world-history another nation. From that time onward the first nation has lost absolute interest, absorbs the higher principle positively, it may be, and fashions itself in accordance with it, but is, after all, only a recipient, and has no indwelling vitality and freshness. Perhaps it loses its independence, perhaps continues to drag itself on as a particular state or circle of states, and spends itself in various random civil enterprises and foreign broils.

348. At the summit of all actions, including world-historical actions, stand individuals. Each of these individuals is a subjectivity who realizes what is substantive (§279, note). He is a living embodiment of the sub-

stantive deed of the world-spirit, and is, therefore, directly identical with this deed. It is concealed even from himself, and is not his object and end (§344). Thus they do not receive honour and thanks for their acts either from their contemporaries (§344), or from the public opinion of posterity. By this opinion they are viewed merely as formal subjectivities, and, as such, are simply given their part in immortal fame.

349. A people is not as yet a state. The transition from the family, horde, clan, or multitude into a state constitutes the formal realization in it of the idea. If the ethical substance, which every people has implicitly, lacks this form, it is without that objectivity which comes from laws and thought-out regulations. It has neither for itself nor for others any universal or generally admitted reality. It will not be recognized. Its independence, being devoid of objective law or secure realized rationality, is formal only and not a sovereignty.

Note.—From the ordinary point of view we do not call the patriarchal condition a constitution, or a people in this condition a state, or its independence sovereignty. Before the beginning of actual history there are found uninteresting stupid innocence and the bravery arising out of the formal struggle for recognition and out of revenge (§§331, 57, *note*).

350. It is the absolute right of the idea to come visibly forth, and proceeding from marriage and agriculture (§203, *note*) realize itself in laws and objective institutions. This is true whether its realization appears in the form of divine law and beneficence or in the form of force and wrong. This right is the right of heroes to found states.

351. In the same way civilized nations may treat as barbarians the peoples who are behind them in the essential elements of the state. Thus, the rights of mere herdsmen, hunters, and tillers of the soil are inferior, and their independence is merely formal.

Note.—Wars and contests arising under such circumstances are struggles for recognition in behalf of a certain definite content. It is this feature of them which is significant in world-history.

352. The concrete ideas, which embody the national minds or spirits, has its truth in the concrete idea in its absolute universality. This is the spirit of the world, around whose throne stand the other spirits as perfecters of its actuality, and witnesses and ornaments of its splendour. Since it is, as spirit, only the movement of its activity in order to know itself absolutely, to free its consciousness from mere direct naturalness, and to come to itself, the principles of the different forms of its self-consciousness, as they appear in the process of liberation, are four. They are the principles of the four world-historic kingdoms.

353. In its first and direct revelation the world-spirit has as its principle the form of the substantive spirit, in whose identity individuality is in its essence submerged and without explicit justification.

In the second principle the substantive spirit is aware of itself. Here spirit is the positive content and filling, and is also at the same time the living form, which is in its nature self-referred.

The third principle is the retreat into itself of this conscious self-referred existence. There thus arises an abstract universality, and with it an infinite opposition to objectivity, which is regarded as bereft of spirit.

In the fourth principle this opposition of the spirit is overturned in order that spirit may receive into its inner self its truth and concrete essence. It thus becomes at home with objectivity, and the two are reconciled. Because the spirit has come back to its formal substantive reality by returning out of this infinite opposition, it seeks to produce and know its truth as thought, and as a world of established reality.

354. In accordance with these four principles the four world-historic empires are (1) the Oriental, (2) the Greek, (3) the Roman, and (4) the Germanic.

355. (1) THE ORIENTAL EMPIRE:—The first empire is the substantive world-intuition, which proceeds from the natural whole of patriarchal times. It has no internal divisions. Its worldly government is theocracy, its ruler a high priest or God, its constitution and legislation are at the same time its religion, and its civic and legal regulations are religious and moral commands or usages. In the splendour of this totality the individual personality sinks without rights; external nature is directly divine or an ornament of God, and the history of reality is poetry. The distinctions, which develop themselves in customs, government, and the state, serve instead of laws, being converted by mere social usage into clumsy, diffuse, and superstitious ceremonies, the accidents of personal power and arbitrary rule. The division into classes becomes a caste fixed as the laws of nature. Since in the Oriental empire there is nothing stable, or rather what is firm is petrified, it has life only in a movement, which goes on from the outside, and becomes an elemental violence and desolation. Internal repose is merely a private life, which is sunk in feebleness and lassitude.

Note.—The element of substantive natural spirituality is present in the first forming of every state, and constitutes the absolute starting-point of its history. This assertion is presented and historically established by Dr. Stuhr in his well-reasoned and scholarly treatise "Vom Untergange der Naturstaaten" (Berlin, 1812), who, moreover, suggests in this work a rational method of viewing constitutional history and history in general. The principle of subjectivity and self-conscious freedom he ascribes to the German nation. But since the treatise is wholly taken up with the decline of the nature-states, it simply leads to the point at which this modern principle makes its appearance. At that time it assumed in part the guise of restless movement, human caprice, and corruption, in part the particular guise of feeling, not having as yet developed itself into the objectivity of self-conscious substantivity or the condition of organized law.

356. (2) THE GREEK EMPIRE:—This empire still contains the earlier substantive unity of the finite and infinite, but only as a mysterious background, suppressed and kept down in gloomy reminiscence, in caves and in traditional imagery. This background under the influence of the self-distinguishing spirit is recreated into individual spirituality, and exalted into the daylight of consciousness, where it is tempered and clarified into beauty and a free and cheerful ethical life. Here arises the principle of personal individuality, although it is not as yet self-centred, but held in its ideal unity. One result of this incompleteness is that the whole is broken up into a number of particular national minds or spirits. Further, the final decision of will is not as yet intrusted to the subjectivity of the independent self-consciousness, but resides in a power, which is higher than, and lies beyond it (§279, *note*). Moreover, the particularity, which is found in wants, is not yet taken up into freedom, but segregated in a class of slaves.

357. (3) THE ROMAN EMPIRE:—In this empire the distinctions of spirit are carried to the length of an infinite rupture of the ethical life into two extremes, personal private self-consciousness, and abstract universality. The antagonism, arising between the substantive intuition of an aristocracy and the principle of free personality in democratic form, developed on the side of the aristocracy into superstition and the retention of cold self-seeking power, and on the side of the democracy into the corrupt mass. The dissolution of the whole culminates in universal misfortune, ethical life dies, national individualities, having merely the bond of union of a Pantheon, perish, and individuals are degraded to the level of that equality, in which they are merely private persons and have only formal rights.

358. (4) THE GERMAN EMPIRE:—Owing to the loss of itself and its world, and to the infinite pain caused by it, a loss of which the Jewish people were already held to be the type, spirit is pressed back into itself, and finds itself in the extreme of absolute negativity. But this extreme is the absolute turning-point, and in it spirit finds the infinite and yet positive nature of its own inner being. This new discovery is the unity of the divine and the human. By means of it objective truth is reconciled with freedom, and that, too, inside of self-consciousness and subjectivity. This new basis, infinite and yet positive, it has been charged upon the northern principle of the Germanic nations to bring to completion.

359. The internal aspect of this northern principle exists in feeling as faith, love, and hope. Although it is in this form still abstract, it is the reconciliation and solution of all contradiction. It proceeds to unfold its content in order to raise it to reality and self-conscious rationality. It thus constructs a kingdom of this world, based upon the feeling, trust, and fel-

lowship of free men. This kingdom in this its subjectivity is an actual kingdom of rude caprice and barbarism in contrast with the world beyond. It is an intellectual empire, whose content is indeed the truth of its spirit. But as it is yet not thought out, and still is veiled in the barbarism of picture-thinking, it exists as a spiritual force, which exercises over the actual mind a despotic and tyrannical influence.

360. These kingdoms are based upon the distinction, which has now won the form of absolute antagonism, and yet at the same time are rooted in a single unity and idea. In the obdurate struggle, which thus ensues, the spiritual has to lower its heaven to the level of an earthly and temporal condition, to common worldliness, and to ordinary life and thought. On the other hand the abstract actuality of the worldly is exalted to thought, to the principle of rational being and knowing, and to the rationality of right and law. As a result of these two tendencies, the contradiction has become a marrowless phantasm. The present has stripped off its barbarism and its lawless caprice, and truth has stripped off its beyond and its casualness. The true atonement and reconciliation has become objective, and unfolds the state as the image and reality of reason. In the state, self-consciousness finds the organic development of its real substantive knowing and will, in religion it finds in the form of ideal essence the feeling and the vision of this its truth, and in science it finds the free conceived knowledge of this truth, seeing it to be one and the same in all its mutually completing manifestations, namely, the state, nature, and the ideal world.

THE END.

INDEX OF WORDS

(The figures refer to the page and the line.)

INDEX OF SUBJECTS

(*n.* = note, *add.* = addition; the figures refer to the paragraph, and the figures in parentheses to the page; thus—273, *n.* (159), means that portion of the note to paragraph 273 which is found on page 159).

209